Romancing God

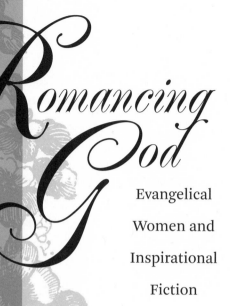

Romancing God

Evangelical
Women and
Inspirational
Fiction

LYNN S. NEAL

The University *of*
North Carolina Press
Chapel Hill

Designed by Kimberly Bryant
Set in Arnhem by Tseng Information Systems, Inc.
Manufactured in the United States of America

The paper in this book meets the guidelines for permanence
and durability of the Committee on Production Guidelines
for Book Longevity of the Council on Library Resources.

Library of Congress Cataloging-in-Publication Data
Neal, Lynn S.
Romancing God : evangelical women and inspirational fiction / Lynn S. Neal
p. cm.
Includes bibliographical references and index.

ISBN-13: 978-0-8078-2998-1 (cloth : alk. paper)
ISBN-10: 0-8078-2998-6 (cloth : alk. paper)
ISBN-13: 978-0-8078-5670-3 (pbk. : alk. paper)
ISBN-10: 0-8078-5670-3 (pbk. : alk. paper)
1. Christian fiction, American—History and criticism. 2. American fiction—
Christian authors—History and criticism. 3. American fiction—Women
authors—History and criticism. 4. Love stories, American—History and
criticism. 5. Christianity and literature—United States. 6. Women and
literature—United States. 7. Evangelicalism—United States.
8. Evangelicalism in literature. I. Title.
PS374.C48.N43 2006
813'.085083822—dc22   2005022332

cloth   10 09 08 07 06   5 4 3 2 1
paper   10 09 08 07 06   5 4 3 2 1

To my parents

CONTENTS

ILLUSTRATIONS

ACKNOWLEDGMENTS

Researching and writing a book teaches one to be grateful for any and all kindnesses, and I have many kindnesses for which to be grateful. This project rests on the many evangelical women who graciously volunteered their time and articulated their insights. Without their willingness to speak to a stranger with a blue clipboard and two tape recorders, this study would not exist. The generosity of these authors and readers continues to amaze me. Throughout the process, their thoughtful answers challenged my presuppositions and stimulated my thinking about evangelical romance novels. While they may not always agree with my interpretations, I trust they will recognize themselves and hear their voices in these pages. In addition, I am particularly indebted to five authors—Shari MacDonald, Irene Brand, Peggy Stoks, Terry Blackstock, and Robin Lee Hatcher—who shared portions of their fan mail with me. These letters proved to be an invaluable resource for interpreting evangelical women's reading practices.

I am also thankful for the teachers who have advised and mentored me through the many transformations, personal and professional, this project has entailed. John Tyson has dispensed wisdom and provided support from my undergraduate days to the present. I am also grateful to Tom Tweed, my graduate advisor, for his loyalty as a mentor and his example as a teacher. His commitment to excellence inspires me. Kate Joyce has shown me the importance of priorities in a profession that makes so many demands; the echoes of Grant Wacker's "so what question" have permeated my research and my teaching; and Laurie Maffly-Kipp and Christian Smith's keen analytical abilities continue to challenge me. I must also express my gratitude to the Louisville Institute and its support for academic inquiry on the nature of everyday religious life. The Institute supported this project in the early stages with a dissertation fellowship. And lastly, I am grateful to my reviewers and my editor, Elaine Maisner, at the University of North Carolina Press. They supported this project in its last stages and challenged me to be a better scholar. To all, my thanks.

On a more personal note, friends and family have sustained me throughout all the stages of this project. They helped me find readers, listened to my theories, and, when needed, supplied me with doses of reality. In particular, Gayle Hoffee, Susan Bales, and Kathryn Lofton have modeled the meaning of friendship. In addition to supportive friends, my family—parents, siblings, nieces, and nephews—consistently provided motivation. Their frequent questioning, "Are you done yet?," bespoke a confidence in my abilities that inspired consistent progress. Lastly, I recognize the love and encouragement provided by my parents, who remain my greatest teachers. This book is dedicated to them.

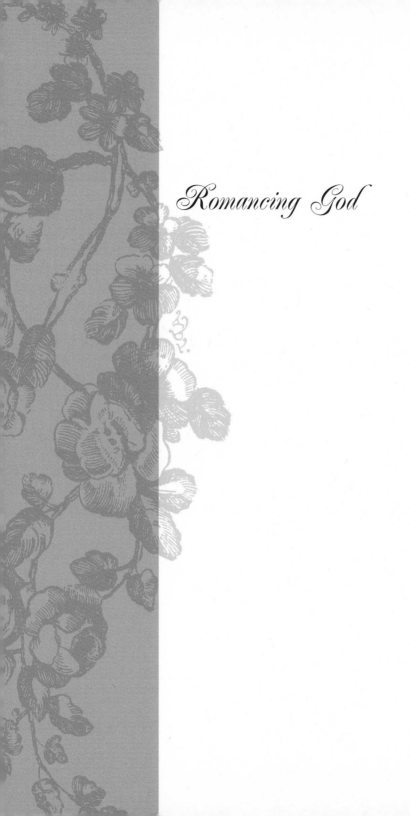

Romancing God

"My family," David said. "They've come." The Indian chief nodded, then smiled. He touched a hand to David's shoulder and gave it a slow squeeze.

"David!"

Louisa?

"David! David?"

"Louisa!" he screamed. He could see her now, with her blue cape and something in her arms. Hobbling over the barnacles, his toes getting scraped over the sharp edges in his haste, he splashed into the water. "Louisa! Louisa!" he shouted with energy he didn't know he had.

She handed her bundle to Mary Ann, then bent to gather her skirts and cape. But as she splashed into a tidal pool—the first of several that lay in narrow strips between long humps of sand—she let them go to run open-armed toward David.

The throbbing of his head forced him to shut his eyes a moment. Pain flashed down his cheek and through his jaw. "Louisa!" he shouted again, then went into the water deeper, feeling the cold go up over his ankles. "Louisa!" He crossed a sandbar and saw her smile. She was laughing!

Then he had her! They swayed as one, their arms locked. His breath came in gulps, painful and searing, and he could feel her warmth against him. The hood of her cape fell and he buried his nose in the coolness of her hair.

"Oh, David!" she cried, clinging to him, sobbing, and laughing at the same time. Suddenly she let go and pushed him from her.

Her eyes flashed. "Let me see you!" she cried.
"Just let me see you!"

"I'm glad you're here," he said, remembering for some reason his last night's visitors.
"The skunks. They've taken all my food."

"Skunks? Oh, David!" She laughed again,
music after so long, and pulled him close.
He held her, kissed her, touched his lips to
her tears. She had come to him. They stared a
moment, lost in their oneness.[1]

After having been separated by disapproving
parents, David Denny and Louisa Boren reunited on the shores of the
Duwamish River in the early days of Seattle. Step-siblings (Louisa's
mother married David's father), Louisa and David found love on the
journey west, but faced parental disapproval because of their age difference. Louisa was twenty-four and David twenty. Together, they
endured travel miseries, jealous misunderstandings, parental objec-
tions, and long separations. However, throughout the story, Louisa
and David remained steadfast in their commitment to be together,
to respect their parents, and to honor their God. Their emotional re-
union marks a turning point in their relationship: the Denny family's
tacit approval of David and Louisa's love. Sixty-five pages later, the
couple marries and moves into the cabin David built and modeled
after King Solomon's palace with its "beams of cedar" and "rafters
of fir." The novel, *Sweetbriar*, by Brenda Wilbee, recounts David and
Louisa's love story and the Dennys' settlement of Seattle. A fictional-
ized story based on historical figures and events, the novel promises
to deliver, as it states on the cover, "history at its best."

From the start, Wilbee firmly positions her story in history. She begins with an introduction that places the Denny family in historical
context and ends with a bibliography of historical sources on Seattle
and the Dennys. Throughout the novel she situates David and Louisa
in historical frames—sections and chapters that open with historical quotes—that emphasize their pioneer faith. For example, part one

features a quote from the historical Louisa Boren: "What a book the story of my life would make!" And part two opens with the words of the historical David Denny: "In looking back over my pioneer life I can see many places where I would do differently if I had the chance to pass that way again, but knowing what I do now I would have come to Puget Sound, to Elliott Bay, and located just as I did before . . . that I would marry the same woman, join the same church, but endeavor to be a better Christian." In her interweaving of Western history, romantic intrigue, and Christian faith, Wilbee narrates "the beginnings of an empire and the story of a remarkable love."[2]

While not all evangelical romance novels fictionalize the lives of historical figures, they all recount stories of "remarkable love." The genre uses a "traditional" romance formula, which scholar Kay Mussell describes this way: "the romantic novel or romantic story, in popular fiction, is a story about a love relationship, a courtship, and a marriage." There are two general forms—the journey from love to marriage or from troubled marriage to triumphant marriage.[3] In these chronicles of secular romance, hero and heroine love one another, but misunderstandings on both sides keep them apart until the end of the story. For example, in Elizabeth Boyle's *One Night of Passion*, heroine Georgie and hero Colin meet at a "Cyprian's Ball," a promiscuous fete outside the moral strictures of the ton, in 1799 London. Wanting to avoid her arranged marriage to the evil Lord Harris, Georgie attends the Ball to lose her virginity and escape her marital fate. Enter Colin. Instantly attracted to one another, Colin and Georgie share "one night of passion," after which Georgie flees without a word and Colin sets sail upon his ship. A year later, both still haunted by the magic of that night, they meet again aboard Colin's ship. Georgie, traveling with her young daughter (the product of their night together) and her sister, is fleeing Italy in the face of the French and none too happy to realize that the man she loves, Colin, is Lord Danvers, the guardian who arranged her marriage to Lord Harris. The misunderstandings continue as Colin suspects Georgie of being a French spy and Georgie doubts Colin's love after finding a picture of his supposedly "former" fiancée. Despite the numerous miscues,

Georgie and Colin's love for one another endures and the novel ends with their reconciliation as well as an epilogue set in 1814 that assures readers that their love continues and happiness persists.[4]

The problems between Georgie and Colin, as well as those between other heroes and heroines in secular romance novels, arise from various sources—misinformation, distrust, or jealousy. Janice Radway, in her seminal study *Reading the Romance*, delineates the thirteen-point narrative plot structure of these romance novels, from the beginning when the heroine is cast adrift by various circumstances—an accident, unemployment, or travel—through a back and forth series of tender and hurtful interactions with the hero, until at the end the couple reconciles and revels in their love for one another. At times, Radway notes, the reconciliation is hard to understand: "No action on the part of the hero or, for that matter, on the part of any other character can be said to cause or explain the magic transformation of his cruelty and indifference into tender care."[5] While cruelty often characterized the heroes of the 1970s (the period Radway studies), today's secular romance hero more resembles Colin, a man of good intentions hindered by an inability to trust until he meets the right woman.

Evangelical romance novels like *Sweetbriar* overlay this basic plot structure with the fundamentals of conservative Christian faith. In these fictional worlds, the obstacles that keep hero and heroine apart emerge from their religious beliefs (or lack thereof). For example, David and Louisa love each other from the opening scene but remain apart because their Christian beliefs demand they honor their parents, who disapprove of their relationship. As they try to gain familial approval, both Louisa and David must confront spiritual difficulties. David, jealous of his brother James's love for Louisa, realizes the sinfulness of this emotion and seeks to correct it by memorizing the biblical book of James. Louisa, in turn, wants to defy her parents and marry David without their consent. She responds to this spiritual dilemma through the practice of prayer and the cultivation of patience. Similar themes of religious strife emerge in Judy Baer's contemporary novel *Shadows Along the Ice*, featuring heroine Pamela Warren and hero Ty Evans. New to Winnipeg, sports reporter Pamela meets hockey star Ty. As the two begin dating, Pamela's Christian beliefs are tested as she falls in love with her non-Christian hero. Confronted by the biblical injunction recorded in 2 Corinthians 6:14—"Do not be yoked with unbelievers," commonly interpreted within evangelicalism as a command for Christians to marry other Christians—Pamela comes to an unwelcome conclusion. Baer describes her heroine's conflicted thoughts: "In that moment came the dawning realization of the love she had for him. And the fruitlessness of that love if Ty could not share her love of the Lord with her. She could not tear herself asunder—serving God and loving a man who couldn't understand that call. Pain and joy mingled within her. Unless Ty grew to share her faith, she would have to make a choice. And that choice would not include the irreverent golden man she loved so deeply." Pamela remains committed to putting God first, even if it costs her the man she loves. However, as the novel ends, Pamela's patience and trust in God is rewarded as Ty "impressed by her quiet faith" reaches out and establishes a relationship with God.[6] Many evangelical romances, like Baer's, feature the necessity of conversion; others resemble Wilbee's *Sweetbriar* with its Christian hero and heroine learning how to address religious problems and conflicts. In the genre and in evangelicalism, problems—whether one's attitude or a family crisis—represent symptoms of a deeper spiritual malaise. The cure, in these fictional worlds, necessitates a religious action, such as conversion, forgiveness, or obedience. Whether historical narratives or contemporary renderings, evangelical romances place one's relationship with God before all other relationships. This in turn becomes the necessary foundation for a successful heterosexual relationship. The transformation that seems "magical" in secular romances is explained by divinely sparked spiritual growth in their evangelical counterparts. There are no heroes or heroines magically reconciled, but rather characters transformed and brought together by the power of God's love.

The genre of evangelical romance, also referred to as inspirational fiction, constitutes a vital part of the vast romance-publishing industry. Romance novels are big business. "The world's largest publisher of romances, Harlequin Enterprises, has reported annual sales of over 190 million books worldwide. These books are translated into over twenty languages, including Japanese, Greek, and Swedish." The popularity of romance novels transcends cultural differences and is evidenced by their dominance of fiction sales. In 1999, romance constituted "58.2 percent of all popular mass market fiction sales, 38.8 percent of all popular fiction sales, and over $1.35 billion in sales." The size of this industry has attracted many scholars, including Janice Radway, Tania Modleski, and Carol Thurston, who examined this genre's appeal to and effect upon women. These studies have helpfully explored the terrain of secular romance novels and their readers, but an examination of religious romances like *Sweetbriar* remains absent, despite the genre's increasingly important niche in romance publishing. The year 2000 saw the publication of 2,056 romance novels and of that number "inspirational romance" held a 6.1 percent share.[7] "The most successful religious fiction today," reports Nick Harrison in *Publishers Weekly*, "comes from evangelical Protestant Christian publishers. Although they are published by conservative Christian houses and have been sold mainly through Christian bookstores, such novels have racked up impressive sales and are increasingly making a strong showing in general trade stores and in nonbook outlets like the major discounters."[8] Through its layering of romantic elements and conservative Christian beliefs, evangelicals have hit upon an increasingly popular formula. Today a woman can find dozens of evangelical romance titles on the shelves of her local Christian bookstore. Increasingly, however, she can also find some as she shops in K-Mart and Wal-Mart, as well as Barnes and Noble and Walden Books.

As I first imagined it, this project would be about the novels' plots and prescriptions. I would analyze gender depictions, historical descriptions, and evangelical prescriptions. It would be a study about the novels' contents. The power of the romance "formula" captured my initial focus as a scholar. However, as I began to sketch out the parameters of this research, the imagined woman shopping for evangelical romances at her local Barnes and Noble or Family Christian

Store demanded my attention. Why did she read evangelical romance novels? How did she understand her reading practice and its relationship to her religious life? The questions continued, a different approach emerged, and an alternative story surfaced.

Using work in audience, media, and popular culture studies as models, including Janice Radway's *Reading the Romance*, as well as Henry Jenkins's study of television fandom in *Textual Poachers* and Ien Ang's analysis of melodrama devotees in *Watching Dallas*, my approach moved from textual examination to semi-structured interviews. While informed by ethnographic models, this method uses discrete interviews, rather than sustained fieldwork, to understand people's beliefs and practices related to a specific television show, media form, or popular culture product. Despite its chronological and geographical limits, this approach offers a way to elicit consultants' views on a particular topic at a particular time. "Personal narratives," sociologist Wade Clark Roof writes, "are rich in meaning and nuance, a means of exploring the many webs of cultural meaning that people spin." [9] Talking with women who read and write evangelical romance novels, then, offered a fruitful way to learn how these women understand their reading practices and spin a web of everyday religious life. These women cannot be reduced to their reading, but their devotion to it illuminates the complicated ways they construct and negotiate evangelicalism on a daily basis. To supplement these women's narratives, I also analyzed one hundred letters from readers to authors. While their contents ranged from teenage girls' dreams to adult women's pain, these missives not only afforded insight into a wider range of readers, geographically and demographically, but they also highlighted how readers became writers of their own spiritual stories. Together, the interviews and letters provided an array of views on inspirational romance novel reading, and the story of why some women read these novels emerged.

This is not the book I thought I would write, but it became the story I had to tell. As I spent thirteen months interviewing fifty readers and twenty authors, plots and prescriptions remained important parts of the tale, but the evangelical women with whom I spoke became the central characters. While a few of my consultants mentioned making their husbands read a particular passage or novel, and one fan letter came from a man, the evidence led me to a story about evangelical women. They dominate the pages of the novels as well as the authorship and readership of the genre. This study, then, is about how these women interpret their reading practices in relation to their religious lives—their fictional devotion.

While the women interviewed for this book were not always easy to locate, once I found them they eagerly volunteered to participate in the study. (Not surprisingly, authors proved easier to find than readers. I interviewed twenty of them over the phone, via e-mail, or in person.) To discover readers, I employed the snowball method, an approach in which I asked each reader interviewed to refer me to another reader whom they knew. After each meeting, I also asked them to complete a brief survey to supply demographic data and to discern reading patterns. In the end, I talked with readers from nine states, with the majority, thirty-two, being from North Carolina.[10] There was diversity among the readers (they ranged in age from twenty-three to seventy-four), but a social profile emerged. The average reader was forty-three years old, white, female, married, with at least one child, a college education, and an annual income between $50,000 and $74,999.[11] Twenty-three readers affiliated with Baptist churches— Southern, Free Will, and Independent. My consultants included five United Methodists and five Presbyterians. There were four Pentecostals, three Roman Catholics, and a few from nondenominational churches, as well as one Moravian and one Evangelical Covenant reader. Although United Methodists, Presbyterians, and Roman Catholics might not immediately be identified with evangelicalism, these women often saw themselves (and their churches) as advocates of evangelicalism amidst nonevangelical denominations.

In addition, the women's church attendance patterns placed them further within this religious subculture. Of the forty-two who answered the survey question on church attendance, forty of them—95 percent—attended church once a week or more. This accords with Christian Smith's findings in *American Evangelicalism* that 80 percent of evangelicals attend services once a week or more and that "among committed American Christians, evangelicals by far and away display the highest levels of church attendance." Not surprisingly, these women also shared the church attendance patterns of consumers at Christian bookstores—one of the main distributors of evangelical romances. Christian bookstore shoppers are also predominantly white women, and 97 percent of them attend church once a week or more.[12] While this study remains limited to those interviewed, these statistics and patterns reveal the evangelical ties exhibited by my consultants, as well as the ways these women resemble other evangelicals who may or may not read evangelical romance novels. Put another way, the women I interviewed do not represent the fringes of evangelical life or the margins of the subculture. In church attendance, theological affirmations, and consumer patterns they are like other evangelical women and men, except that they read evangelical romance novels.

While the women I talked with identified themselves as "evangelicals," for scholars the term *evangelicalism* continues to elude easy definition. Some try to capture contemporary evangelicalism through metaphors, and some attempt to delineate evangelical beliefs. The common metaphors include mosaic, kaleidoscope, quilt, and family; in addition, scholars have pointed to several defining evangelical tenets. For example, Mark Ellingsen lists three main beliefs—the authority of the Bible, a personal conversion experience, and witnessing to one's faith—while George Marsden highlights five: salvation through Christ, living a spiritually transformed life, the authority of the Bible, a cosmic view of history, and the importance of witnessing. Unlike Catholics who "acknowledge a common authority," or the "vestigial ethnicity that unites" many Lutherans, Randall Balmer theorizes that evangelicals emphasize belief because it serves "as the basis for whatever cohesion exists among them."[13] Given the centrality of belief in evangelicalism, scholars have attended to this emphasis with great care, and these attempts to define and understand evangelicalism help make sense of the identities and practices of the women I interviewed. Readers emphasized the importance of the Bible, spoke of "personal" relationships with God, shared their efforts to live "spiritually transformed lives," viewed God as active in history, and sometimes mentioned evangelism. These definitions reflected women's beliefs and helped situate them within evangelicalism, but at the same time they essentialize evangelicalism, downplay its dynamism, and dismiss its diversity. Focusing only on evangelical beliefs neglects evangelical practices, elevates the church over the home, and as a result obscures women's lives and the audibility of their voices. In addition, this emphasis often divorces religion from daily life, separating evangelicalism from emotion and religion from recreation. Consequently, these scholarly definitions and accounts fail to adequately capture how evangelicals attempt to live a religion that they see as permeating every aspect of life. While the women I interviewed affirmed the theology identified above, they struggled with how to practice their faith amidst the ordinariness of life. Focusing on evangelical romance reading illuminates one aspect of this complex and dynamic piety by providing a glimpse into these women's everyday religious lives and the ways readers used evangelical romance on a daily basis.

Taking my consultants' narratives seriously shifts our focus from the church and the pew to the home and the sofa. From this perspective, the struggles of parenting, the demands on women, and the difficulties of evangelicalism become visible. Using this lens defies simple dichotomies of liberation and oppression or reductionist theories of delusion and repression. These women's reading represents more than this—it is intertwined with the tactics of everyday life and the survival of what is most important to them—their faith. Rather than lament how these women's lives would be better if only they would read and believe differently, I analyze how my consultants maintain their religious commitments through evangelical romance reading. This does not mean a lapse into recovery history or a celebration of romance reading, but rather a critical yet empathetic exploration of these women's religious lives. This approach, as R. Marie Griffith notes, leaves one vulnerable to feminist critics and evangelical opponents; however, it more fully reveals the complicated piety of ordinary people. Griffith writes, "The heated responses that I have occasionally received in progressive academic settings—responses bidding me to censure evangelical notions of Christian womanhood and, by necessary extension, the masses of women who claim such patterns for their lives—suggest the hazards of this endeavor, including the ease with which it may be mistakenly construed as antifeminist. Still, I remain convinced of the need to bridge disparate worlds, to translate the lives of evangelical women in terms nonevangelicals can understand, insofar as such an enterprise is possible."[14] In *Visual Piety*, David Morgan takes a similar approach: "What I propose in this opening chapter is not a refutation of theological opinion. People are entitled to the theologies they choose, and I am neither qualified nor interested in changing their minds. Instead, following the lead of many scholars working in communication and media studies, popular culture, and the sociology of religion, I would like to examine why believers are positively attracted to devotional imagery, what they believe it offers them, and how scholars might understand this appeal in terms of a popular aesthetic of religious images."[15] Like these and other scholars in religion and popular culture, I focus on how and why evangelical romance novels elicit the devotion of these women.

This is thus a study of evangelical women's devotional lives, of the ways romantic fiction both configures and reflects their daily practice of religion. Evangelical romance reading emerges from and leads back to the evangelical subculture. However, at the same time women's reading narratives reveal the negotiations, inconsistencies, and disjunctures of evangelical living. Amidst doubts and uncertainties, evangelical romance reading "sutures the gaps that appear as the fabric of a world wears thin."[16] As J. Hillis Miller writes, "If we need stories to make sense of our experience, we need the same stories over and over to reinforce that sense making." In this view, popular culture in general and evangelical romances in particular are neither radical nor revolutionary; rather, they contain both regressive and progressive elements that challenge us to examine "the micropolitics of everyday life."[17] Through examining these women's stories, the intersection of religion, reading, and daily life becomes visible. Amidst the demands of ordinary life or a challenge to faith, the genre offers a

respite from problems and a time for fun, as well as a means to cultivate piety. For these women, the genre works on various levels and fulfills diverse needs. Their narratives demonstrate how readers maintain and negotiate their faith from Sunday to Wednesday and from
Wednesday to Sunday.

Throughout this study, I employ the phrase "fictional devotion" to
capture the complexity of the relationship between reader and text.
The term denotes how my consultants are both devoted *to* and *through*
the genre in ways that reflect and configure the contours of their conservative Christian piety. Their reading decisions embody a religious
choice. Within this devotion a variety of themes emerge, including
gender, leisure, theology, and aesthetics, which help explain the attraction and salience of evangelical romance.

The fictional devotion exhibited by these women, I suggest, revolves around three related loci. First, these women read (and write)
evangelical romance novels as a way to demonstrate and maintain
their religious identities. Choosing this genre sets them apart from
nonevangelicals, even as it affords them ways to indulge in the fun
of romantic fiction. Sociologist Christian Smith, through his "subcultural identity theory," argues that this ability to combine engagement with distinction explains evangelical strength: "In a pluralistic
society, those religious groups will be relatively stronger which better
possess and employ the cultural tools needed to create both clear
distinction from and significant engagement and tension with other
relevant outgroups, short of becoming genuinely countercultural."[18]
Evangelical romance reading, then, becomes a way for women to assert their evangelical identities even as the novels provide them with
ways to improve and sustain their conservative piety. Second, the
genre, while upholding contemporary evangelical ideas about gender, transports these women from the periphery to the center of evangelical life. By foregrounding women's spiritual lives, as well as their
concerns about marriage and family, the genre validates women's
experience of evangelicalism and their roles as wives and mothers,
friends and leaders. In a subculture where men continue to dominate
religious leadership, the genre offers fictional worlds where women

occupy center stage. Third, evangelical romance novels elicit these women's devotion through their theological aesthetics. These love stories invoke larger narratives predicated on God's use of the arts, his acting in history, and his romance with humanity. In this grand sacred romance, problems occur and difficulties arise, but as in the evangelical romance formula itself, the happy ending remains assured. Through the novels, readers maintain a theology of hope as they realize the power of God's love amidst the struggles of daily life. For them, a relationship with God represents the ultimate happy ending, an ending that evangelical romances reflect and help them achieve.

The three components of this fictional devotion are interwoven throughout this study. In Chapter One, I explore the historical emergence of evangelical romance novels, which represents one byproduct of evangelicalism's long love affair with the media. As the genre has emerged it has built on the past and established boundaries within the present. These parameters, in turn, influence how some women come to read evangelical romances. Chapters Two and Three analyze how religious and gender socialization affect women's reading choices and narrative evaluations. Chapter Two examines the ways evangelical gender ideology shapes my consultants' views of leisure and fun, while Chapter Three reveals the diverse interpretive schemes and narrative expectations these women employ. In a general way, then, these chapters emphasize women's devotion *to* the novels, while the remaining chapters highlight women's devotion *through* the novels: my consultants are not only committed *to* the genre, but they view it as a means *through* which they can achieve spiritual sustenance. Accordingly, Chapter Four considers the consensus between authors and readers on framing evangelical romance as a ministry through which God works. The following two chapters examine how readers narrate this experience of the divine. Chapter Five investigates the ways that women's identification with and inspiration by the heroine elicits the reader's spiritual maintenance and growth. Relatedly, Chapter Six reveals the ways evangelical romances invoke larger historical and sacred narratives. The sense of divine immanence and intimacy, the experience of a romancing God, gives rise to a larger evangelical narrative that transcends the pages of a novel.

This study remains one of many possible stories about evangelical romances and their devotees. It is neither the first word nor the last. Others, I trust, will tell tales and spin stories that further illuminate this complicated nexus between religion and daily life, women and literature, evangelicalism and romance. Given this, I hope *Romancing God* will contribute to these ongoing conversations in helpful and provocative ways. Understanding the power of these women's narratives, how "storytelling is crucial to both religion and the human condition," can help us as scholars and as citizens to tell more complicated, textured stories.[19]

CHAPTER 1

*The History
of Evangelical
Romance*

"But your people, Jean?"

"My people all love you and honor you," said Jean, with shining eyes. "They think you are magnificent! They cannot say enough about you. But, Jasper, listen, if every one in this wide world were against you, even my dear people, I should marry you anyway and stay with you! I couldn't live any longer without you!"

He looked into her eyes, and he drank in her trust and loveliness, and beautiful self-surrender as if it had been some life-giving draught; then he laid his hand upon her hair and pressed her closer to him.

"Oh, you wonderful woman!" he said.

So when it was announced most informally that a wedding would take place no one was surprised. Indeed, Jean's girl friends had been embroidering and chattering away over wedding gifts for a week before it was whispered officially that they would be needed.

. . . It was sunset again, gold and ruby sunset, when they went home to his house, after the wedding supper. The sky was broad and clear translucent gold, with a deep heart of pure ruby blazing out behind the rose-wreathed cottage when Jean saw it for the first time. There alone at last together in their own home they stood with ruby and golden light from the sunset windows mingling with the soft flicker of fire light, and looked into each other's eyes and knew that their heavenly Father had been good to them.[1]

In the closing scenes of Grace Livingston Hill's *The Finding of Jasper Holt*, Jean and Jasper finally surmount the obstacles keeping them apart and marry, secure in their love and the love of God. Kept apart by Jasper's bad reputation (largely undeserved) and Jean's family, the couple reconciles in the last four pages of the novel. Having rescued Jean's nephew from being trampled by a bull, Jasper sustains life-threatening injuries, but redeems himself in the eyes of Hawk Valley and Jean's family. As Jean keeps vigil at his side, Jasper begins to recover and they affirm their love for each other. In the end, their faithfulness to God and each other is rewarded as they wed with the approval of family and friends. For Hill, a successful romance depended upon both hero and heroine having a personal relationship with God. Often viewed as a redeemed or baptized version of a secular romance novel, what is perhaps most surprising about this story is its original date of publication: 1915.

Finding Grace: Remembering the Evangelical Romance

Frequently overlooked in the annals of American Protestantism, the writing of Grace Livingston Hill (1865–1947) blends faith with fiction in ways that reflect aspects of a Protestant past while revealing glimpses of an evangelical future. Hill's prolific writing and sales success exemplify evangelicalism's long and intimate involvement with various media forms. Simultaneously, Hill's work itself represents the offspring of this involvement—evangelical romance novels—and provides one of the reasons for its emergence as a genre in the late 1970s and early 1980s. Her combination of religion and romance illustrates how evangelical women have navigated the contested terrain of popular culture as creators of products, arbiters of taste, and makers of meaning.

Economic necessity and evangelical desire transformed Grace Livingston Hill from amateur writer into professional scribe. She enjoyed writing from an early age and found inspiration in her aunt Isabella Alden, who authored the "Chautauqua Girls" series. However, it was the deaths of Hill's husband and father, combined with the need to support her family, that eventually provided the catalyst for her career. Having already authored poems, Sunday School lessons, and short stories, she then turned to her writing with clear goals for her literary future. Hill wanted to find an established company to market her work, an expert editor to improve her writing, and a respected publisher willing to include her salvation message. According to her grandson and biographer, Robert Munce, "At family prayer time each night, the family asked for guidance for Grace in her writing and in choosing a publisher." Their prayers were answered in the form of J. B. Lippincott who began publishing Hill's combination of "religious inspiration blended with boy-meets-girl romance" in 1908. Over the course of her life she wrote 105 novels, which are still published and read today. In 1946, interviewer James M. Neville wrote, "Mrs. Hill's romances hold to a steady 16,000 copies. Her reprint sales are more than double that number, leading the field, according to a recent survey, with a total of 76 titles to date. Each reprint sells 33,000 copies, or more. She publishes three novels a year." [2]

Like other Christian authors, Hill viewed her work as an extension of her religious life. She told Neville, "I have attempted to convey, in my own way, and through my novels, a message which God has given, and to convey that message with whatever abilities were given to me." Crediting God with both her talent and her message, Hill felt obliged to use her skills and employed the romance formula as her evangelistic medium. For Grace Livingston Hill and other conservative Protestants, a God-given gift should not be ignored or disregarded, a belief drawn from interpretation of biblical passages such as Matthew 25, the parable of the talents. In this tale, the master entrusts three of his servants with talents or coins. Honoring their master, the first servant turns his five talents into ten and the second makes two into four. Both servants cared for and built on their gifts and were rewarded accordingly by their master. In contrast, the fearful third servant buried his one talent in the ground and returned it alone to his master. He hid his talent and as a result earned his master's condemnation: expulsion to a place where tears fall and teeth gnash. Like the two loyal servants, Hill, a faithful steward of her abilities, honored her

God and honed her gift through writing religious romance. For her and other evangelicals, the medium, be it romance or radio, remained neutral. The message conveyed shaped the artistic form into a force for good or ill. Implicitly, this attitude, exemplified in Hill's interpretation of her vocation, exhibits a utilitarian attitude toward the arts— "the view," according to J. I. Packer, "that the value of anything is to be found in the extent to which it is useful and productive as a means to an end beyond itself." The end, for conservative Protestants, meant a Christian or more Christian life. Rejecting the notion of art for art's sake, novels like *The Finding of Jasper Holt* served not the gods of literature, but rather, in Hill's view, the God of life.[3]

Grace Livingston Hill's goals reflected common evangelical ideas about the utility of media and the arts. Conservative Protestants had long used existing cultural forms and invented new genres in their efforts to evangelize the world. Media analyst Quentin Schultze states that "from the founding of the Plymouth colonies to the present, the United States has been an incredible laboratory in which evangelicals have been able to experiment with every imaginable form and medium of communication" and historian Leonard Sweet documents "evangelical mastery of the media" from the Great Awakening to Oral Roberts. In the mid-eighteenth century evangelicals established the first American religious periodical, *Christian History*, and revivalist George Whitefield helped create the "evangelical newspaper and magazine." In the nineteenth century, technological developments made the printing of novels, newspapers, and magazines more affordable and accessible. With the increasing popularity of the printed word, evangelicals expanded their experiments with publishing. Recognizing the power of print while encountering texts that did not endorse their values or beliefs, evangelicals "entered the very market they feared, and in some ways they mastered it." Fighting fire with fire, evangelicals established publishing houses, tract societies (most notably the American Tract Society) and became "key developers of new technologies of print."[4]

Throughout this history, evangelistic intentions legitimized these media efforts and indeed became a criterion of evangelical aesthetic judgments. However, in the realm of fiction, literature and religion forged an uneasy alliance. Utilitarian concerns for evangelism governed evangelical literary efforts; nevertheless, even as they experimented with fiction's redemptive possibilities, such fiction remained suspect. Unlike other types of media, novels directly juxtaposed the truth of Christianity with the falsehood of fiction. Departing from truth, unleashing the imagination, promoting idleness (and perhaps even idolatry), fiction was an unwieldy weapon at best in the war for lost souls. Leland Ryken, evangelical literary critic, states: "Christians have traditionally found it difficult to grant integrity to this world of the imagination and have responded in two directions. One tendency has been to discredit imagination and fantasy as being untruthful, frivolous, a waste of time, dangerous escapism and something to be left behind in childhood. The other tendency has been to suppress the imaginary element in literature and to act as if literature is a direct replica of life, in effect abolishing the world of the imagination and merging it with empirical reality."[5] Fears about fiction also reflected doubts about women. Their domination of novel reading raised concerns about the "nature" of woman and her ability to handle imaginative material. In her study *The Woman Reader, 1837–1914*, Kate Flint recounts, "First, the argument ran, certain texts might corrupt her innocent mind, hence diminishing her value as a woman. Second, it was often put forward that she, as woman, was peculiarly susceptible to emotionally provocative material." Flint cites warnings written as far back as 1566 about women reading romance novels and demonstrates how "these Renaissance prescriptive remarks concerning women's reading were remarkably close, in outline, to ones which were repeated during the next three centuries."[6] Despite anxiety about both fiction and women, for some in the early and mid-nineteenth century, evangelistic potential trumped these fears. They began to claim imaginative literature as a vehicle for religious instruction and "the reading of novels crept gradually into the range of permitted activities because the content of many of them indicated the market could be made to respond to moral concerns."[7]

This acceptance occurred, in part, through the work of female authors, including Susan Warner, Harriet Beecher Stowe, and E. D. E. N. Southworth. Many scholars have excavated the importance of this literature. Studies range from examining how these nineteenth-century authors and characters subverted gender roles to analyses of the opposition between women's "sentimental" fiction and men's "literary" fiction. Fewer treatments explore the relationship between this literature and its contemporary counterparts, a relationship that constitutes an important element in the emergence of evangelical romance novels. Drawing on domestic ideology, which touted the power of women's pious influence in the home and in the world, and an evangelical aesthetic, which legitimated fiction through its faith-based message, nineteenth-century women like Stowe and Warner forged simultaneous literary careers and Christian ministries. They wrote, according to literary scholar Jane Tompkins, "for edification's sake," and "the highest function of any art, for Warner as for most of her contemporaries, was the bringing of souls to Christ." To achieve this, they composed sentimental novels for and about women that celebrated conservative Protestant piety as well as love and the home. As Mary Kelly notes of the authors and their subsequent work, "their perspective was private and familial, their allegiance was to the domestic sphere," and they were, Nina Baym adds, "profoundly oriented toward women."[8] While romance did not always drive these nineteenth-century plots, it often remained an integral part of the story. In *Uncle Tom's Cabin*, Stowe narrates the love between George and Eliza and their eventual triumph in establishing a free Christian family. *The Minister's Wooing* even more explicitly celebrates romantic love with the story of James and Mary, and Susan Warner's best-selling *Wide, Wide World* emphasizes Ellen's love with John as well as her growth in Christianity.[9]

Even as sentimental fiction declined in popularity in the late nineteenth century, Hill built on this foundation as she constructed her vision of the Christian romance. Indeed both evangelical and secular romances trace their lineage back to these nineteenth-century novels. In *Fantasy and Reconciliation*, Kay Mussell proposes that "today, romance formulas differ from their eighteenth- and nineteenth-century predecessors because each era finds its own models for the familiar tale; and yet the fictional world they describe remains remarkably unchanged over time." The works of each "era," past and present, center around "the course and culmination of one woman's love story" or, as another scholar put it, "the formation and assertion of feminine ego."[10] However, only Grace Livingston Hill and the subsequent evangelical romance preserved the nineteenth-century emphasis on God and Protestant faith. Like those from earlier novels, Hill's heroines radiate evangelical purity and piety—the hallmarks of domestic ideology—but romance drives the plot as her heroes respond immediately to this feminine influence. For example, upon first seeing Jean, in *The Finding of Jasper Holt*, Jasper thinks: "She was the sudden startling revelation of some pure dream of his childhood, the reality of which he had come to doubt." The description continues, "Her face was wonderfully pure, free from self-consciousness and pride, yet she looked as if she knew her own mind and could stand like a rock for a principle." This purity and steadfastness inspires Jasper Holt to convert and live a life worthy of Jean's love.[11]

At the same time that Hill drew on the past to augment her literary success, conservative Protestantism looked to an uncertain future. Foes, in the form of "higher criticism" and Darwinism, forced evangelicals to define and defend the fundamentals of their faith. Gender norms and popular culture provided the battlegrounds for this emerging conflict. Even as these "militantly anti-modernist Protestant evangelicals"—to quote historian George Marsden—upheld Victorian gender ideology, they sought to diminish women's power in the church and discredit the dominance of their emotional piety. In this war with modernism, the emerging voice of fundamentalists "promoted a manly Christianity to replace the perspective and practices of feminized evangelical Protestantism." Armed with the doctrines of biblical inerrancy and premillennial dispensationalism, conservative Protestants shifted the focus of faith from women to men, and from heart to head. Deeming women's faith too emotional and unintellectual, this militant and manly Christianity sought respectability even as it retreated from previous ways of engaging with "the world."[12]

After 1925, as many scholars have documented, the once prominent and respected evangelicals became the parochial and ridiculed fundamentalists. They built their own institutions—publishing houses, Bible institutes, and Christian colleges—and created, according to Joel Carpenter, "a distinct religious movement," one concerned about women and wary of the arts. "Fundamentalists of the first half of our century," argues Roger Lundin, "wrote almost no essays of significance on the arts. When the arts are mentioned in fundamentalist works, either their value or their use is called into question."[13] During this period of retreat and regrouping, the "material Christianity" so pervasive in the previous century became a liability. Colleen McDannell writes, "What in the nineteenth century was considered tasteful and pious, in the twentieth came to be seen as tacky and irreligious." Associated with women, owning Christian things signaled a believer's weakness, and perhaps even her worldliness.[14] Advocating "muscular Christianity" and a "Christ against culture" position, fundamentalists became increasingly suspicious of women, fiction, and the arts in general. Grace Livingston Hill, however, while remaining a committed conservative Protestant, continued to write her brand of fiction. Evangelistic goals and her call from God superseded fundamentalist fears.

Hill honed the evangelical romance formula, boy plus girl plus conservative Protestant Christianity equals a happy marriage, and navigated her way through the less-than-hospitable waters of the era. In writing salvation into her stories, Hill's work complied with the demands for evangelism. However, her novels contained elements of the formulaic feminized faith that made fundamentalists afraid for their masculinity and modernists anxious for the arts. Her emphasis on women's faith challenged the rise of a more manly Protestantism. The power of pure heroines, like Jean, over less pious heroes continued the nineteenth-century tradition of elevating women's spiritual status over that of men. At the same time, Hill's formulaic style defied modernist concerns. In an artistic world where novelty, intellect, and realism increasingly guided aesthetic taste, Hill's novels constituted an unhealthy diet of predictable plots and happy endings. Invariably Hill's novels end happily with the couple, like Jasper and Jean, united in faith and matrimony. As one woman described it, "When I found the stories, in the early 60s, I thought them terribly quaint; to the modern reader they may seem hopelessly so. Still, there's something about them." Hill's literary critics were not so impressed. Quaint for some readers meant escapist and unrealistic for others. Too sentimental, too predictable, and too saccharine, Hill's work embodied the "kitsch" of womanly Protestantism, in contrast to the "art" of manly Christianity.[15]

In the 1940s, during the twilight of Hill's career, fundamentalism became increasingly divided over its rigid separatism from the wider culture, a position that novels like *The Finding of Jasper Holt* defied. A more moderate evangelical leadership, including Harold Ockenga, Carl Henry, and Billy Graham, emerged with a vision of Christianity as "engaged orthodoxy." Sociologist Christian Smith describes these new leaders thus: "In keeping with their nineteenth-century Protestant heritage, they were fully committed to maintaining and promoting confidently traditional, orthodox Protestant theology and belief, while at the same time becoming confidently and proactively engaged in the intellectual, cultural, social, and political life of the nation."[16] With the formation of the National Association of Evangelicals in 1942, the establishment of Fuller Theological Seminary in 1947, and the increasing popularity of Billy Graham, these new evangelicals created an infrastructure to advance their cause—a cause that Hill's work had always embodied. The new generation of leaders "called for a holistic gospel that would make a difference in every realm of one's life" and they used radio, television, and the book to do it.[17]

In 1950, these new evangelicals took a step toward the creation of this gospel and established the Christian Booksellers Association (CBA) as a "trade association for anyone selling Christian literature."[18] Building on postwar economic growth and the evangelical tradition of media usage, CBA supported the "holistic gospel" through the marketing of Christian books as well as other religious products. Just as their nineteenth-century predecessors used technology to advance the gospel, CBA provided an organizational resource for producers and retailers to do the same. As a result, many publishers today belong to CBA and view their products as a ministry that generates profits to fund yet other evangelistic and devotional endeavors. For example, Bethany House, which emerged in 1956 from Bethany Fellowship International (a ministry-training and missionary-sending agency), declares that their goal "is to help Christians apply biblical truth in all areas of life—whether through a well-told story, a challenging devotional, or the message of an illustrated children's book." The president and CEO of prominent Christian publisher Zondervan (established in 1931 and now a division of HarperCollins) frames the company as a provider of "resources for people of every age and in every stage of life as they seek a richer, more fervent, more enlightened relationship with Jesus Christ."[19]

Despite evangelicalism's newfound theological and entrepreneurial commitment to the "holistic gospel," Hill's novels remained one of the only sources of Christian romance during this time. However, the broader market for religious books experienced growth and these books sold well in the 1940s. One industry observer reported, "Ink has been a favorite and powerful weapon of religion through the centuries. Ever since the first printing of Gutenberg's Bible, religion and the printing press have been inseparable allies. That historic alliance has never been more productive than during the year 1949, and, indeed, during the decade just closed." This success continued in 1950s with Norman Vincent Peale's *The Power of Positive Thinking* and Billy Graham's *Peace with God*, but fiction remained secondary and parochial. In contrast to Grace Livingston Hill's focus on the laity and love, many of the religious novels of the 1950s revolved around ministers and Bible stories. For example, *The Brand New Parson* by Sara Jenkins tells "the story of a young preacher," Victor MacClure's *A Certain Woman* revolves around Mary of Bethany, and Faith Baldwin's *The Whole Armor* chronicles a young pastor's first year of ministry.[20] Throughout the 1950s and 1960s, religious books continued to meet with success, but during this time Catherine Marshall was one of the few to join Grace Livingston Hill in the field of evangelical romance.[21]

Catherine Marshall (1915–83) had successfully published her late husband's sermons in *A Man Called Peter* and had published some other nonfiction titles as well before McGraw Hill issued her novel *Christy* in 1967. The book chronicles the love story of Christy Huddleston, a young woman called by God to teach school in the Appalachian Mountains of North Carolina. In this isolated mountain area, Christy encounters superstition, hostility, and two handsome men. She endures the hardship of the mountains, grows in her faith, and eventually chooses the fiery Doctor MacNeill over minister David Grantland. This combination of religion and romance, like Hill's, met with success. By December 1967, *Christy* occupied third place on the bestseller list with 121,000 copies in print.[22]

Emerging Love: Reclaiming the Evangelical Romance

Despite the reprinting of Hill's novels and *Christy*'s popularity, romance, and fiction as a whole, remained a small segment of the Christian bookselling industry. The rhetoric of "engaged orthodoxy" lauded by this new brand of conservative Protestantism would seemingly embrace inspirational romance, but in reality many evangelicals remained suspicious of fictional formulas and their female authors and fans. Author Carol Gift Page recalls of the mid-1970s, "I knew the Lord had called me to write Christian fiction, but there were no Christian novels, there were virtually no publishers, no Christian publishers that were publishing fiction."[23] Not until later in the decade did this begin to change.

In the late 1970s, evangelical publishing houses established in the 1950s and 1960s, including Bethany House and Tyndale, began to grow and gain success in selling the holistic gospel. For example, Tyndale's publication of *The Living Bible* reaped huge sales; by 1978, it had sold over twenty-three million copies, while Bethany's *The Christian Family* sold a modest one million.[24] An increase in the number of Christian bookstores supported this growth. In the late 1970s, the number of religious bookstores rose to 2,751 (by 1985, they totaled 4,142, and by the mid-1990s, the number leveled around 4,000).[25] The

1970s also saw the unprecedented success of six evangelical books. John P. Ferré reports that "each sold over two million copies, one of each to at least every one hundred Americans. Those remarkable best sellers were *Prison to Praise* and *Power in Praise* by Merlin Carothers, *The Late Great Planet Earth* and *Satan is Alive and Well on Planet Earth* by Hal Lindsey, *Angels* by Billy Graham, and *Joni* by Joni Earekson." The success of these entrepreneurial endeavors reflected a desire to infuse every part of one's life with religious meaning. As scholar Colleen McDannell explains, "Christian retailing is possible because consumers refuse to separate the sacred from the profane, the extraordinary from the ordinary, the pious from the trivial. For these consumers, Christianity is intimately bound up in the day-to-day life of the family and its goods."[26] However, while the above list contains no fiction titles and only one female author, this "boom in evangelical book publishing" provided an opportunity for change. It paved the way for new evangelistic and entrepreneurial endeavors, in areas as diverse as bumper stickers, rock music, and love stories.

The 1970s also witnessed a rise in the popularity of secular romance novels and forced publishers (both secular and Christian) to recognize women as powerful consumers. In 1972, Avon Books published *The Flame and the Flower*, by Kathleen Woodiwiss, and changed the face of the romance industry. Janice Radway reports that "the house's extraordinary success with Woodiwiss's novel soon caused industrywide reconsideration of the possibilities of paperback originals as potential bestsellers." Rather than a gothic romance where the heroine can never quite be sure if her protagonist is hero or villain, Woodiwiss wrote an epic historical romance of the tumultuous love between Heather and Brandon. Full of unwitting misunderstandings, murderous intrigue, and love scenes, her book sparked romance sales and more than previous romances opened the door to graphic sexuality.[27]

It was during this time that evangelical Janette Oke moved from reader to writer. At the age of forty-two, after much prayer and with four teenagers in the house, she transformed her lifelong love of writing into a career. She describes the transition this way: "There wasn't much being done in fiction in the Christian market at all. In fact, this was one of the things that sort of spurred me on. I was a reader of fiction, and I really wasn't finding anything to read on the secular shelves." In response, she wrote *Love Comes Softly*. Always interested in the settlement of the West and impressed by the "deep religious faith" of its early settlers, Oke wove this history into the novel. Like Grace Livingston Hill, she combined evangelical Christianity, the Western prairie, and a romantic plot. She wrote of the love between Marty and Clark, a story that contained an evangelical message as faithful Christian Clark shared the gospel with and prayed for his wife, heroine Marty. Her eventual conversion demonstrates the steps to salvation and fulfills, like Hill's earlier work, evangelical aesthetic demands for witnessing. In the preface, Oke writes, "I have shared my thoughts with you in the hope that you will feel inspired to reach out to the all-knowing God." [28]

Initially wanting to market the novel beyond the Christian subculture, Oke sent it to Bantam Books, who promptly returned it. Not deterred, Oke decided to learn more about publishers and publishing. During this period, she recounts, "One day in my devotional time I drew a prayer promise from a little promise box, asking the Lord for direction, and the verse was a very common verse that I had learned as a child. But on the flip side was a little four-line poem, and in the middle of that poem was the word fellowship, but the strange thing about it was that it was capitalized." Unable to understand why it was capitalized in the middle of a sentence, Oke searched for publishing houses with the name fellowship. She found Bethany Fellowship (later Bethany House Publishers) and editor Carol Johnson. [29]

Oke attributes her success to God, an important belief to understand; however, historical developments also explain why Bethany House was willing to take a chance on her prairie romance manuscript. The long history of evangelical media usage, its unprecedented achievements in the 1970s, and the rising popularity of secular romances all contributed to Oke's success. *Love Comes Softly* reflects the heritage of sentimental fiction, the legacy of Hill's religious romance, and the commitment of evangelicals to using media for ministerial

LOVE
COMES
SOFTLY

JANETTE OKE

A tragic accident, a grief-stricken
young widow, a lonely father
and child—a tender story
of two hearts
broken by
despair finding
wholeness
through
patience,
loyalty,
and faith
in God.

Cover of *Love Comes Softly* (1979), by Janette Oke. Reprinted by
permission of Bethany House, a division of Baker Publishing Group.

purposes. In addition, Oke's evangelical romance offered publishers a way to build on the existing sales boom, provided readers with an alternative to increasingly sexual secular romances, and maintained the subcultural boundaries surrounding evangelicalism. Bethany's Carol Johnson recalled, "Our first fiction piece that really got attention was Janette Oke's *Love Comes Softly*, which we published in 1979. When it came to us, we were not seeing much happening in Christian fiction in the CBA market. Some Grace Livingston Hills had been around for awhile, and some Catherine Marshalls." With the house's literary efforts dominated by male authors and theological topics, Oke relates that editors Carol Johnson and Jean Mikkelson "had to do a real sell job to get the other members of the committee, which were basically men, to agree to give this book a try." She continues, "It was not the type of thing they had been doing at all, and at that point, no one knew if Christian fiction would sell well." It did. To date, Oke has written over two dozen books and sold over sixteen million copies. Just as Kathleen Woodiwiss revolutionized the secular romance novel industry, Janette Oke transformed the landscape of Christian fiction as she inaugurated the contemporary form of evangelical romance.[30]

In many ways Oke's prairie romances echo Grace Livingston Hill's earlier stories with their handsome heroes, pious but struggling heroines, and happy endings, but unlike Hill, Oke met with a success and popularity that paved the way for other women to enter evangelical romance writing. The difference, it seems, between these two women's impact is time. Hill wrote her novels espousing conservative Protestantism while fundamentalist leaders grappled with the arts and struggled to rebuild their identity. She penned her stories without the benefit of a religious subculture theologically or institutionally committed to her vision. In contrast, the holistic gospel promulgated in the late 1940s had met with unprecedented success by the late 1970s when Oke went to market her manuscript. Not only was the movement growing, but its rising political power and economic potential harked back to the prefundamentalist days of public prominence. These achievements fueled further endeavors in popular culture and growing confidence in its redemptive potential. Consequently, Oke, unlike Hill, found the theological and practical support that helped make her work successful and allowed other women to follow in her footsteps.

In the wake of Oke's success, other publishers began to venture into evangelical romance and target female readers. Bethany House continued to publish Oke's novels, as well as edited versions of George MacDonald's historical romances, including *The Baronet's Song* in 1983. In 1985, Harvest House began publishing the prairie romances of June Masters Bacher, and Victor published George MacDonald's *The Vicar's Daughter*, "edited for today's reader."[31] However, in 1984 Zondervan took the lead with the launch of their Serenade romance line. Featuring both contemporary and historical novels (in the Serenade/Serenata series and the Serenade/Saga series, respectively), Zondervan set out to publish "romance with a difference." Emphasizing the exotic locales and glamour of "Serenatas" and the evangelical simplicity and courage in "Sagas," Zondervan assured publishers and readers of their "solid Christian standards" and how the novels "radiate the love of God . . . and reveal the harmony of lives united in Him." As seen in their advertisements, Zondervan touted their reasonable prices, attractive characters, and many titles.[32] Other publishers in the late 1980s and into the 1990s followed this pattern and established their own evangelical romance lines—Palisades by Multnomah, HeartQuest by Tyndale, and Heartsong by Barbour.

As these companies embraced the genre and met with success, they carefully integrated inspirational fiction into their corporate and Christian publishing visions. Publishers' statements articulate a rationale for evangelical romance and echo the evangelistic utilitarianism of the past. For example, Tyndale House is animated by a corporate aim "to minister to the spiritual needs of people, primarily through literature consistent with biblical principles." However, their justification of evangelical romance goes into more elaborate detail as it combines specific views about women, evangelization, and fiction. According to their Web site, "the form [of romance] has several characteristics that make it a natural vehicle for conveying Christian

truths and ministering to women readers. Women are relationship-oriented, and romance novels are about relationships." The rationale also lauds the optimism of romance novels and explains that "the romance novel with a Christian foundation and worldview provides a wonderful opportunity for sharing biblical truths about love (both human and divine), relationships, family, and the necessity for a person to have a relationship with God through Jesus Christ." Rather than merely baptizing secular romance novels, Tyndale desires to infuse their books with "clear Christian content that will minister to [readers] in a specific way."[33] Setting themselves apart from the competition and drawing on a heritage of evangelistic media usage, as well as Hill's earlier endeavors and Oke's more recent efforts, Tyndale and other houses successfully tapped this emerging market—evangelical women who read romantic fiction and buy Christian products.

In the world of evangelical popular culture, women wield the almighty dollar. They constitute the overwhelming majority of Christian bookstore consumers. John P. Ferré reports, "The typical reader is a married evangelical woman, 25–49, who lives in the Sun Belt from California to Georgia." Colleen McDannell's statistics on Christian retailing yield similar demographic data. Women between ages twenty-five and fifty-four comprised 75 percent of Christian bookstore customers. In addition, these women are usually white, married, and attend church at least once a week; half of them had an income between $20,000 and $40,000. For these women, Christian products, including evangelical romance novels, provide a way to bolster their faith, a way to cultivate Christianity in all areas of their lives. Historian Michael Hamilton's breakdown of evangelical spending further demonstrates women's commitment to the "holistic gospel." He found that "for every dollar evangelicals spend on political organizations, they spend almost $12 on foreign missions and international relief and development; they spend another $13 in evangelical book and music stores; they spend almost $25 on evangelical higher education; and they spend almost $31 on private elementary and secondary schools."[34] Hamilton's statistics show just how much of evangelicals' funds go toward instilling faith in one's family. Through products and schooling, parents hope to enhance their own beliefs and pass them on to their children.

As the religious bestseller lists attest, conservative Protestant women read and evangelical romances sell. In March 1987, despite competition from popular male authors such as James Dobson, C. S. Lewis, and Charles Swindoll, Janette Oke's *When Hope Springs New* occupied first place among paperback religious bestsellers. Similarly, in 1989, Janette Oke occupied second and fifth place with her novels *Love Takes Wing* and *Winter Is Not Forever*. The genre's success continued in the 1990s. The religious book publishing industry saw a 6.3 percent increase in sales between 1987 and 1996, a 4 percent increase between 1997 and 1998, and another 3.3 percent increase in 1999.[35] While the growth rate may have slowed during the 1990s, the industry continues to do well. In 1994, coinciding with the advent of the *Christy* television series, consumers purchased over a million copies of the reprinted novel. In 1995, Oke's *A Gown of Spanish Lace* sold over 100,000 copies; a year later sales of her *Drums of Change* totaled over 200,000, and *Return to Harmony*, co-authored with T. David Bunn, sold more than 180,000 copies. In 1996 Lori Wick also reached a measure of popularity as readers bought over 100,000 copies of *Where the Wild Rose Blooms* and 80,000 copies of *Whispers of Moonlight*.[36] In 1997 Beverly Lewis joined Oke and Wick at the top of evangelical romance sales with *The Shunning* (over 100,000 copies sold). *The Confession*, also by Lewis, sold in excess of 75,000 the same year, and another 178,000 in 1998, a number matched by her novel *The Reckoning*. 1997 also saw the success of Francine Rivers's *Redeeming Love*, as readers purchased more than 55,000 copies. And in 1999, two of Lori Wick's novels, *Princess* and *Every Little Thing About You*, passed the 100,000 mark. Furthermore, Janette Oke, Beverly Lewis, and Lori Wick all had titles among the top ten best-selling Christian fiction books of 2000.[37]

Negotiating Faith: Reexamining the Evangelical Romance

Despite the popularity of evangelical romances, in many ways they remain, like Hill's earlier work, overlooked or invisible in the evangelical subculture. For example, an examination of *Christianity Today* reveals numerous articles relevant to evangelical women's lives, including marriage, abortion, genetics, and homosexuality, but few treatments, other than brief reviews, of evangelical romance. Even though Oke had been published for over ten years, a 1991 review of her novel *A Woman Named Damaris* seemed unfamiliar with and uncertain about her work. Struggling to categorize the novel, the reviewer calls it "a sort of woman's western" and spells Oke's first name incorrectly (Janet instead of Janette). Further, in an April 2002 article on the success of evangelical publishing, entitled "No Longer Left Behind," the genre is virtually absent. Oke's work garners only one paragraph in an eight-page spread. Overshadowed by the male-authored "Left Behind" series, as well as the works of Frank Peretti and Bruce Wilkinson, female authors and evangelical romances barely merit a mention. The genre receives equally little attention in the evangelical periodical *Today's Christian Woman*. Despite numerous articles on sex and marriage, including "He's Lost that Lovin' Feeling" and "Five Questions Women Ask About Sex," there is scant mention of evangelical romance novels.[38]

In addition to enduring industry silence, the genre also faces a stigma. Evangelical romance authors have expressed their frustration with how other conservative Protestants view their literary endeavors. One author simply states, "Romance is just looked down on." Another refers to it as the "stepchild" of Christian fiction, and Janette Oke relates, "I think there are a number who still feel that what we should be spending our time reading is nonfiction, self-help, and devotional study books." Similarly, when asked what she would change about the Christian romance-publishing industry, author Robin Jones Gunn answered: "the perception of the genre." She continued, "We got mail, verses quoted at us, what a degradation we were to the industry." This stigma also revealed itself as she led a CBA workshop featuring a panel of evangelical romance authors. According to Gunn, one workshop participant asked author Lori Wick why she was on the panel, implying that her work was not romance, that it was "too good for that." Although Wick replied, "My books are romances, they're love stories," the participant responded to the effect of, "No, we highly value you, and we wouldn't lower you to that genre."[39]

Despite the novels' popularity and their embodiment of the holistic gospel, the genre remains suspect, its authors ignored, and its readers absent. Why have industry observers focused on the success of "Left Behind," rather than *Love Comes Softly*? Why is the genre ignored in *Today's Christian Woman*, and why must its authors defend their vocation? A quick answer might simply invoke the gender hierarchy that pervades evangelicalism. Whether in charge of the pulpit or the pen, men continue to occupy the visible and audible leadership roles in the subculture. As a result, a genre dominated by women as authors and readers remains unnoticed and seemingly unimportant. While compelling on one level, this explanation obscures the complicated ways that art, theology, and gender combine to make the genre at once successful and suspect.

Uncertainties about the arts as a whole do not account for the suspicions facing the genre, as evangelicals — from their mid-century emergence as a subculture — have used the Bible to establish a positive view of the arts. Prominent evangelicals, including Frank Gaebelein and Francis Schaeffer, established a theology of the arts that continues to guide the movement today. The arts, they argued, are biblical. From the beginning of the Bible, God showed himself to be a creator. God made the world and it was good, beautiful, and functional.[40] Further, humanity, as a part of creation and a reflection of God, shares in this ability. Gaebelein wrote, "Art belongs to the only creature made in the image of God, the only creature to whom is given in a limited but real extent the gift of creativity, even though the gift is marred in fallen human nature." He continued, "The image of God in us has its 'creative' or 'making' aspect."[41] These theologians argued that a doctrine of stewardship also justifies artistic endeavors. The idea of stewardship — caring for and cultivating that which one has been given — governs a believer's talents and time. As a result, *imago dei* demands the nurture and use of one's gifts, whether preaching sermons or writing poetry, just as the faithful servants of Matthew 25 multiplied their talents. Further, recognizing that involvement with the arts generally accompanies the presence of free time, evangelicals insisted upon the goodness of leisure and the necessity of using it wisely. In this, they again appealed to Genesis, specifically to God's rest during the seventh day. According to Leland Ryken, "God's rest after creation sanctified the aesthetic acts of celebration and enjoyment." However, given humanity's fallen state, faithful Christians need to use their time and talents wisely: "Always there goes with stewardship the inevitability of finally giving an account of what has been committed to us and being judged on how we have used it." [42] This mandate demands, according to these evangelical upholders of the arts, the best of one's self. "The compelling motive for Christian action in the field of aesthetics lies in the nature of God. Christians are obligated to excellence because God himself is supremely excellent." [43]

Evangelical excellence, however, is not an uncontested terrain. While many conservative Protestants revel in the plethora of products that affirm or expand their faith, others within the subculture find it a morass of mediocrity. Franky Schaeffer, in *Addicted to Mediocrity*, laments the present state of evangelical popular culture and indicts its betrayal of Christian obligations to excellence and stewardship. He writes, "One could sum it up by saying that the modern Christian world and what is known as evangelicalism in general is marked, in the area of arts and cultural endeavor, by one outstanding feature, and that is its addiction to mediocrity." He continues, "The price is the ludicrous defacing of God's image before the world. The price is abusing and manipulating God-given talents by turning them into mere useful tools." Similarly, Frank Gaebelein asked, "Where are the first-rate Christian novels and poems?" He continued, "If there is, as we have seen, tension between many evangelicals and the aesthetic aspect of life, the reason lies in a contented ignorance of much that is aesthetically worthy and satisfaction with the mediocre because it is familiar." [44] According to these standards, contemporary evangelical romance novels represent mediocre literature, one more example of evangelicalism's artistic weaknesses.

For these aestheticians, artistic failures point to even more seri-ous spiritual flaws. Whether criticizing "second-rate" rock and roll or "formulaic" romantic fiction, evangelical theologians of the arts claim that these endeavors not only deny God's excellence, but also God's truth. First, they argue, "All truth is God's truth," and its mani-festations may not always occur through Christians and their artis-tic endeavors. Accordingly, the so-called evangelical ghetto, the ten-dency to partake only of the subculture's products, at least implicitly denies the universality of God's truth and the integrity of God's reve-lation: "There is no Christian world, no secular world," writes Franky Schaeffer, "these are just words. There is only one world—the world God made."[45] Second, evangelical critics argue that substandard art is inherently a lie. Not only does mediocrity inhibit excellence, but it also falsifies and misrepresents reality. "Art that distorts the truth is no more pleasing to God than any other kind of untruth," Gaebelein argued. He went on to state, "We must see the real distinction is be-tween the true and the false, which means in the arts the distinction between what has integrity and so speaks truly and what is preten-tious or sentimental, vulgar or shoddy, and thus is false."[46]

For critics, evangelical or otherwise, the combination of a roman-tic formula and an optimistic faith mean sentimentality, a "perverse perfection" that denies the realities and complexities of life. At best, this combination exhibits a lack of aesthetic taste; at worst it repre-sents a failure of moral judgment. In his article "On Kitsch and Senti-mentality" Robert Solomon explores the relationship between these two concepts and cites six main criticisms of sentimental kitsch. According to Solomon, four of the six indictments revolve around emotion, ranging from claims that sentimental kitsch manipulates emotions to charges that it provokes excessive, false, and easy emo-tions. Criticisms five and six charge that sentimental kitsch is "self-indulgent and interferes with appropriate behavior" and that it "dis-torts our perceptions and interferes with rational thought and an adequate understanding of the world."[47] In this view, popular culture becomes an agent of pacification and oppression.

Previous studies of the romance novel reveal traces of these criticisms. On an aesthetic level, scholars have never lauded the literary excellence of contemporary romance novels, and on a practical level, many have argued that they may inhibit women's power and prevent social change. For example, Kay Mussell maintains that through reading romance novels women "escape from powerlessness, from meaninglessness, and from lack of self-esteem and identity." Their escape, however, is limited: "Romance novels work as a conservative force, palliating and ameliorating the effects of chaos and change by portraying traditional modes of being and aspiration as more fulfilling and exciting than they may seem in reality." Similarly, Tania Modleski writes, "Women escape, disappear into the world of Harlequin Romances, which, like the real one, insists upon and rewards feminine selflessness." And early in her monograph, Modleski states, "In exploring female romantic fantasies, I want to look at the varied and complex strategies women use to adapt to circumscribed lives and to convince themselves that limitations are really opportunities."[48] Further, in *Reading the Romance*, Janice Radway gives a careful and balanced interpretation of romance reading, but concludes that "the women who seek out ideal novels in order to construct such a vision again and again are reading not out of contentment but out of dissatisfaction, longing, and protest." She goes on to suggest that reading itself "may be cathartic" but "it is tempting to suggest that romantic fiction must be an active agent in the maintenance of the ideological status quo because it ultimately reconciles women to patriarchal society and reintegrates them with its institutions."[49]

These criticisms and explanations illuminate one dimension of the complicated story that is evangelical romance. The novels do not exhibit literary excellence, embrace a feminist politics, or encourage a liberal faith. Rather, they rely on formulaic plots, reaffirm heterosexual marriage, and revere evangelical piety. However, it is the unique combination of these very components that sets the genre apart within evangelicalism (and from other types of romance) and demands our attention. In contrast to other more unisex products, such as contemporary Christian music or children's Christian videos, and unlike the religio-artistic ideals proposed by men like Frank Gaebelein, the evangelical romance offers a distinctly female devotion in both its form and its faith. Not only is the genre written and read by women, but it also utilizes a fictional formula and a sentimental piety designated as feminine. It is this combination that makes the novels problematic for evangelical aestheticians and some academics while simultaneously popular with many evangelical women.

The stories, like their nineteenth-century predecessors and Hill's transitional endeavors, focus on women's lives and experiences. They foreground the ideals and institutions that, while contested, continue to shape the lives of American evangelical women: romantic love, heterosexual marriage, and conservative piety. While perhaps predictable in their plots and pedestrian in their execution, the novels appeal to women by affirming the reality of heterosexual love and happy endings. Overlaying this plot with sentimental piety further encodes these narratives as feminine. Just as the love story ends happily, so too does the religious plot end triumphantly. Sinful heroes convert, bitter heroines forgive, and struggling Christians succeed. Erling Jorstad describes the pattern this way: "The key virtue seems to be patience with the understanding through religious faith that all things will work to the good of those who follow God's way for them." [50] In effect, the novels apply Romans 8:28—"And we know that in all things God works for the good of those who love him"—to the romantic and religious lives of evangelical women. The genre upholds the belief that in the end everything will work out.

Throughout the history of these combinations of Christianity and romance, a religio-romantic happy ending has remained constant. For example, in nineteenth-century sentimental novels, the heroine has "the guarantee that God will provide her with inner strength if she turns to him." Similarly, when questioned about her ever-optimistic endings, Grace Livingston Hill replied, "I feel that there is enough sadness in the world. So I try to end all of my books as beautifully as possible, since that is God's way—and the best way." [51] Even as Hill acknowledged the reality of sorrow, and experienced it in her own life with her first husband's death and her second husband's desertion, she wrote novels that celebrated temporal happiness and an eternal hope. Such a vision likewise permeates Janette Oke's *Love Comes Softly*. Not only does Marty convert, but together, Marty and Clark rear their family in the faith and see their children find Christian spouses —a journey readers can follow in subsequent volumes in the series, including *Love's Long Journey* and *Love's Unending Legacy*. For these authors, the very aesthetic condemned by critics is the one they feel called by God to convey.

The theology of "all things work for good" conveyed through romantic fiction may also explain, in part, why some women do not read the novels. For some evangelical women, the novels simply do not appeal to them artistically or theologically. It seems a divide exists between those who read romance novels and those who do not. As secular romance author Jayne Ann Krentz writes, "No one who reads or writes romance expects to be able to teach critics to appreciate the novels. As any romance reader or writer will tell you, a reader either enjoys the novels or she does not." [52] In addition, the genre's commitment to religio-romantic triumph may explain, in part, the racial divide that characterizes the genre's authorship and readership. Evangelical romance, as well as evangelical popular culture as a whole, is predominantly white. Not surprisingly then, many of the African American churches I called and African American women I talked with did not know that evangelical romances existed. However, for many of those African American women who do frequent the Christian bookstore, the genre's emphasis on success and triumph, as well as its covers featuring white heroes and heroines, may simply be too unrealistic, too divergent from their experiences. [53]

Some have never heard of evangelical romance, some criticize it, while others refuse to read it. In light of these varied responses and the stigma characterizing the genre, the question remains: why do some evangelical women choose to read these novels? The following chapters address this question as they explore the complicated rationale for my consultants' fictional devotion. Rather than condemn the novels for their literary weaknesses or feminist failings, this study examines how and why women read evangelical romance novels. Taking their answers to these questions seriously illuminates not only the complex relationship between reader and text but also how these women negotiate everyday evangelical life through the act of reading.

The days managed to crawl by, one by one. Soon Missie was down to day eighteen. Her eyes kept searching the distant hills. She hoped that by some miracle Willie would complete his tasks in less time than antici- pated and be home early.

One afternoon as Missie's eyes again swept over the hills visible through her window, she was surprised to see a lone rider heading directly toward the house.

Who could that be? she puzzled. It's sure not Clem or Sandy. As the rider neared the house, Missie let out a gasp of unbelief.

"It's a woman!" she exclaimed aloud, bursting through the door and waking small Nathan with her sharp cry and rush of activity. Tears ran down Missie's cheeks as she ran toward the rider. She hadn't realized just how starved she was for the company of a woman. Oh, to talk, to laugh, to visit, to sip tea—oh the joy of it.

Missie's visitor was hardly more than a girl, with dusky skin, long, loose-flowing dark hair, and black eyes. Her full lips suggested that they liked to laugh. Missie felt drawn to her new friend immediately.

"Oh," she cried, "I'm so glad to see you." She rushed forward and threw her arms around the girl, laughing and crying at the same time. The stranger responded and Missie received a warm hug in return.[1]

Shortly after this greeting, Missie discovered that her new friend, Maria, spoke Spanish, not English. Despite the language barrier, during their first visit the two women shared tea, learned each other's names, and bonded over Missie's son Nathan. Missie and Maria also prayed together before they parted. Kneeling side by side, Missie thanked God for the gift of friendship, voiced her hopes for another visit, and shared her desire to learn Maria's language. After Missie's petition, Maria prayed in Spanish for Missie and Nathan (the only words Missie recognized) and then departed. As she left, Missie felt reassured that "surely God himself had sent Maria."[2] For Missie, who was isolated on the barren Western prairie, another woman's friendship eased her loneliness as it afforded a measure of forgetfulness and assurance of God's care.

Forgetfulness, friendship, and God: a powerful combination not only for Missie, but also for the women I interviewed. The decision to read, most simply, reflects a desire for the combination of fun and forgetfulness embodied in popular culture entertainment. In this bazaar featuring film, television, literature, sports, and more, the choice of amusements rests with the individual and her desires. As Nancy told me, "If I don't think it's going to be interesting or really, really good, I just don't go on with that book."[3] However, Nancy's choice of evangelical romances also reflects aspects of her identity as an evangelical woman. Her fictional devotion, like that of my other consultants, rests on a series of constantly negotiated relationships between escape and entertainment, forgetfulness and attention, faith and friendship, religion and recreation. This devotion fulfills a variety of readers' needs for enjoyment and leisure, but at the same time it remains firmly within the boundaries of evangelicalism.

Evangelical Women's Leisure: The Fun of Forgetting

On a typical day, Debbie works in a lab at Duke University. After work, she comes home, cares for her animals, makes supper, and then perhaps picks up *Love's Long Journey* or another evangelical romance. She is forty-six, single, white, and college-educated, with an income between $25,000 and $49,999 a year. A shy person (she declined to be tape recorded), Debbie reads approximately seven evangelical romances a month, 50 percent of her overall reading. For this Presbyterian woman, reading romances is an escape, a relaxing form of entertainment. In contrast to Debbie's single status, Jenna, a vivacious strawberry blond, is married and a mother of three. She works as a secretary, and her husband works in construction. They have a combined household income of $25,000 to $49,999 and attend an Assemblies of God church. Jenna reads three evangelical romances a month, and these romances constitute 98 percent of her reading repertoire. Like Debbie, she finds the novels full of fun and faith. On average, evangelical romances make up about half (56 percent) of my consultants' overall reading. While not all of my consultants read this much, some read even more, as many as ten or twelve evangelical romances every month. One letter writer reported that she sat down with five to ten novels every week![4] These women are clearly devoted to evangelical romance novels, but the question of what shapes the contours of their reading choices remains.

When asked why they liked evangelical romances, almost all the readers I interviewed—with astonishing continuity among them—mentioned two words: escape and entertainment. For example, Betty stated simply, "It's entertainment, it's an escape," while Evelyn told me, "I do it for my entertainment, it has to be fun." Like other leisure activities, such as sports, film, or television, reading evangelical romance novels provides pleasure and entertainment. The novels, women told me, were "brain candy," a "brain break," and "better than television." Seeking a respite, readers hoped to enter fictional worlds that would "take them away," as they explored romance, history, and religion. They wanted to get "lost in a book," "caught in the whirlwind of the story," and "immersed in imagining [the heroine's] world." "The books take you somewhere," as Jane told me—to an evangelical world where everything works out in the end.[5]

For these women, the definition of fun (and entertainment more broadly) remained inseparable from their faith. Just as many evangelicals reject the notion of art for art's sake, doctrines of stewardship and accountability fence in the terrain of fun. Evangelical popular culture, from the "Left Behind" films to Christian rock music, rests on this combination of religion and recreation. For those within the subculture, this redemption of popular culture affords opportunities for leisure and enjoyment, which are enhanced by the knowledge that these products affirm Christian values. Charlotte's story illuminates this combination. As we discussed the novels at her kitchen table (near the bookcase that housed her Christian romance collection), and the children played in the other room, Charlotte framed her reading practice as "wholesome entertainment," as a small way to strengthen her faith and claim some fun: "I think it is honoring God to pick that as a form of recreation because you are still . . . I think it is pleasing to him because it has Scripture, it is clean. There are so many other books that you have to either skim over something, or you might read it and wish you hadn't and it might stick in your mind. I think it is a Godly way of self-entertainment. I think the Bible says to think on these things, whatever is pure. When you are reading, to me, when I read something it really stays with me."[6] Charlotte seamlessly combines entertainment and God in a way that reveals the pervasiveness of evangelical ideas about sacralizing all of life. The novels direct her attention to God and enable her to forget those books that may deter that focus. In *Visual Piety*, scholar David Morgan argues that "forgetting is therefore as important as remembering in the social economy of everyday life." He continues, "I have more broadly in mind forgetting as the enablement of attention."[7] Employing this idea, we see how the genre allows Charlotte to forget about the "impure" books out there that offer danger rather than safety, filth rather than wholesome fun. In addition to forgetting "sinful" alternatives, reading Christian romances helps Charlotte escape some of her other demands. As a mother of three who also watches children in her home, she finds that reading helps her cope: "I kind of relish it. I look forward to it when the mornings are crazy. I think, it won't be too long and I'll put [the children] to bed and I can put my feet up and read." Evangelical romances, then, afford Charlotte and other women I interviewed an opportunity to combine their love of reading with their love of God. The concept of fun remains subservient to the criterion of faith, but forgetfulness remains a vital component of their reading pleasure.

Like Charlotte, many of my consultants mentioned that part of the joy of reading evangelical romance derives from the escape it affords. Reading temporarily frees them from the demands of everyday life and offers a chance, albeit a limited one, to forget about domestic responsibilities. Heidi, a wife, mother, and full-time teacher, echoed Charlotte's comments, but as a mother of older children she does not have to wait for them to go to bed. We sat in her family room, amidst neatly stacked and folded laundry, while she recounted her unspoken reading rule: "Don't bother me until it's done. Don't ask for food. Don't ask me for anything." For Heidi, reading is *her* time, a time to forget all else and focus on herself and her need to relax. Whether they are parenting teenagers or toddlers, reading provides these women with a way to temporarily block out everything else and claim a loved hobby, spiritual enrichment, and personal time.[8]

For these women, escape means an outlet when "you are stressed and just need a brain break." Gail, an office manager, made evangelical romance reading part of her nightly routine: "I read myself to sleep every night just to get my brain off of whatever is going on in the day." Another woman stated similarly: "[Reading] takes my mind off everything else that is going on."[9] The novels allow forgetfulness and provide relaxation. To both her pleasure and her dismay, sixty-three-year-old Evelyn finds the novels so relaxing that she falls asleep reading them. Reading helps others escape sleeplessness and depression. Cathy, who suffers from bouts of these problems, "just wanted to read something that was nice and not depressing." A friend lent her some of Janette Oke's novels, and Cathy would read all day and on into the night, as she said, "to get my mind off things." Not only did reading help her forget her problems for a time, but it also prevented her from doing things, including housework. Cathy described her reaction coming home from the church library one day with two new novels: "I was like, 'Oh dear, the house isn't clean and I can see it's not going to get clean!'"[10] In this moment, Cathy gained the illicit pleasure of avoiding her housework and the enjoyment of escaping her problems.

For others, reading provides one of the few leisure activities they can enjoy, as it enables them to escape from lives confined by illness or defined by loneliness. Lillian, on dialysis fifteen hours a week, wrote to author Peggy Stoks that "I read a lot because I can't do much else." Likewise, Paige, suffering from chronic fatigue syndrome and caring for her mother with Crohn's disease, said that "we don't drive so it's kind of hard," but wrote to thank author Shari MacDonald for her books and to tell Shari about her love of reading.[11] For these women, limited by poor health, reading filled the time and helped them at least imaginatively leave home and forget illness. One daughter wrote, "My mother is ninety-two years old, housebound, and reading is her only possible pastime. She enjoyed your book so very much." Similarly, Christy, in a letter to author Irene Brand, described herself this way: "I'm a seventy-four-year-old widow and read a lot." And on stationery decorated with roses on a linen tablecloth, another woman wrote, "My husband died four years ago so I have many hours in which to read and it brings such pleasure."[12]

Over and over, these women told me of their long and passionate relationships with reading. "I have always enjoyed reading," "I have been an avid reader since I could read," and "I love to read" were common remarks.[13] For many of my consultants, evangelical beliefs about stewardship and literature govern their reading choices. Like other evangelicals, they choose products that reinforce, rather than challenge, their faith. However, the broader context of their decision-making process reveals another way evangelicalism shapes and disciplines their fictional devotion.

For many, their choice reflects the influence of a Christian past and a Christian woman, usually a mother. Just as Marty, Oke's heroine from *Love Comes Softly*, reared her stepdaughter Missie (the heroine of *Love's Long Journey*) in the Christian faith, so too did many of my consultants' mothers. For these mothers, evangelical romance novels disciplined their daughters to choose Christian forms of entertainment, particularly a literary formula that emphasizes the virtue of chastity prior to marriage and the necessity of a Christian spouse. In this religious rearing, mothers not only teach their daughters how to read as children, but guide them in what to read as teenagers. For example, Valerie's mother, who worked in their church library, prompted her to begin reading evangelical romance. Speaking of the novels, Valerie happily reported that "my whole family likes them"—her mother, herself, and her sister-in-law. Like Valerie, Janet acquired devotion to these books from her mother: "My mom had them and I just got into it and I loved it."[14]

Mothers, then, not only introduce their daughters to the genre, but they also share their daughters' dedication to it. They teach by example, embodying the practice they want their daughters to learn, the discipline they hope to instill. Often these bonds of faith, fiction, and family occur over the works of the prolific Grace Livingston Hill. Fiona recalled that her mother "had bunches of Grace Livingston Hill books" and remembered that her "first one was *Rainbow Cottage* and I have three copies of that." Rita, an assistant manager of a Christian bookstore as well as a mother and a wife, related a similar story: "I started reading the Grace Livingston Hill books. My mother had them and I think I read every one of those." Like the other women I interviewed, Rita too had her favorite: *Miranda*. A collector like Fiona, Rita owns a copy of it "in a very old hardback." Kate reported that a friend introduced her and her mother to the genre at the same time: "Well, I started when I was a teenager. Me and my mother both were avid readers and somebody loaned us some Grace Livingston Hill books, and I've been hooked on Grace Livingston Hill ever since. I've collected almost every one of her books."[15]

For others, sisters or family friends played pivotal roles in their reading histories. Laura, always an avid reader, described the influence of a friend of her mother: "She lent me *Patricia* by Grace Livingston Hill, so then I started reading all those Grace Livingston Hill ones and the church had them also, so every Sunday I'd get a couple of them out." Reflecting on her reading of this novel as a teenager, Laura told me how of all that she read, *Patricia* made the biggest change in her spiritual life: "I must have read it at the right age, where it made such

A Novel of Enduring Romance by

GRACE LIVINGSTON HILL

A young couple's childhood friendship
ripens into a mature and inspiring love.

PATRICIA

S7247 ★ 75c ★ A BANTAM BOOK

Cover of *Patricia* (1977), by Grace Livingston Hill. Reprinted by
permission of Bantam Books, a division of Random House, Inc.

an impression upon me of how important it was to live a Christian life and to find a Christian spouse." It also changed Laura's reading life: "It opened a whole new world up for reading, even from that moment on, I rarely read anything else but Christian books." For Gail, it was her sister who played the pivotal role in introducing her to Christian romances. In a conversation between the two, Gail expressed her concern that movies and television were not making her a better person. Her sister recommended evangelical romance reading as an alternative, and Gail has been devoted to the genre ever since; it constitutes the vast majority of her overall reading.[16]

Having first learned their fictional devotion from other evangelical women, whether mothers, sisters, or friends, it is not surprising that some of my consultants want to continue this heritage. Sharing their evangelical romance reading with the next generation, they seek to influence their daughters' and granddaughters' ideas about faith and fun, pure and impure. For example, Evelyn, a mother and grandmother, started her library years ago when her son and his family moved in next door. At that time, she started loaning evangelical romances to her daughter-in-law. Though Evelyn's relatives eventually moved further away, their book-swapping continued and her collection expanded. Now, Evelyn's teenage granddaughters love to read, "so grandma's got a library" for them. Speaking of the number of books she has acquired, Evelyn relates, "It's grown from there and now I don't have any place to put them when I get them. My granddaughters that are still home ask if I have any books. They want to read them before I even get a chance."[17] In addition to her granddaughters, Evelyn also lends books to Jenna, her niece, who in turn shares her novels with other family members as well as friends.

Like Evelyn, Lila, who has two daughters, also works on building her own personal library. She told me, "I like buying all those books too because I have young daughters and I want to have good reading material around that they can pick up and read." Similarly, Mary, single and creating her own library, shared, "I've saved some of them specifically thinking about my children . . . I mean these are great books. There is so much trash out there."[18] Nora echoed these sentiments: "I'm real careful about what I let my daughter read. I grew up not with Christian romance, but with Beverly Cleary where Jeanie and Johnny double date and those books. It really warped my idea of what male/female relationships were supposed to be." These women want their daughters to inherit more than a love of reading. They hope that evangelical romances, with their combination of faith and fun, will teach their daughters evangelical lessons in sexuality and marriage.[19] Sharing this fictional devotion also strengthens these women's bonds of family and Christian fellowship. Part of the fun of reading emerges from its connection with other women in the family: mothers, daughters, sisters, and grandmothers. However, at the same time, this fun remains firmly within the boundaries of evangelicalism. In families that read these novels, women learn from an early age that reading and religion are integrally connected.

For women seeking fun and mothers teaching faith, the genre fulfills these needs in a way other evangelical offerings, such as nonfiction devotionals or self-help books, do not. While these other options provide religious instruction and inspiring anecdotes, they afford little in terms of entertainment. Christian music offers entertainment with evangelical values, but does not present a developed narrative or a sustained escape, and evangelical efforts in film tend to be marketed toward children. For my consultants, then, fictional devotion reconciles pleasure and piety, romance stories and religious themes, in ways that speak to these women's lives—their spiritual desires, their leisure longings, and their reading habits—and keeps them tied to evangelicalism.

Given their reading histories and love of things literary, it is not surprising that readers' demands often exceeded authors' supplies. For women reading five to ten novels a month, Christian bookstore shelves may hold few unfamiliar titles. Publishers, attuned to these demands, have increased the quantity of evangelical romances and are offering readers a growing array of choices. Gone are the days when only Grace Livingston Hill and a few Catherine Marshalls filled the shelves. While the contemporary rise of the genre was inaugurated by Janette Oke's Western prairie settings, more and more the plots of evangelical romances vary. Some are historical renderings, while others are contemporary tales. Some authors incorporate a mystery or suspense element, while others include the comedic. Novel length now ranges from one-hundred-page novellas to four-hundred-page sagas.

Not only have the genre's boundaries expanded, but other publishers—Christian and secular—are entering this profitable market. For example, Harlequin, the foremost publisher of secular romance novels, established a new imprint, Steeple Hill, that issues three "inspirational" romances every month under the line title "Love Inspired." Random House established an inspirational fiction division named Waterbrook Press, which publishes evangelical romance and Christian fiction. Further, in 1988, HarperCollins bought Zondervan, a Christian publisher established in the 1930s.[20]

This market growth provides readers with more possibilities to combine faith and fun. Rather than make a trip to the Christian bookstore, readers can obtain Love Inspired books through a subscription service or at any store that carries Harlequins. One woman wrote, "I'm thoroughly enjoying the Love Inspired books published by Steeple Hill. It's nice to open these and know it will be inspirational and free of the foul language that is so offensive in most novels of today. I have just been a subscriber to the Love Inspired books since May, so I hope I will see more of your work. Thanks!" And Audrey, fourteen years old, exclaimed, "I love to read and I am a member of Love Inspired, where I get three books at the end of each month. I love to read Christian romance and your book, *The Test of Love*, was sensational!"[21] For these women, this line offers the ease of home delivery and, perhaps more importantly, a consistent supply of new books.

The creation of Steeple Hill also offered more publishing opportunities for authors. This realization emerged as I asked Carole Gift Page about her decision to write for Harlequin. "Crossing over [into the American Booksellers Association's market]," she told me, is the goal of many Christian romance writers, but "the important thing to remember about crossing over is to carry *the cross* over." This maxim guided her decision to write for Love Inspired. Indeed, the possibility of carrying the cross over to Harlequin may seem questionable to some. Many view the line with suspicion, and it cannot be found on the shelves of the local Christian bookstores I visited. While Page feared criticism by other authors and those within the Christian publishing industry for her choice, she prayed about it and believed writing for Harlequin was the right decision. She explained to me how she has never been asked to dilute the faith component in her work and how Harlequin instituted her practice of putting a Bible verse on the epigraph page of her novels. Page can also express her religious views through a "Dear Reader" letter at the end of every book. For Page, not only does her work witness to those employed at Harlequin, but Harlequin itself has become a missionary enterprise. In her view, the press is able to distribute the gospel message through romance to more countries, more stores, and hence, more readers than would be possible solely through a Christian publisher. Author Irene Brand echoed this as she discussed writing for Love Inspired: "CBA [Christian Booksellers Association] publishers don't have the marketing expertise and the ability to publicize large numbers of books. Steeple Hill has Harlequin/Silhouette publishing machinery behind it, and therefore they can put their books into supermarkets, drugstores, general retail stores, etc., all over the world."[22]

In addition, as they seek new markets, publishers are challenging the racial homogeneity of the genre by actively recruiting minority authors. The three African American authors I interviewed, who had never heard of "Christian fiction," became part of the industry this way. Sharon Ewell Foster, for example, told me, "I always loved writing" but "I didn't really know anything about Christian fiction." This changed one day when she went to the library and looked at Writer's Digest, where she saw an advertisement seeking Christian romances featuring minority characters. She then attended a writers conference where Multnomah Publishers, who took out the advertisement, recruited her.[23] Tyndale House made a similar effort and now features one African American romance author, Angela Benson. While Walkworthy Press, a division of Time Warner, "publishes contemporary fiction that may be of particular interest to African American readers."[24] The emergence of African American Christian fiction, including romance, has opened up new possibilities for readers, both white and black. This change brought Roxanne, a single forty-year-old African American woman with a career in television news, to the genre. As a reader, she "was specifically looking for African American authors," and would not have picked up an evangelical romance by a white author. While she still wishes for more African American titles, the growth in the industry offers her more reading options than in the past. Similarly, another woman told me happily, "I like the variety. I like this historical fiction, I like that one with a spiritual part in it, I like the light one. There is a greater variety of Christian romances out there than there used to be."[25] The genre, like much of evangelical popular culture, represents an alternative to things secular and the publishing industry has fully supported its growth.

While my consultants' concept of fun is both enhanced and limited by evangelical faith, other factors also constrain their recreational opportunities, such as concerns about women and their use of leisure. For some, reading four evangelical romances a month or having the genre represent 95 percent of one's overall reading may be too much fun and too much leisure, despite the genre's religious dimension. Theologians may insist, like Leland Ryken and Frank Gaebelein, that God redeemed rest, but they also caution that Christians must use it wisely. Evangelical romance, for these and other critics, may not seem a wise use of one's time. In addition, many evangelicals, scholar J. I. Packer writes, continue to "emphasize work rather than leisure, activity rather than rest, and life commitments rather than life-style choices."[26] Concerns about the idleness associated with leisure pursuits are further enhanced by evangelical views of the millennium, of the second coming of Christ. The imminent return of Jesus demands that Christians make every minute count for eternity.[27] All choices matter, and with heaven and hell in the balance, a little light reading can be difficult to justify—especially for women.

Studies demonstrate that women indulge in less leisure than men due to lack of time, money, opportunity, and facilities. Furthermore, Susan Shaw, in her article "Gender, Leisure, and Constraint," shows how the socialization of women into an "ethic of care" (or put another way, into "traditional" gender roles) prompts women to place others first and to sacrifice their already scarce leisure. This ethic also limits women's leisure choices, usually to activities designated as feminine, including romance novel reading. Given the prescriptive power of these gender roles in evangelicalism, as well as the demands of working both inside and outside the home, the choice to read these novels reflects not only the gender constraints on women's leisure but also their control over it. Susan Shaw argues, "If leisure experiences represent situations of choice and self-determination for individuals to exercise personal power, such power can be used as a form of resistance to imposed gender-related constraints or restrictions."[28] Similarly, in their study of mass media and escape, Elihu Katz and David Foulkes examine how popular culture affords individuals, male and female, some time to themselves. They argue that exchanges such as " 'Shh, Daddy is reading the newspaper,' or 'Can't you see we're trying to watch this program?' imply that exposure to the media is sufficient to justify a degree of insulation or immunity from other pressures."[29] The fictional devotion of my consultants rests on the interrelationship of faith and fun, but this relationship is shaped by evangelical as well as broader cultural ideas about women and their use of time. Therefore, although women's leisure guarantees at least a little time in which one can stop juggling the roles of wife, mother, and housekeeper to claim that of reader, for some of my consultants, guilt accompanied this forgetfulness.

These evangelical romance readers, like other evangelical women, balance a variety of demands—children and husbands, home and office, religious prescriptions and real-life contingencies. As Sally Gallagher demonstrates in her study *Evangelical Identity and Gendered Family Life*, contemporary evangelicals "move across a range of perspectives and ideas in outlining the contours of work and family life. The whole remains in dynamic balance." While evangelical gender ideals may prescribe male headship, Gallagher argues that in everyday life a "pragmatic egalitarianism" operates, one that includes the sharing of breadwinning duties. In the 1990s, "the question was no longer 'should women work' or 'what are OK motives for working' but how to support families in which husbands and wives were both employed." Accordingly, "about 56 percent of all married evangelical women are now employed, about the same percentage as other women in the United States as well as other religiously committed Protestants." [30] Gallagher's study reveals the reality behind the rhetoric of evangelical gender ideology and shows how these conservative Protestant women, like so many others, face the superwoman syndrome or triple duty dilemma.

This is certainly true of the women I interviewed. They constantly negotiated competing demands and some spoke of "reading guilt." For example, Jane, a white married mother of four who teaches at a local community college, described the fun of reading: "[Books] involve you, engage you to some point and you feel, reading is always part of a fantasy, you are always being taken away from where you are and that is what keeps me reading. I mean, why else would you read? You read for enjoyment. Of course, I have read for my studies and everything like that. I'm reading these to relax." However, even as she highlighted her enjoyment, she also admitted that she used to feel guilty reading. When she read, that meant she was not doing the laundry or cleaning the house. She explained this guilt by locating herself in a generation that associated reading fiction with wasting time. Accordingly, Jane wished for more Christian books on tape, so she could combine housework and "reading." While she referred to her guilt in the past tense, she nevertheless mentioned it in our conversation and still struggled with taking the time to read. Similarly, Lila's mother deemed reading a less-than-worthwhile activity, so as a child Lila would hide with her books. Even now, she occasionally feels guilty when she reads, but that does not deter her. Sometimes, this married mother of two confided, she taunts her mother over the phone, "I'm reading now mom, ha ha." [31]

Given their love of evangelical romance and awareness of its tempting possibilities, many of my interviewees, rather than flaunting their reading, made conscious efforts to restrict it. For example, Gail shared, "I have to discipline myself because I would sit and read all the time."[32] Similarly, Beth and other women who worked as teachers carefully monitored their time and used the summer and school breaks for their literary escapes. Too busy during the school year to read as much as they would like, these women looked forward to the summers. One divinity school student reread her favorite books during the summer, and for others, holidays and vacations provided more time for sitting alone with a novel.[33] As Evelyn told me, "Usually I like to read cover to cover, and usually after the holidays. I take a week or two where I do a lot of reading to catch up, but I never do catch up." Another evangelical woman had more time to read in the winter than in the summer: "Reading is an especially winter treat."[34] Desiring to read but knowing their roles—as wives, mothers, and workers—these women imposed boundaries on their fictional devotion.

Nancy's reading history exemplifies this negotiation. A sixty-five-year-old evangelical from Durham, North Carolina, she could only find the time to indulge in reading after an unexpected injury. "Well, I love to read. When I was a young teenager, I read all the time in the summertime. When I got older and had a family, the time just didn't seem to be there. But I stopped working about a year or so ago and I had some knee surgery this year and someone kept talking about this Mitford series, so while I was not able to get around much, I started reading and got into the habit of reading again." Fostered by a "wonderful" church library, Nancy now regularly reads, shops at Christian bookstores, and makes sure she has a couple of novels for her trips to the beach.[35]

Others, after acknowledging the difficulties of finding time, often use the language of theft and compulsion to describe how they claim it regardless. As one letter writer stated, "I have two grown daughters, and one son, and four beautiful grandchildren. I keep busy with my family and church *and I always find time to read.*" While this writer does not elaborate on how she finds the time, she expresses a sentiment that other readers share and more fully explain. For example, another wrote, "I'm an avid reader, *stealing away* some time here and there from my day of caring for my two little ones."[36] More often, though, readers stated simply, "I couldn't put it down!" Whatever the time constraints, most of the women believed that "sometimes we must do ourselves a favor" and read. They "found the time," and once they started reading, they "couldn't put it down." Using this language of necessity, they often spoke of reading a novel cover to cover, a practice demanding at least a couple of hours of time. Valerie, who prefers longer stories, told me she reads a novel in a day or two, and while she enters this fictional world, "everything stops." Diana even cautioned me about this compulsion. She warned that if I were to read the "Mark of the Lion" books by Francine Rivers, I would be unable to put them down.[37]

Letters from readers, even more than interviews, convey this sense of urgency. The letter writers emphasize their enjoyment of a novel by telling the author how quickly they read it or about their inability to put it down. Whatever the length of time—two days or four and a half hours—women claimed hours for their reading pleasure: "I can't put them down. I look forward to being able to spend time reading!"[38] Some readers stay up until 2 A.M. to finish the novels, while others read until they "can't see anymore." Some hurry home from work to finish reading. As Victoria wrote, "When I came home from work the [mail order] book was there waiting for me. I dove right in, so glad there were no commitments for the night! I finished it before work this A.M."[39]

The language of compulsion provides a way for these women to claim leisure time. It transfers responsibility for their behavior from the self to the story. In the logic of this rationale, the novels exert power over readers and demand that they take the time to read. Portraying themselves as passive before the power of the narrative (in this context), they diminish the significance of their own power—their control over leisure—and thereby ward off criticism from the self or from others of their reading. This understanding enables my consultants to keep reading and to claim leisure. It helps mitigate their guilt and simultaneously demonstrates their enjoyment of the novels, their absorption into these evangelical worlds.

While positive connotations generally accompany the concepts of pleasure, fun, and leisure, the terms escape and compulsion fare less favorably. They evoke images of denial and addiction. In this view, readers, like other types of addicts, are hooked—characterized by their need for novels and their inability to deal with reality. This negative view of escapism, and the concomitant idea of its consumers as passive, pervades perceptions of popular culture. For example, in *Remote Control: Television, Audiences, and Power*, scholars describe how many critics of and commentators on television viewing see it "as an addiction, as a passive, individual activity which precludes direct communication with others." The authors point out that this attitude "is a theory about what television does to other, more vulnerable people."[40] Moviegoers, according to Murray Smith, face similar stereotypes, built on the "characterization of the spectator as a dreamer or the dupe of an illusion."[41] However, when we go beyond this stereotypical image, the complexity of everyday life and the piety of fictional devotion emerge.

As Yi-Fu Tuan asks in *Escapism*, "Who hasn't sometime wanted to escape?" Leonard Pearlin puts it another way: "It can be said without exaggeration that stress is a common feature of modern social life. . . . Just as no society can exist free of stress, it is also likely that there is no society which does not have accepted practices which can function as coping mechanisms for stress."[42] In contemporary American culture, television, film, and literature are common coping mechanisms proffered by popular culture. These escapist avenues are not just the purview of Stark Trek fans, soap opera devotees, or evangelical romance readers. Escape is not a category of the other, but one in which we must include ourselves. Women like Victoria and Diana who read evangelical romance are not any more escapist than you or I, who may be inclined to watch "The Sopranos" rather than a daytime soap opera, or to read Barbara Kingsolver instead of Lori Wick. Perhaps "they" are not so different from "us" after all.

Given that we live in, as Tuan argues, a "culture of escape," unraveling the context and content of readers' escape into evangelical romance remains critical to understanding their devotion. Elihu Katz and David Foulkes urge us to remember that "even if it is true that alienation or deprivation tend to drive people to seek refuge in the mass media, it is not at all self-evident what they find when they get there. . . . A drive, in other words, may well be escapist, but its fulfillment may or may not be." Readers may desire a "brain break," but the question of where that leads remains. Katz and Foulkes continue: "That the media transport one to the world outside of one's immediate environment is the very essence of their function. The better question to ask would seem to be whether these excursions feed back to one's real-life concerns, personal or social." [43] For the women I interviewed, reading evangelical romance displays a desire for fun, shaped by their socialization in faith and gender. In many ways, their forgetfulness and escape revolves around the self, an individual indulging in entertainment. From this perspective, fears about the isolation of popular culture consumers seem justified. However, when the lens widens to look beyond the solitary act of escaping to the whole reading process—acquiring, sharing, discussing, and interpreting novels—relationships with other evangelical women emerge.

Evangelical Women's Networks: The Sharing of Romance

In *Love's Long Journey*, the heroine Missie, the only woman on her husband's ranch in the Western prairie, longs for the friendship of another woman. She finds that friend in the Spanish-speaking Maria, a relationship that she attributes to God. While stories like this help readers escape from their everyday demands into fictional worlds, they also help readers cultivate relationships with other women, much like Missie develops a companionship with Maria. Readers may temporarily forget the stresses of daily life while engrossed in a book, but in reading evangelical romance they also become involved with other women in their local church communities. These relationships "provide bandages, routine emotional support and minor services to help people cope with the stresses and strains of their situations." They supply a "flow of supportive resources" to meet a variety of needs: "emotional aid, material aid, information, companionship." [44] Readers' escape, then, leads not to isolation and alienation; however, neither does it lead to a global village or relationships with random women. Rather, through evangelical romance reading my consultants cultivate involvement with other evangelical women, which in turn enhances both the fun of reading and the practice of faith. This is another way in which the fun of reading remains within the boundaries of evangelical community. These relationships strengthen the evangelical identity of those who are involved in them. As Kevin Hetherington argues, "The creation of conditions of support, friendship, and solidarity are all important issues in understanding the role of a 'structure of feeling' within processes of identity formation." [45] Through their literary connections, these women support one another in their desire to forget demands, enjoy leisure, and grow spiritually.

Given my consultants' enjoyment of the genre, one might expect to find them meeting regularly in book clubs to discuss their favorite authors, lessons learned, or a particularly compelling novel. However, when I asked readers if they had ever heard of an evangelical romance book club, the answer was almost always no. While some had heard of Christian fiction book clubs, they knew that evangelical romance was not the focus of these clubs. When asked, a few expressed their delight in the idea of a book club. For example, retired Nancy said, "I'm not aware of any groups. I think it would be great to have a group like that. I would love to be a part of it." And librarian Jackie echoed this sentiment: "I would like to sit down with people to see how the book affected them. I think it would be more beneficial to me." [46] Only through the help of author Sharon Ewell Foster did I locate a book club—a group of African American women—that read evangelical romance. While I will discuss this group in more detail later, they seemed the exception rather than the rule.

Constraints on the leisure time of evangelical women, along with criticism of the genre, kept readers from forming evangelical romance book clubs. These women "made the time" to read and escape on an individual basis, but they did not seem able or willing to "steal the time" to meet other women for a formal, collective gathering. Gwen, for example, liked the idea of the book club, but also added an important qualifier, "if I could find the time for that." Gail responded similarly. She imagined that other readers were like her—women who are "involved in church and are working or moms who have little time to read anyway unless they are sitting on the john and hopefully the door stays closed long enough." Likewise, Betty told me that "the time factor is a big thing"—big enough to prevent her from going to any type of book club. She also provided another possible reason for the absence of book clubs: the subculture's bias against the genre as too lusty or too lacking in literary quality.[47] During my search for interviewees, when I asked readers to provide the names of other readers, I encountered long pauses, stuttering hesitations, and delaying tactics: "I'll ask them and let you know." Women's reticence in volunteering the names of other readers seemed implicitly to reflect not only a desire to protect their friends' time but also an unwillingness to "out" them as readers.

While tight-knit and organized groups that meet once a month may have seemed a nice idea to some women, most found alternative ways to meet their needs for support and community. Attending church at least once a week, these women set up their reading exchanges in spaces they already occupied—their churches and their homes—and with people they already knew. They established local literary connections through which they reaped multiple rewards without a book club. They cut costs by borrowing novels, conserved time by using church and home, and minimized the criticism a book club might evoke. In addition, these relationships provided fun—the enjoyment of casual conversation, the sharing of a beloved hobby, and a strengthening of evangelical ties—as I learned in an interview with five Baptist women.[48]

A Case Study: Five Baptist Women

I drove to Raleigh, North Carolina, laden with chocolate chip and oatmeal raisin cookies as an expression of my gratitude to my consultants. I was extremely thankful to Tina, an employee at a large Southern Baptist church, who had organized this meeting of five white female readers. The church, situated on a major commercial thoroughfare in Raleigh, stands five or six stories high and used to be a hotel. I drove through the huge parking lot and parked behind the church. Juggling my equipment and snacks, I walked to the door, and was buzzed in by the secretary. Taking the elevator up to the fifth floor, I related my purpose to the secretary, who called my contact person. Tina, a fifty-two-year-old strawberry blond, greeted me with enthusiasm and led me through the maze of hallways to our meeting room — the library workroom.

Upon entering the room, Tina introduced me to Agnes, a senior citizen who assisted at the library and offered to give me a quick tour of their collection. So I set off with Agnes to see the library: two big rooms, one devoted to adult literature and the other to children's. The books were grouped according to topic — theology, fiction, biography — and biblical pictures adorned some of the walls. Agnes proudly told me that their computerized library loaned 250–300 items on an average Sunday morning. After my tour of the library, Agnes led me back to the meeting room, where I put my snacks and tape recorders on the long conference table and Tina introduced me to the other women: Beth, Pamela, and Joan. These three forty-somethings worked as teachers, wives, and mothers. The five women greeted me politely and each other warmly, as they already knew each other. Upon sitting down, they voiced their appreciation for the snacks, Tina said a prayer (asking that we would have a good discussion and expressing gratitude that we could all be together), and I told them about my project before proceeding with my first question: "How did you get started reading evangelical romance?" Smiling and laughing, the women seemed more than happy to talk about their reading practices.[49]

During the course of our conversation, it became apparent that these women already knew something about each other's reading habits. They had discussed evangelical romance before — not as a formal group, but as friends and acquaintances. They often remembered if someone in the group had read a particular novel, asked for book recommendations, and valued others' opinions of different stories. They frequently expressed similar likes and dislikes, but were not afraid to dissent from each other. These women understood various references to authors, books, and ideas. They shared, it seemed, a common evangelical romance vocabulary which allowed for a seamless flow of banter, as well as more in-depth discussions. These five women asked questions of each other, shared their views, and laughed a lot. I recorded at least thirteen different instances of group laughter prompted by "inside jokes" about specific authors or anecdotes. Consider this exchange:

> Agnes: I like Hilda Stahl. Have y'all read any of Hilda Stahl?
> [Beth is laughing in the background at the mention of Stahl]
> Beth: Yes, she has shallow characters. That is my pet peeve. Develop the character! Give them something to identify with, give us something to like or hate about this person instead of a shallow character.
> Tina: Now see, I like thick books and that is probably the reason I do. I never thought about it much before. I don't like those Beverly Lewis books, you kind of have to make up what happens because it is such a shallow character.
> Pamela: They are shallow characters.
> [Interestingly, earlier they spoke of enjoying Lewis.]
> Beth: Because she does . . . what was it? The man goes back and they end up in love and I don't remember any love story there. Where was that written?
> Joan: Yeah, I remember that.
> Tina: They must have talked a few pages and we didn't get the dialogue!

This exchange continued with more laughter. As I spent over an hour with these five Baptist women, I was surprised by their shared views, as well as their familiarity with each other's reading preferences. While the act of reading may be solitary and the desire to read escapist, evangelical romances also foster friendships and engagement with others. Through the church library and through passing conversations on Sundays, these women constituted not a reading group but a literary network that validated each other's reading practices through discussions, swapping, and laughter. They were not best buddies, but rather casual friends and fellow readers. These "weak ties" allowed for a flow of information and ideas, of fun and láughter, as they both maintained and bolstered the women's evangelical bonds.[50]

Just as this Baptist church library played a vital role in connecting these five women, other church libraries function similarly. In churches dominated by male leadership, women often claim the library. As John Fiske argues, "The powerful construct places where they can exercise their power," while "the weak make their own spaces within those places."[51] This description seems apt as ministers (I learned through calling churches to locate readers) knew very little, if anything, about their congregation's reading practices; however, the church librarians I talked with, who were all women, knew their evangelical romance patrons. For example, Nora referred me to three of her main readers: Cathy, Betty, and Debbie. Church librarians, like Nora, provide their friends and acquaintances with reading expertise and guidance. These women offer invaluable advice as they steer readers, who may be leery of trying a new author or uncertain about a novel, toward certain books and away from others. For example, Nora tried to focus her teenage patrons on Janette Oke's novels, because of their reading level and "lightness." She also understood the preferences of her regular customers. For example, she knew that Cathy enjoyed less serious stories and confided that Betty "reads everything. She doesn't just read romances, but she reads everything from the lightest romance to the heaviest fiction." Nora also influenced readers through her careful selection of novels. Unwilling to have just any Christian romance on the library shelves, she solicited her readers' opinions of authors and titles and made book-buying decisions accordingly.[52] Librarians like Nora support, encourage, and guide readers in their choices. Through their shared love of books and in the space of the congregational library, librarians and patrons found a sense of literary support and evangelical community.

Church libraries also connect readers with one another. For example, Cathy fondly remarked on the reading rivalry at her Presbyterian church. Women fight, she told me, over who gets to check out new books first. Similarly, through her church library, Nancy knew of eight to ten other regular readers. She also donated her books to the church library to support her literary friends and other potential readers. She remarked, "They are not just going to sit in my house forever and not be touched again." For Nancy, the library not only linked her to other readers, but it also allowed her to contribute to and possibly expand her reading community through book donation. In Jenna's Assembly of God church, a similar reading community developed. A group of evangelical-romance-reading women came together to share their hobby. They began by swapping novels with each other, but they also wanted to invite others into their informal reading circle. As a result, they brought their books to church and set up a library so "people can read them. As long as we bought them, people might as well enjoy them." [53]

Even in churches without libraries, women share their hobby with acquaintances and friends. It provides a way to build relationships as well as enhance the fun of this fictional devotion. Twenty-four-year-old Janet, for example, related how evangelical romance reading enabled her to bond with both teenage girls and married women in her congregation. She shared, "I was just talking to a girl two weeks ago about Lori Wick and that is something that I can connect with her and talk to her about. I can suggest books to her. Then there are a lot of married ladies that read the books and we can talk about it too." Sixty-three-year-old Evelyn described a similar experience. "Well, we just talk about them sometimes in church when we have socials or whatever. Sometimes we get to talking, have you read this one or that one." Others, like Gwen, give the novels to friends when they have finished them or lend them out. [54] And for Diana, swapping even kept her from sleeping. She told how Lila, a friend and fellow church member, called her up at 11 P.M. one night wanting to borrow the next book in a series by Francine Rivers. Similarly, Laura and Jean shared friendship, church membership, and many novels. I talked with them together at Jean's house. As we conversed, Jean recounted how Laura introduced her to evangelical romance, showed us her recent evangelical romance acquisitions, and asked if Laura wanted to borrow any of them. It seems, one reader remarked, that "quite a circle of us pass our books around."[55] Under the radar of their local churches, so to speak, these women cultivate and enhance their relationships with one another through their shared love of reading.

However, these literary bonds remain limited by church affiliations. A few women I spoke with exchange novels long-distance, but most remain tied to their local religious communities.[56] Gender and religion shaped my consultants' ideas about and enjoyment of leisure, as did race. Friendships, network analysts demonstrate, tend to be homogeneous. They flow through churches, family, and groups of people that are demographically similar. In evangelicalism, Sunday morning segregation intensifies these patterns. Few white readers of the genre connected with African American readers, or vice versa. I encountered only one instance of an interracial evangelical romance reading relationship. At the Durham Public Library, as I talked with Jackie (white), who had organized the evangelical romance collection, she referred me to her friend Tamara (African American), who worked at another branch of the library. In turn, Tamara led me to Jocelyn (also African American), a library patron. But the snowball stopped there. I found Mona's Book Club, a reading group comprised of African American women from suburban Chicago, only through the help of African American author Sharon Ewell Foster. This group of women illuminates some of similarities and differences between African American and white readers.[57]

A Case Study: Mona's Book Club

Unlike the other women I talked with, the members of Mona's Book Club met regularly, every third Saturday of the month from March to November. They had also just started reading the genre, perhaps owing to the recent advent of African American evangelical romance. I am not sure why these women formed a book club rather than rely on less-formalized reading relationships, as did my other consultants. This difference may reflect the historic importance of literacy in the black community. Elizabeth McHenry, who examines nineteenth-century African American literary societies in her monograph *Forgotten Readers*, chronicles how such societies were established "to promote literacy and to ensure that, as a group, they would not be excluded from the benefits associated with reading and literary study." Perhaps Mona's Book Club also signals differences between black and white evangelicals on the concepts of gender or leisure. The club might also reflect excitement over this emerging genre, the influence of "the Oprah Book Club model," or the power of a good leader. In addition, a relative lack of criticism of the genre and of the women's reading practices may also have contributed to the formation of this club. Mona's husband, for example, strongly supported her reading and the group. While we would need more information to arrive at firmer conclusions, what did become clear as I e-mailed Mona, the group's leader, was her enjoyment of evangelical romance and her desire to share it with other women, including me. She arranged the time, logistics, and permissions for my conference call interview with the whole group on May 11, 2001.[58]

I called on Saturday evening, knowing the difficulties that awaited me in interviewing a large group over the phone. While there were some awkward moments (ill-timed questions and brief pauses), we laughed about them and moved on. The interview began when Mona answered the phone and put me on speakerphone. The six women introduced themselves to me, and I began by thanking them and asking for their thoughts on *Ain't No River* by Sharon Ewell Foster, their current book club selection. Bella began the discussion with a question about the relationship between heroine Garvin and her boss Robert that launched a rapid exchange:

> Sharise: They were different races. She had a problem with him because he was very nitpicky with her and judged her, but she didn't want to think it was racial. She wanted to think it was more because I'm a woman, not because I'm a black woman.

Cover of *Ain't No River* (2001), by Sharon Ewell Foster.
Reprinted by permission of Multnomah Publishers.

Bella: So, she knew it was discrimination, but it wasn't that she . . .

Mona: I got that she thought it was more discrimination because her career was going so good. He was jealous because his career didn't go as good.

Bella: She was like top dog?

Sharise: If you think about it, in the current time, what we're going through now is the glass ceiling, where women are being pushed up the ladder more so than men, even white men, because many of them are losing their jobs and many of the women are being sent up, and they'll push a black woman up to be president, before they will a black man.

Dawn: He was riding her real hard and she was trying to go and be a partner, and he wanted to slow her down. He had to slow her down. He figured that if he nitpicked, she'd get tired of it enough that she'd leave.

Unlike my other interviewees, the members of this book club discussed racism, an issue they faced. Mona, a nurse, described the similarity between her work and that described in the novel: "I work with a lot of Caucasian people and when they make certain remarks on things due to the fact [I'm African American] I catch them real quick and I'm like, 'That's unacceptable.'" The group had only read a few African American Christian romances, and seemed unfamiliar with its white counterparts. Whether due to the genre's novelty or the medium we used to communicate (or both), this book club did not evince the same kind of fluid dialogue that I found with the five Baptist women. They lacked, it seemed, the same kind of shared reading history and evangelical romance idiom that the five Baptist women shared. Like the Baptist women, they discussed ideas, plot elements, and asked questions, but their familiarity and knowledge of each other and their reading preferences seemed less evident.

However, while the group members differed in some respects from my white consultants, they also shared similarities in their desire for the forgetfulness and relaxation afforded by entertainment. Callie explained, "Sometimes you just get tired of the everyday hustle and bustle, the same old, same old, you know, so seeing what that other person's doing in that book, you can be sucked in, and it's entertaining enough that you can get away for a little while." Dawn agreed: "I like to read for relaxation, entertainment, too, to learn, to open up my mind to different things. Most of all it relaxes me. It gives me a chance sometimes to escape from my own problems." Just as white consultants employed the language of escape, so did these African American women. However, it seems that the women in this group exerted more power over their leisure time. They met regularly and did not have to "steal" time or use the language of compulsion. However, like others I interviewed, the members of Mona's Book Club remained connected to other women like them and to their local religious and racial community.[59]

Evangelical romance reading reflects the intersection of religion, race, and gender. It does not challenge the societal structures that constrain women's leisure, break down the racial barriers which divide contemporary evangelicalism, or question the religious beliefs that shape women's lives. Amidst the various demands of everyday life, it seems, as David Morgan writes, that "for most people, it is more important to cope with an oppressive or indifferent world than to resist or subvert it."[60] For my consultants, their fictional devotion, their reading of evangelical romance reconciles, to a certain extent, conflicts between faith and fun, escapism and engagement, forgetfulness and attention. It offers them recreational and religious opportunities that otherwise may not exist. Given this, as much as readers portray themselves as passive in their inability to put down novels, they actively assess, as the following chapter demonstrates, each novel's ability to help them through the ups and downs of day-to-day life. In their view, faith not only defines the fun of reading, but the interrelationship between the two becomes the basis for their evaluations of evangelical romance novels.

Garvin shook her head and closed her eyes while Jonee spoke. She couldn't bear to look at her.

"Why is that so unbelievable? Alcoholics get jobs, murderers get jobs, so—racists get jobs too."

"This is 2000."

"And so? You know Gooden has problems. I don't think he likes anyone, not even himself. And yes, I think he has issues with your color, so what? I don't understand why that freaks you out, why it's so unbelievable. It happens all over the world."

"What do you mean?" Garvin looked up at Jonee.

"I remember when I was in Thailand, when I was a little girl, hearing how some Thai people talked about Korean people. Same thing. Same stereotypes. I don't hear it so much anymore. I just don't think it helps to try to pretend it's not there. You shouldn't let it hold you back, but you shouldn't walk around wearing blinders either." Jonee pushed a lock of dark hair behind her ear.

Garvin wanted to be somewhere else. Anywhere but here. Anywhere that would remove her from the pain, from the embarrassment, from the failure.

"I've thought about it a lot, Garvin . . . why you try to deny that it's there. I still haven't figured it out. It's like on some unconscious levels you acknowledge that racism goes on, but then, consciously, you deny it. I'm working on a theory . . . the meat of it is just still out of my grasp."[1]

In *Ain't No River*, having put faith in herself, rather than in Christianity, lawyer Garvin finds that faith shaken after being placed on administrative leave by her racist boss. Stunned, Garvin cannot fathom that her hard work garnered punishment instead of praise and wants to deny the reality of racism. For Garvin, recognizing this reality reveals the fragile foundations of her life. In response, she heads back home and leaves behind Washington, D.C., her DKNY suits, and her fast-paced career, only to confront the faith of her childhood as she stays with her grandmother in North Carolina. In this setting, where Garvin desires to escape her problems, she must in fact face not only her employment troubles but also her relationship with God. Slowly, as she places her life in God's hands, rather than her own, Garvin recovers her faith (and her job), reconnects with friends, and gains a fiancé.

For my consultants, as we have seen in the previous chapter, evangelical romance reading represents a fun activity, a beloved hobby. However, the concept of fun remains defined by evangelical faith, practice, and community. These parameters also configure what readers look for in an evangelical romance and the ways they assess them. Like other forms of evangelical popular culture, the genre attempts to redeem supposedly "secular" elements by combining them with facets of evangelical belief. Such redemption is not confined to literature; evangelicals similarly combine rock rhythms with Christian lyrics and cartoon characters with Bible stories. Attending the 2000 Christian Booksellers Association convention in New Orleans, Louisiana, I realized the enormity of this multi-billion-dollar industry. Standing amidst seven football fields' worth of merchandise ranging from "Bibleman" to "Bible Bars," I wondered if this realization of the "holistic gospel" voiced by Harold Ockenga and Carl Henry in the 1940s has exceeded even their expectations. The vision of infusing all of one's life with religious significance, from coffee mugs to greeting cards, could now for many evangelicals become a reality. While these goods belie the simplistic dichotomy of evangelical and secular, this binary nevertheless shapes how evangelicals assess the vast array of Christian products. For example, listeners expect the latest release from evangelical rock singer Rebecca St. James to provide great music and sound theology without sacrificing either. Similarly, parents buying the latest "Veggie Tale" video for their children evaluate its entertainment value as well as its evangelical attitudes. This vast industry thrives on reconciling artistic endeavors with religious belief, but its success depends upon carefully combining these elements and meeting consumers' expectations.

To the members of Mona's Book Club, as well as to my other consultants, not every novel successfully provides both faith and fun. These consultants disagree, however, on which novels succeed and which fail. Evangelical romance novels feature both struggle and success in religio-romantic issues, and readers' devotion to the genre depends upon its ability to balance these elements. For example, too much tragedy in the plot endangers readers' enjoyment of the story, even as it simultaneously violates their religious expectations. However, at the same time, the novels must also include enough obstacles that readers can find the stories plausible and therefore both entertaining and inspiring. Having too little realism or too few problems fails to draw readers into these fictional worlds and thus diminishes readers' enjoyment of the novels and their ability to learn from them. As active readers, my consultants routinely assess a novel's ability to reconcile these conflicting demands. Failure to attain a proper balance violates readers' interpretive and aesthetic strategies and results in criticism of a particular novel or author. However, while readers share similar expectations, their evaluations reveal a range of views on what constitutes a good read, a spiritual message, and a happy ending. Even as my consultants uphold the boundaries surrounding evangelicalism, their literary evaluations reveal the complexity behind that rhetoric.

Sexual Depictions:
Differentiating the Evangelical and Secular Romance

Not surprisingly, portrayals of romance and sexuality have a major impact on readers' evaluations. My consultants desire a romance storyline, which necessitates some element of sexuality. However, at the same time, they demand that the treatment of this element upholds evangelical beliefs. When a novel achieves this balance, readers can retain the fun of romantic fiction and delight in an entertainment that supports their religious ideals. As a result, their reading further strengthens their evangelical identity as it sets them apart from secular romance readers—a separation that is necessary for their reading pleasure.

Rather than emphasize the historic relationship between evangelicalism and romance, the women I interviewed situated their reading in opposition to the world's secular romance. In this "culture war," romance—as a concept and as a genre—represents an important battleground on which the boundaries of sexuality are fought. "The world," according to my consultants, "has totally distorted it [romance]." The us versus them, subculture versus the world attitude exhibited in this assessment reflects broader evangelical views about their relationship with the wider culture. "The evangelical tradition's entire history, theology, and self-identity," according to sociologist Christian Smith, "presupposes and reflects strong cultural boundaries with nonevangelicals." He continues, "The perception of crisis serves to invigorate and mobilize evangelical vitality rather than to undermine or disintegrate it." [2] Confronted with the crises of homosexuality, promiscuity, and serial monogamy, these evangelical women see the genre as a way to redeem romance and at the same time combat the world's distortions. In their view, the world has reduced romance to sex and divorced sex from marriage. "If things were functioning the way God intended them to be," Melody, a thirty-year-old married mother of two told me, "there wouldn't be all this dating, break up, date somebody else, get married, divorced, marry somebody else." Echoing Melody's charge, Gail stated that "time has perverted it [romance] obviously in our society." It is a loss Lindsay lamented as she wrote to author Irene Brand, "Our society has become so degraded that this subject [Marriage First] is almost taboo." [3]

Nowhere is this distortion more visible, for readers, than in the pages of secular romance novels. Naming sex as the biggest difference between the two genres, my readers indicted the secular and endorsed the evangelical. "Worldly" romances promote relationships based on casual sex, rather than enduring commitment and shared beliefs. Sharise explained it this way: "In secular books, it's like sex, lust, and everything," but in *Ain't No River* by Sharon Ewell Foster, "it's like 'I want to get to know you,' 'Let's get to know God together.'" Lila offered a similar assessment: "[In] a lot of those secular novels, they fall instantly in love and indulge in their passion and they might get married or hang out for a little while and that is usually the end of the book, and that is not life. Life continues after you get married. That is the test of the relationship. It's much harder than the falling in love, that part is easy." The problem for these women revolves around not only the "musical beds" message of secular romance, but also its explicit portrayal. For example, reader Eleanor praised Shari MacDonald's avoidance of this pitfall. She confided in a letter, "I appreciate (not to mention admire) anyone who doesn't write books—please excuse my bluntness—with sex in mind. Have you ever read any of those secular books they have in stores? I bought one once and boy was it bad. I hadn't even got past the first chapter when I had to throw it away."[4] Lila employed the same contrast: "There aren't the sexual scenes [in evangelical romance]. That is the most obnoxious thing that I've read in books. I've read some wonderful books, but the fact that they go into it, explicit sexual scenes, is very offensive to me." For these readers, sexuality belongs in the bedroom, not in the book.[5]

An examination of Lori Wick's evangelical romance *A Gathering of Memories* and Leanne Banks' secular romance *The Lone Rider Takes a Bride* reveals the difference between the two genres' depictions of sexuality. Evangelical heroine Mandy, upon becoming engaged at the end of Wick's novel, exchanges a kiss with her hero Ross: "They leaned toward each other and shared a soft kiss. Mandy's eyes were wet, and she could feel Ross' heart pound." The book ends four pages later. In contrast, in *The Lone Rider Takes a Bride*, an early encounter (one of many) between the dating couple Amelia and Ben quickly becomes sexual: "He pulled her still closer. Her breasts brushed against his chest, and her nipples tightened. She felt annoyed. She felt aroused.

The combination was potent, making her bold." And a few paragraphs later: "He took her lips, plundering her recesses with his tongue. She felt gloriously consumed. Spinning out of control, Amelia held tightly to his strong shoulders and matched his sensuality with her curiosity."[6] For my consultants, plundered lips rather than "soft kisses" and aroused bodies (and body parts) rather than vague sexual "wants" distinguish secular from evangelical in both reading practice and religious belief. These more restrained portrayals of sexuality reinforced their faith and redeemed their reading.

In contrast to the graphic sexuality of secular novels, evangelical romance demonstrates "what good romance should be" and as Diana told me, "It doesn't have to be sex." Rather than promote an "anything for romance impression," the genre emphasizes the importance of friendship and faith in a heterosexual relationship. According to Mary, these ingredients make for a more authentic romance. She described the difference this way: "I think Christian romances have a deeper sense of integrity in their relationships and a deeper sense some way, like providential." For Nancy, the joy of reading evangelical romance came from "knowing that there won't be anything objectionable in there." And other women made the same point: "You know it's going to be a wholesome story, and even when they have the romantic parts, they are done tastefully." Nancy even referred to the books in spatial terms. She described the novels as "a *place* that you can go to read the clean and the wholesome parts [of romance]."[7] My readers' devotion to the genre rests on its ability to portray romance in an evangelical manner. They want stories that, unlike secular romances, affirm their spiritual ideals and offer wholesome entertainment.

Cover art further differentiates my consultants' reading practices. It has become another way to distinguish the "wholesome entertainment" of evangelical romance from the "unclean romantic novels that are out there everywhere." Some women described the covers of Christian novels as "nicely done" and "subtle," but others more explicitly described their standards for the artwork.[8] Not wanting to be classified as a secular romance reader or embarrassed to read a novel with a "bodice-ripper" cover, some told of their gratitude for the novels' artwork. The five Baptist women I interviewed discussed this issue:

> Beth: I just don't want covers that are embarrassing.
>
> Pamela: I want something on the cover that inspires me.
>
> Tina: I don't like them in any way to look like a worldly love and have the girl coming out of her dress, draped over the guy or whatever.
>
> Agnes: Too embarrassing.
>
> Joan: Well, it's not only that. I'm not going to take that into my house and let my children see me reading garbage like that. I like them very mild. I don't have to have anything on the front for me.[9]

For these women, the cover art provided a visible marker of the purity of evangelical romance and further distanced their romance reading from its secular counterpart.

The differences between the two genres prompted some of the women I interviewed to change their reading habits once secular romances no longer provided them an acceptable or fun form of entertainment. As Diana told me, "I used to read Harlequin romances and you just get sick of that and you just don't want to read half of it." Cathy also read secular romances "for a while," until she started reading Janette Oke. And Charlotte, a thirty-three-year-old Southern Baptist, tried to read secular romances, but found them "too uncomfortable" in their graphic sexuality. She was grateful for an evangelical alternative. Marie put this even more strongly in a letter to author Peggy Stoks. She confided, "I have always loved to read and used to read the Harlequin romance books, but God spoke to me one day and said this was not pleasing to him. Now I can hardly wait to purchase inspirational books."[10] Placing their secular romance reading in the past, these women found a welcome alternative in evangelical romance.

Just as readers see attitudes toward sexuality as a dividing line

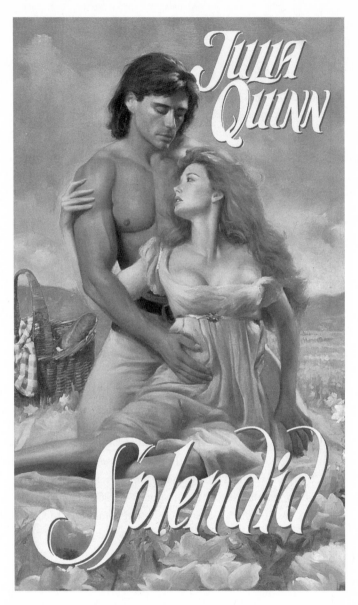

Cover of *Splendid* (1995), a secular romance
novel by Julia Quinn. Copyright Julia Quinn. Reprinted
by permission of HarperCollins Publishers, Inc.

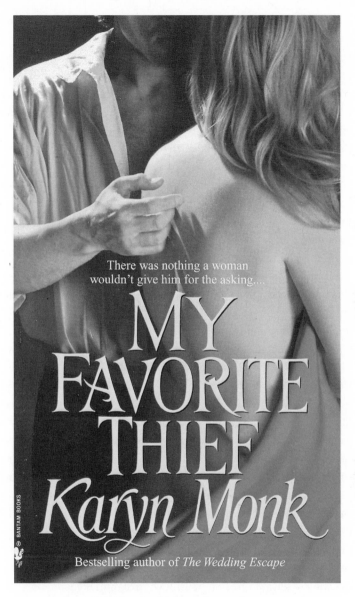

There was nothing a woman
wouldn't give him for the asking....

MY
FAVORITE
THIEF
Karyn Monk

Bestselling author of *The Wedding Escape*

Cover of *My Favorite Thief* (2004), a secular romance
novel by Karyn Monk. Reprinted by permission of Bantam
Books, a division of Random House, Inc.

between themselves and the world, publishers also recognize it as a marker of subcultural distinction—of evangelical versus secular—and ensure that their authors avoid undue depictions of sex. For example, in their submission guidelines, Bethany House writes, "Instead of passionate 'love scenes,' the romance should portray the true meaning of love—commitment and responsibility rather than only emotional and physical attraction." Heartsong Presents, a division of Barbour Books, delineates this even more clearly as it directs authors to "not be overly descriptive when describing how characters feel in a particular romantic moment, for example, kissing, embracing, and so on." The list of don'ts continues, "Kisses are fine (no tongues or heights of arousal, please)." Multnomah's requirements are similar: "Beyond kissing (no French, s'il vous plait) or chaste embraces, avoid the physical arena." Avoiding graphic descriptions, publishers trust that readers' imaginations will remain pure. Tyndale House states this most directly: "Recognizing the prevalence and danger of the sin of lust in the church today, we want to avoid contributing to the problem by titillating our readers."[11]

By emphasizing the contrast between secular and Christian views of sexuality, the novels embody, at least ideally, a perfect combination of romantic elements and religious themes. Not only does the genre potentially impart evangelical values to a perverted world, but it also offers women within the subculture an edifying alternative to the values of that world. In this way, the writing, reading, and producing of the genre becomes a way to exhibit and maintain evangelical identity. However, at the same time, sexuality is not absent. It continues to play a role in the novels and elicits a variety of responses from readers as well as authors. The genre affords women an opportunity to examine, explore, and question the relationship between evangelicalism and sexuality. While readers and authors agree on seeing portrayals of sex as the biggest difference between evangelical and secular novels, they do not always agree on how much sexuality should be present. They exhibit a range of views on this matter that illuminate the complexity of women's interpretations and in some ways belie the rhetoric of subcultural distinction.

For example, some women found that the sexual prohibitions enforced by publishers hindered the love story. Authors such as Peggy Stoks reported finding it difficult to know "how much sexual tension between hero and heroine is okay in a Christian story." Stoks did not want her novel to be "an occasion of sin for a reader," but at times, she felt hero and heroine ended up more like brother and sister, rather than husband and wife. Indeed, this seems true in Janette Oke's *The Calling of Emily Evans*. In this story, heroine Emily and hero Shad hold hands and hug but never kiss. In response to these "holding hands, but no kissing" stories, reader Madeline issued this imperative: "Don't fight what makes it Christian and don't fight what makes it romance!" She professes to want a well-written story that upholds her Christian values while not sacrificing the romantic element. Too often, Madeline and others report, they find the writing lacking and the romance unrealistic.[12]

Lack of realistic sexual chemistry between hero and heroine may also explain why some women continued to read both secular and evangelical romance. While these women disapproved of the graphic sexuality in secular romances and situated evangelical romances in opposition to them, they continued to read them anyway. For example, Betty described how she used a "filter" or a "lens" as she read. "There are some sections that I have to edit out of the secular ones. I like it when I have to do more imagining, but I like a lot of the storylines. I don't forgo them completely, but I moderate them." However, for Betty, not having to wear this "thick skin" proved to be what was most satisfying about reading evangelical romance. She enjoyed "knowing that there won't be anything objectionable in there." Like Betty, Sally also reads both genres and claimed a similar ability to edit: "There's pages that I skip whenever I read a secular one . . . obviously because they are just way too sexually explicit." Her knowledge of which pages to skip, however, depends upon at least skimming the passages to discern their location. At the same time, like Betty, what she enjoyed most about evangelical romance was "seeing how someone applies their Christianity to everyday life, whether it's eighteenth-century, nineteenth-century, or now."[13] While these women enjoyed how evangelical romances integrated their religious beliefs with romantic stories, in some ways they wanted more — more realistic sexuality, more available novels, and more reading freedom.

In contrast, others sometimes found the sexuality in evangelical romance too explicit. Unlike Oke's clasped hands and Wick's soft kiss, Francine Rivers's *Redeeming Love* included substantial detail about the protagonists' sexual relationship as a married couple: "He saw how the pulse raced in her throat and pressed a kiss to it. He heard her soft intake of breath and felt the answering warmth spread swiftly through him. He wanted her. He would always want her. And, praise God, she wanted him as well. He felt it every time he touched her." Readers such as Gail and Jocelyn found Rivers's descriptions too explicit, with "so many sexual images in them, even though they are Christian."[14] For these women, Rivers blurs the boundary between evangelical and secular. Her realistic portrayal jeopardized these readers' religio-romantic expectations; for them Rivers's romance is not Christian enough as it fails to set their reading sufficiently apart from that of the world.

Still others implicitly criticized authors that ignore sexuality as they expressed their gratitude for stories, like *Redeeming Love*, that acknowledge the issue but place it within Christian boundaries. For example, Lila explains, "Francine Rivers is very refreshing because she doesn't ignore it [sex]. A lot of the other ones, they might kiss and it is just not realistic." Kelly agreed: "They don't say, 'Well, you're a Christian so this [sex] doesn't even tempt you.' No, they say 'They're tempted, but with the Lord's help they don't fall into temptation.'"[15] This attitude can be seen in more than one evangelical romance. For example, in *Shadows Along the Ice*, by Judy Baer, Christian heroine Pamela finds herself sexually tempted in her relationship with the as-yet-unconverted hero Ty. Baer writes: "She didn't struggle when Ty stood and picked her up, one arm around her back, the other under her knees and carried her to the couch. He wound exploring fingers in the waterfall of her hair, and his lips surveyed the curves and angles of her face. Pam could hear his breath grow ragged and feel the passion of his kisses increase. 'Pam?' He left the rest of the question unasked, but Pamela knew its meaning. He wanted to stay. And she could not deny that she wanted it too, but her resolve firm, she whispered, 'You have to go now, Ty. Please?'"[16] Ty leaves reluctantly and Pamela remains shaken, yet steadfast, in her faith. In this scene, Baer includes both passion and piety, a scenario that some readers find more realistic than engaged couples who only hold hands. Likewise, in *Where Morning Dawns*, set in the 1580s, Christian heroine Maggie faces a similar dilemma as she falls in love with Native American Towaye. "He kissed her then, and without reservation Maggie surrendered to his caresses. His lips on hers removed any doubt that they were meant for each other. The beating of their hearts made a melody heard only by themselves, and the intensity of their passion cried out for fulfillment. Maggie thought she couldn't muster the strength to put him away, but she did."[17] Again, the heroine upholds the sexual beliefs of her faith and provides readers with a plot both entertaining and inspiring. For some of my consultants, acknowledging sexual desire and temptation while addressing it in an evangelical context makes the novels more practical and more pleasurable. In turn, this realism increases their enjoyment of the genre and enhances the religious learning experience it provides.

The categories "too much romance," "too little romance," and "just enough romance" speak not only to the variety of the evangelical romance genre, but also to the diverse ways readers define the relationship between faith and fun. Despite my consultants' unity on seeing their reading as a form of evangelical entertainment distinct from secular romance reading, they differed in their plot preferences and their romantic evaluations. These differences illustrate the complicated ways women interpret these texts as well as a range of evangelical women's views on sexuality. Some prefer to read only of holding hands, while others expect a few tender kisses, and yet others desire a text that grapples with sexual temptation. Readers (and authors) expressed a variety of views on how to portray romance in an evangelical manner. As a whole, my consultants emphasized the disparities between evangelical and secular romance. However, at the same time, it seems telling that evangelical belief did not prevent many of these women, at one point or another, from reading more erotic literature. They could, it seems, only make the contrast between the two genres if they had read a secular romance novel. These women's reading choices reveal the intricacies of trying to live out the "holistic gospel" and create a distinct subculture. In practice, the boundaries between these women and the world seem not so strong after all.

Publishers may regulate novels' contents, but they cannot control readers' choices or imaginations. Houses like Tyndale and Bethany try to prevent titillation, the "sin of lust," through descriptions of chaste kisses rather than dueling tongues, but their success is not guaranteed. Perhaps, as Ann Barr Snitow argues in "Mass Market Romance: Pornography for Women is Different," the distance between hero and heroine, a plot element in many secular and evangelical romances, heightens the sexual tension: "Distance becomes titillating . . . in romanticized sexuality the pleasure lies in the distance itself. Waiting, anticipation, anxiety—these represent the high point of sexual experience." Similarly, Alison Light suggests that "the reader is left in a permanent state of foreplay, but I would guess that for many women this is the best heterosexual sex they ever get."[18] For the women I interviewed, illicit imaginative possibilities remain a potential consequence of reading romance. Even as some reject secular romances for fear of titillation, evangelical romances contain, it seems, the same imaginative potential, if not the same romantic portrayals.

However, the unity of readers, authors, and publishers on viewing sexuality as something that divides the evangelical from the secular should not be underestimated. This textual difference—veiled marital beds rather than visible "musical" beds—represents an important marker of religious identity. Evangelicals continue to use sexuality as a way to separate themselves from the perceived wider culture. While many conservative Protestants have moderated their views on card playing and bikini wearing, most remain steadfast in defining premarital sex, homosexuality, and pornography as sinful. In this context, evangelical romances become an important site for articulating and defending the subculture's beliefs. Through these narratives, evangelicals challenge the "sinful" sexual ethics portrayed in books or on television and, ideally, offer an alternative. Simultaneously, this spectrum of views on sexuality reveals the subculture's permeability, its ability to absorb and contain a limited diversity. As scholar Randall Balmer notes, "Despite the evangelicals' general insistence on belief, however, they cannot agree on any one configuration of doctrines. And so, paradoxically, their doctrinal precisionism has produced the incredibly diverse evangelical subculture in America."[19] Similarly, for my consultants, even as they agreed generally on viewing evangelical romance as a source of both reading enjoyment and religious growth, their interpretations of the books ranged widely when assessing sexuality—as well as spirituality.

Theological Judgments: Evaluating the Evangelical Romance

Just as readers assess the genre's romantic elements according to their criteria of evangelicalism and enjoyment, they critique the religious components in the same way. Too much evangelicalism or not enough, as well as the amount of biblical content and its application, emerged as vital boundaries monitored by my consultants. Their fictional devotion to the genre rests on its ability to reconcile faith and fun within the framework of subcultural distinction. While they exhibited consensus on these parameters, their evaluations of particular works reveal a variety of views.

Authors supply readers with a variety of spiritual plots from which to choose. From overt evangelical messages of conversion and forgiveness to struggles with loneliness and lack of self-worth, the genre encompasses a range of spiritual storylines. In some ways, the possibilities are endless, as evangelicals perceive all of life in relationship to one's faith. In this view, topics not typically seen as religious, such as weight struggles, work troubles, or attitude problems, become indicators on an evangelical's spiritual barometer. Doubts about self-worth, impatience with a coworker, or angry behavior all reflect a deeper spiritual cause—distance from God. With their insistence on infusing all of life with religious significance, evangelicals view every problem as a gauge of their spiritual status and an opportunity for spiritual growth. However, despite this range of possible topics, the necessity of conversion on the part of the hero or heroine becomes the romantic obstacle and religious message in many of the novels, which are called "missionary romances" in the industry because of their evangelistic emphasis. While authors recognize that many of their readers already espouse evangelicalism, they continue to narrate the conversion experience with the hope of evangelizing the few and ministering to the many.

The plot of Tracie Peterson's *My Valentine* exemplifies the motif of conversion-as-obstacle as religion, not personality conflicts or misunderstandings, keeps hero Pierce Blackwell and heroine Darlene Lewy apart. Set in New York City in the 1830s, the novel depicts the struggles of Darlene, a devout Jew, with the relationship between Judaism and Christianity. Her widowed father Abraham converts to Christianity, raising questions about her faith and inciting the hostility of her Jewish community. Pierce and his father, both evangelical Christians, mentor Abraham, and all three men share their faith with Darlene. During these encounters, Pierce and Darlene fall in love but remain separated by their respective faiths. For Pierce, the divide is insurmountable. He prays, "I love her, God, but I give her to You." By entrusting Darlene's salvation and their relationship to God, Pierce places his love of God ahead of his love for Darlene—and God's desires above his own. Eventually, however, Pierce's prayers are answered. As Darlene talks with her father, he tells her, " 'You must only ask Him into your heart. Ask His forgiveness for your sins, and He will give it to you!' Darlene thought of this for a moment. A peace filled her and she knew in an instant that it was the right thing to do. There was no image of Pierce or her dying father, or the ugliness of her friends and neighbors; there was only this growing sensation that this was the answer she had sought all along. Jesus would fill the void in her heart and take away her loneliness." In her prayer, she denies the influence of others and emphasizes the power of Jesus. Darlene's conversion resolves both her religious and romantic struggles. The novel ends with Pierce and Darlene's Valentine's Day wedding and Darlene's assurance that God would "guide their way." [20]

Other spiritual issues have also become the focus of these love stories. Author Lyn Coleman put it this way: "With each of my stories I try to highlight a spiritual growth issue for each of the primary characters. Whether it be issues of trust, assumptions of knowing God's will, or just getting one's life right with God."[21] Author Lori Wick's novels evince this range of religious topics. While Mandy converts to Christianity in *A Gathering of Memories*, heroine Kate of *Whatever Tomorrow Brings* is a Christian throughout. In this story, Kate struggles to know God's will—what God wants her to do with her life—as she assumes responsibility for her siblings after the death of her mother and her father's decision to stay in the mission field. Disappointed with her father's virtual abandonment and unsure in her new role as family provider, Kate meets fellow Christian Marshall Rigg, but remains uncertain of how to proceed in life and love. Gradually Kate grows in confidence as she discerns God's will and gains Rigg's heart.[22]

While Kate struggles with discerning God's will, others grapple with forgiveness, disappointment, or betrayal. In *Betrayed*, by Lorena McCourtney, devout Christian Rosalyn must face both the loss of her father's company and the marriage of "her best friend and the man she loved. The two strands of betrayal wound like barbed wire around her heart." Despite Rosalyn's faith, doubts about God's care plague her. After an especially painful incident, she questions her faith: "All along she'd depended on the Lord. He would see them through, she'd kept telling herself. But he hadn't! He'd betrayed her too." It takes a while for Rosalyn to deal with this sense of betrayal, but she perseveres. Eventually the love and faith of handsome Christian hero Shea Donahue help her find peace with God. Asking God's forgiveness for her "lapse in faith" and accepting that God "doesn't necessarily answer prayers in the way his people might like or prefer," Rosalyn finds spiritual "serenity" and a man that she truly loves.[23]

Janette Oke's novels also encompass a range of topics, from *Love Comes Softly*, in which heroine Marty becomes a Christian convert, to Missie's struggles with loneliness in *Love's Long Journey*, to Beth's unmet desire for a family in Oke's four-volume series entitled "The Canadian West." The "Canadian West" series assumes the Christianity of the central characters—heroine Beth and her husband Wynn—and the plot revolves not around conversion but rather around Beth's struggle with infertility and the adjustments she faces in following her Canadian Mounty husband to his rural job placements. Lonely, unsure, and sometimes bitter, Beth strives to find contentment with her life as her dreams of children remain unrealized. In the end, Beth and Wynn accept that they will never have biological children, and their faith inspires them to reach out to others and to create the family of their dreams through adoption. Overall, the series celebrates patience, as well as peace with God and one's situation.[24]

Despite the variety of religio-romantic plots, this combination of religious edification and entertainment does not always succeed. Readers find some authors' literary efforts and some novels' religious plots unsatisfactory. As they evaluated each novel, my consultants ranked the novels on a scale that ran from fluffy to gritty and from unreal to real. They labeled those with less religio-romantic depth fluffy or light, and referred to more developed stories as gritty or meaty. However, while many used a similar scale, their rankings and preferences differed. Even as they all expected and desired the genre's happy ending, they disagreed about how much one must go through to achieve it.

Too often, for some women, the stories remained superficial. For example, as I talked with Valerie, a twenty-nine-year-old white woman from North Carolina, she articulated a clear theological vision of spiritual gifts that reflected her own work in music ministry. She viewed her musical talent as a gift from God that she must use for Him, and she expected authors to use the novels in the same way. "If you are going to call it Christian romance," she told me, "then you ought to have a reason behind it." She wanted no plots with a vague spiritual struggle about getting married, "fluff," as she called it, but rather a specific message of salvation. Valerie hoped the authors would "show the way somewhere" and use the novels as tools for God. Others I interviewed echoed Valerie's views. They expected more than Bible verses at the start of each chapter and a few mentions of God.[25]

Often, the lack of realistic spiritual struggle—with characters and plots that are simply "too perfect"—prompted readers to place a novel at the fluffy end of the spiritual spectrum. For example, Jackie remarked that "sometimes they can be too . . . everything falls into place." Lila added, "If the character is so pure, so perfect, I find myself going 'blah,' or like, 'uh huh, sure.'"[26] Knowing their own flaws and how their lives differed from these too-perfect plots, readers labeled these "unrealistic" stories unsatisfying as entertainment items and unhelpful as religious tools. Flawless fictional worlds with too few spiritual problems and superficial characters alienated readers as it denied the reality of their struggles and violated their twofold criteria of enjoyment and edification.

For some of the African American women I interviewed, the obstacles were greater. They struggled with a spiritual issue facing all aspects of evangelicalism, including its novels: racism. These readers confronted a genre dominated by white authors and characters, a dominance overlooked by most of the white women I interviewed. This lack of diversity creates a problem for women like Roxanne and those in Mona's Book Club, who are interested in reading only African American evangelical romance: the problem of finding enough books to read. For African American women who read evangelical romances by white authors that feature white characters, different struggles emerged. As I talked with Tamara, a thirty-six-year-old African American, about the novels in the library where she worked, she raised questions and concerns about race in the novels. She asked, "Why does everyone have to be 6'4" with blue eyes, you know?" The physical perfection and lack of diversity eventually affected her reading choices: "I used to really be into the more historical ones because Lori Wick used to do those historical ones, but after a while I just got tired of the tall good-looking guys with blue eyes . . . sometimes you get tired of it because it does something to your mind after a while. I know that my child will be reading this type of literature at about twelve or thirteen and she will get tired of those things and what will that do to my child's brain?"[27] Troubled by images of flawless white beauty, Tamara struggled to find heroines that reflected her experiences as an African American woman. Madeline also found this lack of diversity troubling: "You can literally count on one hand how many books have black people on the cover if you are in a Christian bookstore." [28] While a few evangelical romances, such as *Ain't No River*, feature successful African American heroines, stories depicting women of color in realistic and relevant ways remain in short supply.

Unrealistic, irrelevant, or superficial may describe the fluffy novels that often disappoint readers' desires for an enjoyable and edifying story, but my consultants disagreed on which authors belonged in this category. The librarians (church and public) that I talked with tended to place the "line romances," Heartsong and Love Inspired, in this category. Stories like *My Valentine*, a Heartsong title, feature little in-depth character development and a simple message of conversion. Of evangelical romance novels, these books most resemble Harlequins in their 180–220–page length, mass-market paperback size, and $3–$5 cost. Other readers poked fun at the works of Hilda Stahl, Beverly Lewis, and Grace Livingston Hill, criticizing their predictability, superficiality, and poor writing. Reader Beth also placed "hokey Janette Oke" on the "light" side of the spectrum. However, even as some criticized these fluffy novels, many others found them satisfying and successful in fulfilling both their entertainment desires and spiritual needs.

Unlike Valerie's desire for a clear-cut missionary romance or Tamara's frustration with flawless heroines, Janet voiced a different wish. She called her reading a "mini-vacation" and preferred the "fluffier," "lighter" stories featuring less-intense spiritual and life struggles. For Janet, relaxation and entertainment weighed more heavily in her literary evaluations. Nevertheless, even Janet still found some spiritual help through reading. Every so often, she said, the novels would make a point that encouraged her spiritually. Another woman echoed this attitude: "They are easy reads usually. I read mainly for enjoyment and if I get a little something out of it, then great. But I'm not reading it like a textbook." [29] These women prefer the fluffy novel because plots that are "too realistic" prevent their escape—the fun of forgetting their problems—and offer too little promise of future happiness. Seeking relaxation in their reading, some found the intensity of the heroine's struggles in more "meaty" novels too dark and depressing, too similar to daily life. After reading a contemporary evangelical romance about issues of evolution, corruption, and church/state relations, Jenna said that "it was okay, it kept my interest, [but] it just seemed like what we are trying to escape from in everyday life." While Jenna finished this novel, Cathy stopped reading one that upset her: "It was real dark and even though I know that is out there, I thought, no, I don't want to read this. It wasn't really vulgar, but there was something about it." She continued, "I don't want anything too heavy." [30] This sentiment accords with other findings in the realm of popular piety. For example, David Morgan writes, "Reassurance or reaffirmation is the principle concern in popular religious art, as in popular art in general." [31] For readers, the novels must carefully balance tragedy and triumph, struggle and success. An imbalance prevents readers' enjoyment of and hence their devotion to the genre.

While Jenna and Cathy dislike novels that are too realistic, others prefer them and label them "deep," "gritty," or "meaty," to indicate spiritual as well as historical depth. As one woman told me, "You can still get the light fluff, but there are things out there now that are more meaty." [32] Most often, readers associated this "meaty" end of the spectrum with two authors—Francine Rivers and Karen Kingsbury—who address topics such as abortion, prostitution, and persecution. Many found this realism rewarding to both their reading pleasure and their spiritual growth. Another woman shared, "One thing I find that Karen [Kingsbury] does that a lot of the authors don't use is allow the main character to fail and I like that because it's about God's grace, not just salvation." Lila said of Rivers, "She writes very down-to-earth, realistic . . . The people are real, they make some bad choices, but ultimately their faith comes down and prevails in their life." [33] These women characterized Rivers as a gifted author who develops three-dimensional characters and addresses everyday religious life. Just as some find Rivers's portrayal of sexuality more realistic and therefore more enjoyable, they view her portrayals of spiritual failure and triumph as more inspiring to their faith. This "meat" not only enhances their reading pleasure, but it also feeds their spiritual growth.[34]

Given the multiple demands on these women's lives examined in the previous chapter, it makes sense that they actively assess each work and remain faithful to authors who deliver good stories, while criticizing those who disappoint. For many, Janette Oke's work dominates their list of favorites, and like Gwen, these readers find her novels realistic: "I think with Janette Oke, she really wants her novels to have the focus on growing with God, rather than satisfying the reader." Others, however, expressed their dissatisfaction with Oke's work and other "light" reads, calling them a "waste of time." Lila, for example, described a particular Oke plot this way: "They were living in some nice little house. I don't think the lady was married, and there was nothing in their life except maybe the dress didn't fit right, nothing ever went wrong. They had no emotional upheavals at all, and I really like to see people work through things." Guarding their leisure time, readers such as this conclude, like Beth, "I don't have enough time to read books like that."[35] As a result, women tend to read authors that they know and like, novels that worked for them religiously and romantically. If a friend recommends a book or if they can flip through it at the library (rather than invest in buying it), they may venture to investigate a new author.[36] However, the women reported being reluctant to try new authors for fear of losing their reading pleasure, religious inspiration, and precious time. Sometimes a new author was not worth the risk.

Women's use of the classification scheme "fluffy" versus "meaty" reveals not only their active approach in reading selection but also the importance they place on the novels' evangelical tenets. Readers expect the novels to include religious elements and assess them accordingly. However, at each end of the spectrum, women discover messages that nourish their spiritual growth. Those who prefer the fluffy formula romances see them as serving a spiritual purpose just as those who read the meaty romances see their choices. Readers' distinctions between fluffy and meaty novels, then, reflect reading preferences as well as the religious relevance readers perceive in the stories. And while readers sometimes employ this distinction to deride lighter novels, more often they express gratitude that the evangelical romance industry now offers such a variety of novels.

Whatever their reading preferences, my consultants expect a religio-romantic happy ending. As Jackie told me, "You only want to read so much sadness." [37] Even those who prefer the more meaty novels spoke of how these realistic plots emphasized the themes of God's grace and faith's triumph. For the novels to succeed as an entertaining devotion, readers need to find elements of realism and inspiration, tragedy and triumph. Any given title must ensure enough reality that readers identify with the circumstances, but at the same time it must also supply an ending that inspires and assures readers of faith's power.

Improperly balanced novels prompt various reactions. Most often, if readers find a story unsatisfying on either level—faith or fun—they stop reading. Just as Cathy stopped reading a plot she described as "too dark," many women simply put down novels that fail to meet their expectations. Others deride novels or authors that fail, as evidenced in Beth's phrase, "hokey Janette Oke." And some readers respond with ready criticism. Most often this occurs when my consultants view a novel as going beyond the spectrum of fluffy versus meaty, real versus unreal, into the unchristian. Author Shari MacDonald, struggling with the genre's purpose, readers' expectations, and publishers' demands, provides an example. MacDonald assumes a Christian readership and believes her audience would find a romance featuring "the four spiritual laws" repetitive. She has adapted her stories accordingly. For example, in her novella *Home for the Heart* only a few vague prayers and a statement of God's love by the heroine mark the story as religious, while the hero's spiritual life remains a mystery.[38] Novels such as this elicit complex reader reactions. For example, Cheryl wrote a letter to MacDonald after reading one of her novels. She called the plot "a good one," but remained "uncomfortable with the constant slamming and verbal combat of the characters." She continued her indictment and questioned MacDonald's vocation—"It [the arguing] was exhausting. I realize that this seems to be common in our world today, but Christian fiction is, I believe, held to a higher standard"—before offering specific ways to improve the novel. Such restrictions frustrate authors like MacDonald, who questions why some evangelicals cannot acknowledge different literary paths to glorifying God. MacDonald expressed the desire to experiment with her writing, to go beyond the evangelical romance genre and write stories that feature "ugliness and imperfection." However, she believes that publisher guidelines and reader reactions may prevent her from doing so, and it seems she may be right.[39]

Readers' demands for both religious inspiration and romantic imagination are so strong that they often try to forget novels that have failed them. When I asked about their least favorite evangelical romances most readers could not recall specific titles but were nevertheless vocal in their critiques of these disappointing works. Beth proved no exception, as she was particularly disturbed over the theology of one novel. In this troubling story, the heroine, experiencing marital troubles, returns to her hometown, sees an old boyfriend, and kisses him. In the end, she returns to her husband but proclaims that a part of her will always love the old boyfriend. Beth, very vocal in the group of Baptist women I interviewed, was not pleased. In her view, "that's just wrong," and she went on to recommend the appropriate course of action: "She should renounce that and leave that completely. She should do away with it." Clearly bothered, Beth expected more of both the novel and the author. "They should be responsible for what they write and *if* they are Christian they should know that." The novel *Temptation*, by Victoria Christopher Murray, prompted similar reflection and criticism from another reader. This story also focused on marital temptation, which, in Madeline's view, the author failed to address in a sufficiently serious spiritual manner. Madeline was unhappy with the book's superficiality and speculated about the author's Christianity. "She knew about [Christianity], but it wasn't in her heart and I think that is something [that appears] in her writing." In both cases, these fictional shortcomings raised questions in the minds of readers about the author's faith.[40] For my consultants, the theology of a novel must resonate with their interpretation

of evangelicalism. Just as narrative portrayals of sexuality differentiate the evangelical from the secular, these woman expect the religious
elements in a novel to do the same.

However, such criticisms of an artist are not unique to evangelical romances. Amy Grant, a popular Christian singer, faced a similar
questioning of her faith when she crossed over into the secular music
market, divorced her husband, and married country musician Vince
Gill. A review of her album, *Behind the Eyes*, charged that "nothing
seems to distinguish Grant's crossover music from secular AC [adult
contemporary] songs." Another reviewer described her music as made
up of "fairly vague lyrics about the personal vicissitudes of the Christian life," and stated, "If Christian music that's identified as such
enters the pop mainstream as, at best, mildly edifying entertainment
that makes no moral waves, then Christianity itself is trivialized."
While these reviewers queried what makes Christian music Christian, concerned evangelical journalist and nonfiction author Wendy
Murray Zoba mounted a more serious indictment. For Zoba, Grant's
questionable crossover music reflected equally poor choices in her
personal and spiritual life. Grant's divorce, Zoba insisted, "should
give us all pause. But neither Grant nor the Christian marketing industry, in promoting her concerts and albums has missed a beat."
Holding Christian leaders to "a higher moral standard," Zoba stated
that the lack of reflection on this issue, by Grant and the Christian
music industry, defied Christian beliefs about marriage.[41]

The evangelical popular culture industry, then, must in the eyes
of its purchasers properly combine secular and religious elements.
Evangelical consumers expect artists to seamlessly weave the two together and offer products that are neither too preachy nor too wishy-
washy. These religious goods must also be accompanied by excellence
in form or artistry. Rejecting art for art's sake and fun for fun's sake,
this industry is predicated not on modernist ideas of excellence or
hedonist concepts of pleasure, but rather on mediocrity. According
to the *Oxford English Dictionary*, historically the word "mediocre" has
meant the "quality or condition of being intermediate between two
extremes," or a "quality or position equally removed from two oppo-

site extremes; a mean." Evangelicalism and its popular culture succeed, in part, by taking this mean or mediocre position of being in, but not of, the world—of engaging with distinction. Their religious identity thrives on a constant movement back and forth between a perceived Christianity and a perceived outside culture. Or to employ Michel de Certeau's terminology, many evangelicals poach on the terrain of popular culture and appropriate it for their own purposes. On a daily basis, these conservative Protestants use Christian products as a way to construct an "in-between" religious identity—a mean position between the perceived extremes of fundamentalism and liberalism. Occupying this middle ground, evangelicals combine and redeem elements of these seemingly disparate worlds.[42]

However, my consultants' struggles with some "inappropriate" storylines, as well as the variety of their assessments, reflect larger conflicts that characterize the relationship between evangelicalism and the arts. Historically, despite its redemption of creativity, evangelicalism has struggled with how to combine its religious mission with forms of art and entertainment. While evangelistic utilitarianism usually overrides artistic concerns, questions about appropriate subjects and proper depictions linger. Evangelical Leland Ryken writes in "The Creative Arts" that "at the heart of the Christian world view is a balance or tension between good and evil, hope and despair, optimism and pessimism." [43] Part of the evangelical "art of being in-between," of being "in but not of the world," thrives on this tension of recognizing evil but emphasizing good, of experiencing despair yet remaining hopeful. In evangelical literature generally, the question of how to portray this tension frequently arises. How does one depict the hope of evangelical faith amidst the tragedies of everyday life? As Thomas Howard asks, "Does there come a point at which the artistic portrayal of evil crosses a certain line and itself begins to participate in the very evil it is portraying?" [44] Given evangelical beliefs that "what goes into a mind comes out in a life"—a CBA slogan—evangelical authors and readers carefully monitor the artistic line between good and evil. Too often, according to critics, evangelical authors and artists fail in their balancing of these dimensions. Critics assert that creators of evangelical popular culture, afraid of participating in evil, err on the side of good, and as a result, produce lamentable sentimental piety, as well as substandard, formulaic art. This sentimentality prompts evangelical critic Rene Frank to wonder "whether the church of Christ shall indiscriminately be satisfied with the sentimental and effeminate art that for the most part adorns our walls, books, greeting cards, and educational helps."[45] Similarly, evangelical Rolland Hein states, "He cannot be a true artist, he cannot be a significant writer, if his vision does not include the whole of human life, the depths of depravity as well as the heights of aspiration." Hein continues, "Not only is the Christian novelist limited in his selection of material; he is forced to handle even the properly selected material in a prudish and unrealistic manner."[46] For these aestheticians, evangelical romances represent kitsch, rather than "true art," as they revel in femininity and sentimentality, predictability and prudery.

While heroine Garvin wants to deny racism's effect on her life, some fear that evangelical romance encourages a similar escapism among its readers. Critics such as Frank and Hein see evangelical literature, including romance, as mired in denial. Rather than encompass the "whole of human life," the novels consistently uphold a happy ending, the idea that "all things work for good" in the end. Evangelical romance publishers' guidelines reinforce this impression. They instruct writers to avoid "sticky topics" and certain subjects remain absent: homosexual children, unconverted heroes, and unforgiving heroines. Barbour Books reminds authors, "Remember, Heartsong Presents readers are conservative Christians who want a good love story. They don't want to be reminded of the evils in our modern world; they are reading to escape this world. They want to read about characters they can relate to, who face similar situations and deal with similar emotions." Multnomah addresses this same issue in its guidelines for heroines. Readers are "looking for engaging, likable, passionate, independent, strong yet vulnerable, true-to-life women . . . these women have to be someone with whom readers will identify."[47] Publishers, understanding readers' desires, strive to maintain the sentimentality of the genre, to the dismay of critics.

Authors, to a certain extent, uphold these guidelines. For example, the mother of the genre, Janette Oke, knows she "has many young readers" and consequently avoids certain topics. She told *Writers' Digest*, "There are also some issues that I have very strong feelings about, such as sexual orientation or coming of age or physical abuse, that I choose not to address in my writings. There are other Christian writers who are tackling these 'prickly' issues in a more direct way." Similarly, Lori Wick recalled her desire to include a scene that included some sexuality or violence, but given the youth of many of her readers, her editor questioned this decision. Wick described the disagreement with her editor thus: "I said, 'I don't write these for kids.' She said, 'Nevertheless, they read them.'" Wick eventually acquiesced to her editor's decision and eliminated the scene. Youth may be one reason authors avoid certain topics, but the fear of participating in evil, as well as the goal of meeting readers' desire for fun, also shapes such editorial choices. Shari MacDonald described her experience with this tension. Despite her desire to write "deeper stuff" with "more conflicted characters," MacDonald knows that "readers are looking for that happy ending, and the lightness of it."[48]

The imperative to write "light" books with a happy ending reveals the sentimentality of the evangelical romance genre. Historically defined as a "refined and elevated feeling," according to the *Oxford English Dictionary*, "sentimentality" now refers to an "indulgence in superficial emotion." Or, as Robert Solomon writes of sentimental kitsch, "from the aesthetic point of view it is the 'perverse perfection' that is so offensive and cloying, the absence of any ambiguity or dissonance on the part of the viewer, but most important it is the manipulation of emotion, the evocation of 'cheap,' 'false' emotions that makes this otherwise 'perfect' [work of art] perverse."[49] To critics of evangelical romance, the "all things work for good" framework fosters an immature hopefulness and denies the suffering and evil so evident in the world. At best, this tendency represents naïve optimism, a childish fantasy—at worst, evil's redemption. How is it that grown women with jobs, families, and education escape into a happily-ever-after fictional world, rather than deal with the reality of everyday life?

For some, psychological and developmental theories best explain such escapism. From these perspectives, choosing sentimentality represents a troublesome act and reveals psychological issues. According to Robert Solomon's analysis, for many, "sentimentality and kitsch reveal not only a woefully inadequate aesthetic sense but a deep moral flaw of character." Aesthetician Frank Burch Brown employs this explanation, at times reluctantly, in his analysis of the Precious Moments Chapel created by Samuel Butcher outside Carthage, Missouri. Throughout the chapel, adorned with murals featuring biblical scenes in the Precious Moments style—children with teardrop eyes painted in soft pastel colors—Brown compares Michelangelo's depiction of the Last Judgment with that of Butcher. He writes, "Butcher gives us a kinder, gentler gospel: the mildest possible image of heavenly rewards, in a setting more placid than inspiring. That sin could possibly have dire consequences is never visualized at all, even if it is somehow presumed." The emphasis on gentleness rather than brutality, good rather than evil, prompts Burch Brown to question the maturity of the place and its practitioners: "The Precious Moments Chapel could appear not merely childlike but somewhat childish in its spirituality and theology." Even as Burch Brown struggles against artistic elitism, traces of it emerge as he seeks to understand the Chapel and the patrons who seemingly lack "normal" adult religio-aesthetic judgment. Burch Brown's inability to escape this approach continues as he indicts the cheap and false emotions evoked by the Chapel, thereby establishing its sentimentality and placing it under the purview of kitsch rather than art. He writes, "These are formulas that trigger a predictably tearful or heartwarming response but that offer no new insight, and in fact tend to trivialize genuine religious feeling, and so to profane what is sacred." Denigrating the integrity of the chapel's art and dismissing its visitors' emotion, Burch Brown relies on the language of childhood and immaturity to describe responses to the Chapel.

Similarly, while describing Catholic women's devotional culture, in *Thank You, St. Jude*, historian Robert Orsi distances himself from, but ultimately relies on, a similar rationale. Struggling to make sense of fidelity to the patron saint of lost causes, Orsi does not fully endorse how psychological explanations situate women's devotion to St. Jude in an infantile stage of faith, but he seems unable, in the end, to escape them. Attributing something of a "delusional quality" to the women's devotional practice, Orsi states, "Like children, these women were mistaking their wishes for the world; they closed their eyes, and everything turned out all right. But also like children, the devout were trapped in an odd conjecture of contradictory feelings of magical agency and resignation." Seeing their devotion as "childish" and "the renunciation of their adult selves," Orsi concludes that while their devotion may offer some compensation, ultimately these women's faith has betrayed them: "Jude turns out to have been Judas after all." [50] The psychological explanations of both Brown and Orsi cast the participants in a less-than-favorable light.

From a similar viewpoint, evangelical romance novel reading represents a childish act of an immature faith—one that escapes and denies problems of real life through fictional plots that ensure happy endings. God embodies not so much an omnipotent ruler or wrathful judge but rather a gift-giving Santa Claus.[51] From this vantage point, these women, unable to handle the tragedies of life, even in fiction, retreat to a world of make-believe and feel-good emotions. It is a world where, to quote Frank Burch Brown, "there is not the faintest hint of shit." As a result, readers deny the injustice and evil that characterize daily life and neglect to change the world in which they live. At this point, the sentimental choice becomes an immoral act.[52] Proponents of this interpretation fear that the escapist impulses and sentimental endings of the genre foster a dangerous apathy in regard to the real world. Rather than change the circumstances of their lives, the situations that often lead to their escapist desires, these women do not seemingly recognize evil's power or challenge oppressive systems. Their reality becomes skewed, their anger minimal, and their actions minuscule.

On some levels, this approach offers a persuasive explanation, especially if my consultants' stories about their reading stopped here. If their reading led only to fictional worlds, and perhaps to a few family and friends, then this explanation might make sense. However, these women's stories continued and many questions remain. What does it mean to term the religious practice of some women childish? What is the task of the religion scholar? Why, in the field of American religion, have scholars sought to emphasize the agency of new religious movement members, only to cast the shadow of passivity over female devotees of popular religion? And, as Robert Solomon asks, "Why in particular condemn the focus on innocence and cuteness as a 'fiction' when every form of enthusiasm or emotion betrays some particular focus or concern? What is the alternative?" [53] These questions necessitate going deeper into the context, content, and consequences of these women's fictional devotion.

Placing my consultants' reading amidst the broader background of evangelicalism helps situate the practice. These women are evangelicals, and like other evangelicals they emphasize the individual and her relationship with God. That personal relationship with God, in their view, takes precedence over everything else. It represents the foremost priority in one's life and the ultimate opportunity for change. The result, according to Mark A. Noll and Cassandra Niemczyk, is a belief "that social reform comes only through the conversion of individuals." [54] Or, as Christian Smith notes in terms of political involvement, evangelicals focus not on "procedural changes" or on "a Christian view of political justice," but rather "view government in exaggerated personalistic terms" and employ an individualistic strategy "to elect good Christians to political office." The evangelical romance genre reinforces this message of individualism, but does not prevent real-life action. Evangelical political and social activism reflects the same participation rates (or higher) as mainline, liberal, and nonreligious groups. [55] Given this context, we must remember that these women cannot simply be reduced to the romance novels that they read, since this genre represent only one aspect of their religious lives.

However, we also should not underestimate the importance of evangelical romances for understanding how women practice their evangelical identity on a daily basis. These novels represent a favored genre that helps us better understand these women's everyday religious lives. For my consultants, the most powerful type of change comes not through political action or social activity, but rather through religious devotion that inspires individual spiritual change. As I talked with these women, they narrated stories of how evangelical romance novels help them achieve that goal. Their fictional devotion *to* evangelical romance novels rests on their view of the novels as a devotion *through* which they realize spiritual change. Their reading is not solely a denial of evil or an escape from life, but along with their religious practices makes up a more complicated collage. They know bad things happen. They have lived through tragedies and sadness. Like other people, whether women or men, evangelical or not, these women sometimes wish to temporarily escape this pain and have devised ways of doing so. Given this, their reading represents an awareness of this often sad reality and of their faith's fragility when faced with crisis. Through their reading choices, they hope to combat that despair with a theology of hope and perseverance. If we take these women's voices and their religious beliefs seriously, the decision to read becomes not the act of a child but that of a woman trying to maintain her faith amidst the ups and downs of daily life. And if the ultimate change for these women is religious, then the question of whether or not reading evangelical romance results in spiritual transformation emerges. The following chapter examines how the authors and readers I interviewed understand the genre's religious purpose and function.

"Please help me to know You. The Bible says we all sin and I can see now that it's true. I do sin." The words were whispered on the wind and for the first time Mandy felt like God was listening.

"Did you really die for everyone, God—for me too?" These words came on a sob and Mandy's tears fell on the grass beneath her. She told God everything through those tears, her doubts and fears, her pride and stubbornness, but mostly how much she wanted to know Him and how afraid she was that He would turn her away.

She sat up when she had finished praying and stared up at the sky. She wasn't sure why but she suddenly knew that God would never reject her.

No words would come then, but she realized she had crossed over the barrier in her mind. Verses Ross had quoted came to her, and every time one did she said yes to God. Yes to believing on His Son. Yes to eternal life. Yes to confessing her sin. And yes to being his child for evermore.

Her tears were spent as a deep peace settled within her. She looked up at the clouds and thought how God Himself had made them. She was on her feet in the next instant and running for the house.[1]

CHAPTER 4

The Ministry of Romantic Fiction

Mandy, heroine of Lori Wick's *A Gathering of Memories*, ran into the house to share the good news of her salvation with her foster family. They greeted their new sister in Christ with tears and salutations: "Welcome home, Mandy."[2] Mandy and her siblings, orphaned by the death of their mother and desertion by their father, found a home with Amy and Silas Cameron. Committed Christians (and the subjects of a previous book in the series), the couple shared the gospel, attended church, and prayed for their new family. God rewarded their evangelical efforts as one by one Mandy and her siblings accepted Jesus Christ as their savior. The scene featuring Mandy's salvation describes a pivotal moment in the life of evangelical Christians and a common element in the plots of evangelical romances. However, the novel does not end with her conversion. It also chronicles Mandy's struggles as she continues in her Christian walk and eventually finds love with Ross Beckett. While the novel ends happily, it demonstrates the hardships that characterize evangelical life.

Mandy-like heroines and their love stories fill the fiction shelves at local Christian bookstores and the reading lists of the women I interviewed. Readers often resemble Laura, a thirty-eight-year-old, white, married woman who does accounting for her husband's electrical business and works as the primary caregiver to their three children. She is a United Methodist, a college graduate, and a reader of Janette Oke and Lori Wick. Or picture Jocelyn, who I interviewed at her favorite branch of the Durham County Public Library. She is forty-eight, African American, widowed, and a mother of four. She attends her United Pentecostal church more than once a week, works nights as a lead supervisor to support her family, and reads, on average, four evangelical romances a month. Jocelyn and Laura, as well as the other women I interviewed, are devoted *to* the genre, as it provides a source of evangelical entertainment. However, their devotion also rests on how they imagine evangelical romance reading as a devotional practice *through* which to articulate a women's faith and a women's ministry. The genre becomes an instrument for the performance and composition of evangelical women's everyday religious lives. In viewing the novels as a devotional tool, as well as a source of wholesome fun, they set themselves apart from their non-evangelical romance-reading counterparts, as well as from evangelical men.[3]

While conservative Protestant men participate in church services, attend Promise Keeper rallies, play in church softball leagues, or lead family devotions, there seems to be no readily apparent male equivalent to the evangelical romance. Subsequent studies, I hope, will illuminate this gap in our knowledge of male devotional life; however, the current invisibility of their practice stands in stark contrast to women's consumption/production of evangelical romance and evangelical popular culture in general. This contrast often casts an unfavorable light upon women's devotion. They appear, unlike their male counterparts, to need more help sustaining their faith. They are, in this view, weak and spiritually vulnerable.[4] However, changing the theoretical lens from deprivation to production reveals not weakness, but rather strength. "The basis of a theory of everyday life," argues John Fiske, "is not the products, the system that distributes them, or the consumer information, but the concrete specific uses they are put to, the individual acts of consumption-production, the creativities produced from commodities."[5] The crucial task, then, is to understand what religious uses evangelical romances serve in the everyday lives of their readers. In this framework, my consultants "make do" with the options available and actively seek ways to fortify their faith.[6]

Evangelical Women's Ministry: Using Evangelical Romance

When one surveys the multi-billion-dollar evangelical popular culture industry, she will encounter the evangelistic utilitarianism of the past in this plethora of contemporary products—Testamints (evangelistic candies), "Jesus is My Homeboy" t-shirts, and games like Bibleopoly. While Christian stores often market these items as evangelistic tools, viewing them solely in these terms obscures the multiplicity of their religious functions. When seen only as witnessing aids, evangelical efforts inevitably appear to fail as most of the products are purchased not by "nonbelievers," but by those already professing conservative Protestant piety. If evangelistic success serves as the standard for judgment, then, too many products simply preach to the choir. In my research, none of the women I interviewed and only one of the letters I analyzed described a conversion prompted by evangelical romance reading. If evangelism is the criterion of success, then the novels fail to achieve their goal, at least on any large scale. However, moving beyond the rhetoric of evangelism, or put another way, shifting the focus away from conversion, reveals a world of women's religious devotion, a space where romance novels become instruments of faith. It is a world where women minister to other women and preaching to the choir is more than just a cliché.

Drawing on the heritage of evangelicalism and the arts, my consultants (both authors and readers) overwhelmingly agree on the purpose of evangelical romances: the novels represent a ministry by, for, and about women. Of the twenty authors I interviewed, all imagined their writing in utilitarian terms, as a ministry through which God works. Just as the characters Silas and Amy taught heroine Mandy, authors use their romance formulas as a way to teach others—whether Christian or not—about evangelical Christianity. With the pulpit and the pastorate (as well as other church leadership roles) closed to them, these evangelical women found in the genre a vehicle and a resource for their spiritual desires. And in its ability to hold together seemingly disparate elements—women and ministry, faith and fiction—evangelical romance offered the authors I interviewed a way to express their spiritual ideas that other evangelical activities did not.

Aware of the unfavorable light thrown upon their novels by some evangelicals and other critics, these authors readily provided a two-fold justification for their work: the example of Jesus and a calling by God. The first part of this defense unfolded as I attended a Christian Booksellers Association workshop entitled "Trends in Christian Fiction." The leaders, two evangelical romance authors, highlighted the stellar heritage of Christian fiction and placed their work in the lineage of Austen, Dickens, Stowe, and (Grace Livingston) Hill. While the workshop leaders surely hoped these names provided some legitimacy, they sealed their case with a claim to the divine. Using Eugene Peterson's *The Message: The New Testament in Contemporary Language*, they read from the Gospel of Matthew, Chapter 13: "The disciples came up [to Jesus] and asked, 'Why do you tell stories?' He replied, 'You've been given insight into God's kingdom. You know how it works. Not everybody has this gift, this insight; it hasn't been given to them. Whenever someone has a ready heart for this, the insights and understandings flow freely. But if there is no readiness, any trace of receptiveness soon disappears. That's why I tell stories: to create readiness, to nudge the people toward receptive insight.'"[7] Like Jesus, these authors would use stories to minister, thereby finding divine inspiration for writing the evangelical romance.

When faced with critics, the mother of the genre, Janette Oke, appeals to this defense. She argues, "Jesus used stories all the time in his ministry." Echoing Jesus's words in Matthew 13, Oke explains how stories reach people in a way that other approaches do not: "We have learned that spiritual lessons can be told by fictional characters and the reader does not feel confronted." She continued, "It's very rewarding to hear from these people and realize that God through his Holy Spirit can take the reader past the words I have written to deal with something in their own life."[8] In these statements, the language of divine utility emerges: stories are *used* by Jesus, and the Holy Spirit takes some readers *through* the written page. Novels become a conduit for an experience of the divine. David Morgan discovered a similar attitude, which he describes in *Visual Piety*, his examination of religious material and artistic culture. He writes: "The point behind the visual culture of popular piety is not principally an admiration of skill which pertains to the manipulation of a medium, but admiration for the object of representation, that is, what is seen *through* the medium."[9] Rejecting writing for writing's sake, evangelical romance authors like Oke defend the utility of love stories through an appeal to the divine. While both men and women in evangelicalism look to the example of Jesus, for women seeking to legitimate their literary efforts and resulting leadership roles, Jesus provides a biblical example strong enough to silence critics.[10]

The second part of the authors' defense, like the first, also appeals to the divine—a calling by God. This justification has a long history of inspiring conservative Protestant men and women to evangelistic action. A divine calling validates one's religious vocation. For men, it offers further support, in addition to the Bible, to pursue religious leadership; however, for women it offers an alternative to the Bible and thereby affords women new opportunities to do the same. Historically, as Catherine Brekus so aptly demonstrates in *Strangers and Pilgrims: Female Preachers in America*, the voice of God supersedes narrow biblical interpretation regarding women's religious roles. For conservative Protestant women today, as in the past, claiming Jesus and being called by God outweigh injunctions against women as ministers, or more specifically, women as ministers with romance novels as their pulpit.[11] In this view, God can use anyone or anything, whether male or female, romantic fiction or religious parable, to accomplish Christian goals.

Following the path established by Janette Oke and, before her, Grace Livingston Hill, evangelical romance authors have established their claim to Christian ministry. As I talked with Robin Jones Gunn, she described the emergence of her calling. On a campout with a youth group, Gunn realized that the teenage girls were in their tents reading secular romance novels. Concerned by this, she went out and bought them Janette Oke and Carole Gift Page novels. However, the supply did not keep up with the reading demand of her teenagers. "They said, 'Why don't you write a book? You write children's books. It'll be easy, we'll tell you what to write.'" They became her focus group and her critics, and the resulting novel, *Summer Promise*, started Gunn's "Christy Miller" series. The books in this series have sold over 1.5 million copies around the world (and been translated into three languages). Speaking of the letters she receives from all over the globe, Gunn said, "What astounds me continually is that we are going to meet these young hearts in heaven because of a novel, because of a romance, because of a fiction story—a character that they related to and the gospel made clear to them. I found a quote from C. S. Lewis—everybody has a favorite C. S. Lewis quote—mine is from a letter he wrote to Arthur Greaves in 1939, and it said, 'Any amount of theology can now be smuggled into people's minds under the cover of romance without their knowing it.' That's what I want to do as I write: smuggle the truth in under cover of romance." In describing this desire, Gunn emphasized her surprise that God would use her, as well as a romance novel, to convert people. Her amazement highlights the religious utility of evangelical romance novels and perhaps silences some critics. She also hopes, it seems, that some unsuspecting readers (non-Christians) will be surprised and transformed when they pick up a romance novel that they do not know contains a Christian message. Here, Gunn provides a rationale that affirms the certainty of her calling by proving the instrumentality of her writing.[12]

Other authors with stories like Gunn's invoked the language of calling and ministry as they discussed their vocational certainty. Tracie Peterson remembered, "When I accepted Christ as my Savior, I knew that he was calling me to do something for him. Turned out to be writing Christian fiction." Similarly, Debra White Smith stated simply, "I knew I had a call to write," and Robin Lee Hatcher explained that "there's a call on my heart and I don't have any option." Likewise, Doris Elaine Fell, a former missionary with Wycliffe Bible Translators, told me, "I feel as called to writing as I was to the mission field."[13] And for Peggy Stoks, who considers herself an "evangelical Catholic," her calling is twofold: "In addition to working to advance the Gospel through my writing, perhaps I am also in the place I am to bear witness to a different type of Catholic than to which people are accustomed. While I am far from being an erudite, expert Catholic apologist, I have many opportunities to explain the Catholic faith to my Protestant brothers and sisters as I answer their questions and clear up misunderstandings."[14] Amidst restrictions on women's leadership in evangelicalism (and Catholicism) and despite doubts about the value of the genre, these women created an instrument for their voices and a rationale for their compositions.

Using evangelical romance as an instrument, these authors communicate spiritual lessons to their reading congregation. As Lori Wick described, "I have a faith in Jesus Christ that pretty much permeates my life and who I am. And I can't take this vehicle, this 350-page vehicle, and not somewhere in this book let people know that they can have the same hope that I have." For these authors, distinct literary standards and goals apply. Bestsellers and critical acclaim may be the dream for some writers, but these authors want to craft stories through which readers encounter the divine. Their success depends not on themselves, but on God. The power of the divine animates their work and ensures their literary achievements. Wick explained it this way: "God takes our very frail efforts—he can do remarkable things with ugly clay pots that are willing to be shaped by him—and he takes sometimes the most puny effort and turns it into something that glorifies him. And I do see fiction as a powerful vehicle for that." Shari MacDonald echoed these sentiments as she asked, "It's just me writing a sweet little story, what possible power can there be in that?" She went on to offer her own answer, as she claimed that "God can use anything. God can use a romance novel."[15] For these authors, God uses their "puny efforts" just as he uses the novels themselves. They, as much as their writing, become instruments of God in this evangelical ministry.

However, authors' divine call to write evangelical romance does not translate into total creative freedom in one's storylines. Houses utilize stringent guidelines regarding the novels' religious content. Bethany House wants authors to deliver "one main scriptural teaching skillfully incorporated into the story without being either 'preachy' or too obscure." Multnomah acknowledges that "people express their faith in unique ways," but insists that "both hero and heroine need to be believers to avoid the 'unequally yoked' issue." Barbour Books offers even more detailed guidelines, stating that the topics of divorce, drinking, and dancing should be avoided. In addition, authors should "steer clear of sticky topics," including the intricacies of baptism (water and spirit), speaking in tongues, the end times, and women's ordination. They state specifically, "No woman character should be ordained," and they will not consider manuscripts if the heroine is a pastor or youth pastor.[16] Ironically, even as publishers eliminate the possibility of women's ministry *in* fiction, they provide the opportunity for women's ministry *through* fiction.

The religious plots of evangelical romantic novels often emerge from the authors' spiritual journeys and further situate this fictional devotion within the realm of women. Telling the story of the heroine, as well as the author, the novels chronicle the spiritual lives of women. On a typical Sunday morning, most, if not all, of my consultants attend church services that, in typical Protestant fashion, feature the spoken word, the sermon. Women may give announcements, sing in the choir, or perhaps read the scriptural passage, but in evangelicalism, the sermon remains the center of the service and under the purview of men. As a result, as Brenda Brasher shows in her study *Godly Women*, these orations "tend to draw illustrative stories from the range of life experiences encouraged by male socialization processes rather than female ones." Put another way, "In sermons, women's ideas and experiences are marginalized." In contrast, evangelical romances offer a ministry drawn from the struggles and experiences of women.[17]

Using life experiences encouraged by female socialization processes, to paraphrase Brasher, women minister to other women. The novels become a way for authors to voice their religious ideas and for readers to increase their spiritual repertoire. This emerged quite powerfully as I talked with Robin Lee Hatcher. Having experienced the pain of marital infidelity and divorce, Hatcher drew on these life lessons to help other women in her novel *The Forgiving Hour*. Referring to it as "God's book," Hatcher penned the story of heroine Claire, who faces a bitter dilemma. Divorced, due to her husband's infidelity, Claire must decide how to respond when her son becomes engaged to her ex-husband's former mistress. In addition to the story, Hatcher includes a letter at the end of the novel to further reach out to her readers. She writes, "While not truly autobiographical, I do know firsthand the heartbreak of an unfaithful spouse, and I also know what it is like to be called upon by our heavenly Father to forgive all parties involved."[18] Here, Hatcher tackles topics—adultery and divorce—not often featured or discussed from a female perspective in Sunday morning sermons. While not a typical romance, many read it within that framework and, as we will see throughout this study, benefit from what Hatcher has learned.

Other authors also use personal experience to fuel their literary ministries. For example, Shari MacDonald debated whether or not God can handle, in her words, "the tough questions." After resolving this dilemma, she wrote an evangelical romance entitled *Sierra*, which she describes this way: "Really, if there was a theme to the book it was that God's big enough to handle your questions." Her subsequent novels also reflect spiritual issues she has worked through. Terry Blackstock has developed the same method: "I like to show characters—both believing and unbelieving—in crisis, and I often take them through the same types of lessons the Lord has taken me through. In the end, the reader can see growth in the characters, and hopefully that will challenge the reader to grow as well." [19] For these authors, not only can God use their writing, but through these literary efforts they can narrate their spiritual struggles and successes.

By framing their writing as a ministry and sharing their own stories, authors hope to script a plot that makes the divine present to readers. Through the novels, they want readers to reach out to God and grow in their personal relationships with him, one of the hallmarks of evangelicalism. To elicit this response, they do not write stories of a distant, disinterested deity, but rather tales that tell of God's closeness with humanity. Author Maureen Pratt describes her literary hopes for readers, that they will "have a stronger sense of the active presence of the Lord in their lives." [20] Evangelical romances narrate God's involvement in daily situations and his desire to participate in readers' lives. Robin Lee Hatcher voiced a clear vision of how this divine presence appears. She realized how much God's voice permeated her own life and wanted readers to learn that God is "always there." To illustrate this, she writes God's words in lower case, italicized letters to set them apart. She uses this technique to make readers pause and listen for God's voice in their daily lives. In her view, God speaks to us all the time, but too often television or radio drowns out his voice. For authors, the reality of God's presence indicates another divine attribute: his providential and personal nature. If God is always there, then God is there for a reason. Authors seek to reassure readers that "God has a plan for each person" and that he cares about the details of their lives, from "the smallest things—getting a parking space—to the largest of things—healing." By focusing on God's attention to everyday details, as well as his presence and planning, authors hope that through their novels readers will experience God.[21]

Authorial intent, however, does not guarantee reader response. As reader-response theory has developed, scholarship has moved from studies focused solely on writers' intentions to the "ideal" reader imagined by authors (or scholars) to analysis of how actual readers interpret texts. This focus reveals how readers, while guided by the parameters of the text, often appropriate it for their purposes and interpret it according to their interests. "Reading," to quote Janice Radway, "is not eating."[22] Recognizing readers' interpretive power, many current literary theories emphasize the contrast between author intention and reader response. However, in the realm of evangelical romance, I discovered a surprising continuity between authors and readers on the religious purposes of the novel. Readers shared authors' utilitarian vision of evangelical romance. They believed in God's calling of authors and his use of their writing. In their descriptions, my consultants often invoked the same vocabulary as authors. For example, before reading a novel by Robin Lee Hatcher, Elsie, a Christian for over twenty-five years, "would have never believed before that God could send you a message in a book," while Tracy wrote, "Thank you dear sister, for an incredible, powerful book that God continues to use in the hearts of his children."[23] Like authors, readers repeatedly expressed God's *use* of these women and their writings. Through their fictional devotion they not only gained the enjoyment of reading, but also the power of God. One woman wrote, "Thank you for being a part of helping me get going in the right direction," and another stated, "I thank God for the powerful way he is using you in my life."[24] For readers, these evangelical romance narratives become a channel through which they can experience the divine.

Authors hope to elicit this experience by striking a chord in readers' memories. They do not introduce radical theology or marginal religious topics, but rather emphasize familiar spiritual subjects important to women and to evangelicalism as a whole. The novels' plots include oft-heard lessons on God's love and the necessity of conversion. Women, like Laura and Jocelyn, already Christian, read of heroines like Mandy, who convert and grow in the evangelical faith. It is not a new story for them, nor is it an unfamiliar one. Similarly, while Robin Lee Hatcher's narrative about marital infidelity offers an innovative treatment of the issue, her message of forgiveness should ring a few bells in the evangelical mind. For some, this preaching to the choir makes no sense given the already-converted Christian status of the audience.

However, just as Grace Livingston Hill rejected the art for art's sake credo of her time and built on the past, contemporary evangelical romance writers do the same. Their literary aims defy the artistic achievements lauded by modern art. "Modernist aesthetics," according to artist Odd Nerdrum, are "based on the idea that artwork must be complex, surprising, innovative and exciting." The enemy of this aesthetic, according to Nerdrum, is kitsch. "Kitsch became the unified concept for all that wasn't intellectual and new, for all that was conceived as brown, old-fashioned, sentimental, melodramatic and pathetic."[25] It is this aesthetic division that leads evangelicals such as critic Franky Schaeffer to describe conservative Protestant popular culture as kitsch, as "the same idle rehash of acceptable spiritual slogans, endlessly recycled as pabulum for the tone-deaf, TV-softened brains of our present-day Christians."[26] However, for evangelical romance authors, what literary critics would call pedestrian writing represents pious devotion and what Schaeffer would label recycled sloganeering embodies women's spirituality.

It is these familiar and rehashed spiritual struggles, drawn from the experiences of female authors and portrayed through fictional heroines, which my consultants use to help sustain their religious commitments. Whether a plot features a heroine's rebirth into Christianity or a problem she encounters later in her spiritual journey, readers I interviewed use these fictional stories to maintain their faith. Their religious identity is not static or intrinsic, but rather formed and maintained in everyday life, in part, through evangelical romance reading. Preaching to the choir, then, is precisely the point. It represents part of "a dynamic, processual, and contextual phenomenon" through which my consultants constantly remember, relearn, and, in turn, live their faith.[27]

Readers frequently used the language of memory to describe the relationship between their reading and religious lives. As Lila explained, reading the novels "reminds you of what you have and encourages you to persevere." Another told me, "They remind me that I do have the strength to overcome things." Rachel, in a letter to Robin Lee Hatcher, wrote, "I enjoyed *The Shepherd's Voice*. What a beautiful story of God's love, grace and forgiveness! And what an important reminder that it's God's will, not our own that matters." Susannah remembered a similar lesson: "Your book," she told Hatcher, "reminded me to give the whole problem over to God."[28] In these statements, the fragility and fluidity of these women's faith becomes clear. For these readers, it seems that other evangelical practices, such as attending church or teaching Sunday School, do not suffice. As a result, they create an additional way to maintain their religious identity. Through their fictional devotion, readers retain or regain the reality of their faith. "All commodities," as theorist John Fiske writes, "can be used by the consumer to construct meanings of self, of social identity and social relations."[29] For my consultants, evangelical romance reading becomes a tool in the construction of their religious identities. Writing and reading evangelical romance becomes a spiritual practice, a devotional act, for the women I interviewed. Laura said it this way: "I guess if I can walk away and it gives me more strength to live the way I should then I think that is probably the best thing. It uplifts me spiritually and gives me a boost, you know, closer to God and to live that way. I look at a lot of it as more of a *devotional* thing, besides pleasure. I do feel that I get closer to God out of reading them." Similarly, Jean stated, "If I can't get to my devotion or I can't get to Scripture, I always find something in here that helps me with my walk."[30] Amidst the multiple demands of everyday life, the genre provides a vehicle for escape, an avenue of fun, and a path to God.

The agreement between authors and readers on the religious utility of the genre, its devotional purpose, reflects their power as an interpretive community—a group, according to literary critic Stanley Fish, "made up of those who share interpretive strategies not for reading (in the conventional sense) but for writing texts, for constituting their properties and assigning their intentions. In other words, these strategies exist prior to the act of reading and therefore determine the shape of what is read rather than, as is usually assumed, the other way around." [31] As women, as evangelicals, and as evangelical romance devotees, these readers "know their way of doing things; they know a customary mode of thought and performance." [32] United in their vision of the novels, these readers and writers have created a community of women bound together by their interpretive strategies and more.

Evangelical Women's Community: Narrating Faith and Friendship

The strength and scope of the evangelical romance community goes beyond shared interpretive strategies and the pages of any given novel. For these readers, fictional devotion also means female relationships. Their reading practices connect them not only to female members of their families and churches, as discussed previously, but also to female authors. Lila described this shared feeling: "I think the fact that the author is writing about these things encourages you too. The fact that they are thinking it through and putting it down on paper, that they were probably going through the same kind of troubles." [33] This sharing of faith, fiction, and misfortune creates bonds between authors and readers that reinforce this woman-centered ministry. While the women I interviewed expressed appreciation of this bond to me, its importance emerged even more strongly in readers' letters to authors. When readers become writers, they, like the women to whom they write, narrate their spiritual struggles and successes. They reveal facets of their religious lives—their hopes, their dreams, their failures. Through their letters, they extend the reach of authors' ministries and ask for more, whether support, advice, or friendship.[34]

In this section I focus on fan mail to illuminate additional uses of evangelical romance novels. Through the writing of fan mail, the novels become a means not only for authors to articulate their spiritual stories, but also for readers to voice their religious trials and triumphs. Readers narrate their own spiritual lives and establish a dispersed female community with authors. This community, in turn, shares joys and sorrows, offers guidance and solace, and provides validation and assurance.

In the process of establishing a bond with authors, a common letter writing pattern emerges. The initial greetings typically revolve around a statement of gratitude for and enjoyment of a particular novel (and author). For example, in a typed letter, Marie opened with, "Just wanted to say I enjoyed *The Sound of the Water*. It was such a delightful story. I am so thankful for the writers who love the Lord, and have been given the talent to put their thoughts into words." Similarly, Elena greeted novelist Robin Lee Hatcher with the following: "I just wanted to write you, to say thank you. I believe when someone does something for you, you should say thank you." Letter-writers often closed their missives the same way—with thanks.[35] However, many also added specific wishes for the authors. "May God bless you and your work," is a common refrain, while others offered additional encouragement, such as "Be strong in the Lord and have faith always!" and "Thank you for listening and may God our Father give you His insight, His strength, and His many blessings on you and your work."[36] In between the opening salutations and closing wishes, women usually narrate their stories—how or why they connected with the novel and the author—and many times voice a request.[37] In the intervening paragraphs, the significance of these dispersed literary communities (for fans, as well as authors) emerged. Through these missives, readers hope for a relationship with authors that will strengthen the bonds of their fictional friendships, as well as their evangelical commitments.

As letter-writers penned their stories, they often chronicled a spiritual lesson learned or a connection made with the novels' characters or plot. Like authors, these women became narrators of their spiritual experiences and desires. For example, in a note to Shari

MacDonald, Marsha explained how she became involved in Christian ministry because of Shari's writing; Pamela wrote about how Robin Lee Hatcher's *Whispers from Yesterday* helped her as she struggled "to find that special relationship with God." Other letters took a lighter tone and commented more on the novels' plots. For example, many younger readers connected with Shari Macdonald's novel *Diamonds*, featuring romance in a baseball setting. Twelve-year-old Stephanie wrote on lined notebook paper that she "would like to play softball" and enjoys going to baseball games, closing her brief letter (as others did) with an expression of gratitude: "Thank you for writing *Diamonds*. I enjoyed it a lot." Similarly, Nicole, in college and "the biggest baseball fan ever," explained how the novel echoed her dream proposal and wedding. She wanted her boyfriend, a baseball catcher, "to propose on the field during a game, but not in a mascot's outfit [as in the book], in his uniform. I also want to be married on a baseball field." [38] As letter writers pen their missives to authors—including similar interests, related events, a shared faith—they emphasize their bond with these authors. As one woman wrote, "I feel like I know you after reading." Viewing the writing and reading process as one of Christian kinship and female connection, readers ask authors into their lives in a variety of ways. [39]

Requests that readers make of authors range from personal information to professional advice and spiritual assistance. For example, Loretta, intrigued by Irene Brand's travels, proceeded to ask a litany of questions: "I saw that you and your husband have traveled to forty-nine of the fifty states. Which one haven't you been to? I also read that you've visited thirty-two foreign countries. What is it like to travel abroad?" The list of questions continued, and Loretta closed with "I think it would be a huge thrill if you could respond personally!" Having enjoyed a recipe listed in Peggy Stoks's book, Emily requested more recipes; in a different vein, Lily, who admired Shari MacDonald's book dedication to her mother-in-law, wrote, "I bet you have a really neat husband too, with such a mother?! I'd like to see a picture of you both—just a snapshot if you have one." Sharon also asked for a picture of MacDonald, as well as a list of her books. [40]

Sharon was not alone in requesting more information on an author's publications. Some simply asked, "What's next?," while others seemed to expect authors to automatically supply the desired information. Grace aimed to complete her "full collection" of Robin Lee Hatcher novels, but needed a list of books published since *The Forgiving Hour*. She wrote, "Please could you send me a printout of those that you have made since." Carol wanted to make sure she didn't miss any new novels, so she asked, "Please let me know if any more books in this series come out."[41] Others desired information on where and how to acquire specific titles. Carrie, on the lookout for Peggy Stoks's next novels, wrote "I have been looking for *Romy's Walk* and *Elena's Song* in Christian bookstores but no one has them. Have these books been published yet and if so how/where can I buy a copy?" Similarly, Bonnie, who owns all of Shari MacDonald's books with the exception of *The Garden*, "thought maybe you could suggest how to get it." And Courtney seemed to demand similar information of Irene Brand: "I would like for you to tell me where I can get the other four [novels]."[42] Courtney's underlining emphasizes the importance of reading in her life, but also her sense of entitlement and expectation—emotions that seem to emerge from her perceived relationship with Irene Brand. Invoking their shared faith and love of evangelical romance, women asked authors to help them fulfill their needs for support (reading and otherwise).

Others sought to establish bonds with authors based on their common Christianity and love of writing. Accordingly, these letter writers requested information on literary careers and publishing opportunities. For example, fifteen-year-old Carly requested a favor of Shari MacDonald "from one writer to another." Hoping to develop her writing skills, she asked, "Would you be willing to send me a small note back just telling me one simple and small thing—your favorite book that YOU have written and why!?" She went on to thank MacDonald, assured her that "I will pray for you each time that I remember," and stated, "You can pray for me, also, and my blossoming, God-given desire of writing!"[43] Older women also sought writing advice. Jennifer explained to MacDonald, "I felt compelled to write to you because I appreciate your work and also because you were published as an unmarried person." Jennifer then described her two novels and voiced her desire for publishing advice. Phoebe's request echoed Jennifer's: "I was hoping you would be able to help me find some Christian publishers and editors that would be able to help me." A slightly different request came from Roberta, a married stay-at-home mother of one. She wrote, "My dream job, besides raising my son, is to be able to get paid for reading Christian books and either reviewing them or proofreading them. I find too many errors in already published books and think that it is a shame." She concluded this paragraph with a series of questions: "How do dependable people get chosen for a job like this? What kind of educational background do they require? Do you think you could in any way, shape, or form, help me find some information on this?" [44]

While some chronicled their dreams of weddings on baseball fields or desires for careers in Christian publishing, others wrote of their hopes for Christian friendship and guidance. One of the most moving letters that I read came from Danielle. Dated January 20, 1998, she wrote to Shari MacDonald in shaky script on stationery featuring violets, butterflies, and a Bible verse, Philippians 4:25, which reads, "The grace of our Lord Jesus Christ be with you." In her letter, Danielle confided how she suffered a disabling stroke on May 29, 1987, and could only read, write, and watch television. The bright spots in her life seemed to be her "dear husband" who cared for her and the bookmobile's monthly delivery of novels for her to read. After signing her name, and adding a postscript wishing the author "good luck" in her future writing, two wobbly little words conveyed Danielle's request of Shari MacDonald: "Write me." [45] Echoing off the page, these words reveal the importance of this relationship, this sense of community, to a woman imprisoned by poor health.

Similarly, Caroline, literally in prison, wrote to Irene Brand requesting guidance. "You must have a wonderful spirituality about you. I can feel the peace and serenity, even in your writing. I need someone to correspond with—to possibly teach me about Scriptures. It would be wonderful if you could write me once in a while." Later, she requested a list of other novels written by Irene Brand and added, "If you could find the time to at least answer my letter I'd be truly grateful. Its very lonely in places like these—a letter is like gold." For these two women, confined by different circumstances, letters became a way to reach out to others, a means to cultivate Christian relationships. The letters provide "emotional support" and are in some ways "the only outlet available for the expression of care, affection, and intimacy."[46]

Like Caroline, many other women requested additional spiritual assistance from authors. After reading *Whispers from Yesterday*, Pamela wrote to its author, "Can I ask you a question? Do you have the kind of faith as Sophia and Esther [characters in the novel]? Is it possible to attain that special kind of relationship with our Creator or is it all a pipe-dream and just the makings of a 'true-to-life' Christian fictional book? I wish I could meet you I have so many questions to ask." In contrast to Pamela's typed, polished missive, Gemma handwrote her letter on plain white paper. Referring to a previous exchange, Gemma related the significance of a letter from Irene Brand. "The one highlight of March," the month when Gemma's husband of thirty-six years died and her daughter with spina bifida had four surgeries, "was a letter from you. I read it often as it is a real life line for me." She continued, "I am now asking for your prayers as my doctor found a growth on my right ovary that he says is the size of a honeydew melon and is going to do surgery." Hoping to escort her oldest daughter down the aisle after the surgery, she requested of Irene, "Pray all goes well and I'll be able to walk down that aisle with her."[47] Through their fictional devotion, women like Caroline and Gemma gain a way to articulate their spiritual struggles and a sense of female community, a community that shares their faith, their misfortunes, and at the same time offers a helping hand and a listening ear.

Jocelyn, the forty-eight-year-old African American widow mentioned earlier in the chapter, who reads four evangelical romances a month, also found a confidant and mentor in author Karen Kingsbury. As we talked, Jocelyn described how God reached her through Kingsbury's novels. For Jocelyn, "God has always spoken to me through things that I read," and after discovering Kingsbury's work, she proceeded to reach out to the author through e-mail in response. "I just wrote out what I was feeling," Jocelyn told me, "and how this book affected my life and she just happened to be on the computer." Their correspondence has continued and Jocelyn seeks Karen's spiritual advice: "Karen always talks about being a prayer warrior and actually I was going to e-mail her this past week—in fact, I'll do that when I go home—it has got me to the place of looking at my spiritual walk and wanting to grow and even more to the point where I want to write to her and just see what worked in her life to get her to a higher plane." Like Gemma, Jocelyn sought and found spiritual guidance in more than a novel. For many readers, fictional devotion means more than wholesome fun; it also involves creating relationships with authors willing to dispense religious support, as well as finding a way to voice the struggles and successes of their faith.[48]

For the writers of evangelical romance, readers' letters constitute a vital element in their writing careers. When I asked authors about the most rewarding part of their writing, many replied: "the letters." Tracie Peterson, for example, answered the question, "The letters I get show that often people have rethought painful situations, dealt with crisis, found hope or joy, or in general felt reaffirmed in their own faith and beliefs. That leaves me believing I'm doing something right." Similarly, Peggy Stoks replied, "Learning that a reader's heart has been touched or even changed by something I wrote. Most often this happens through letters I receive in the mail."[49] Fan letters affirm authors' calls to write, the effectiveness of their literary endeavors, and God's use of their "puny efforts." Through the letters, they can see how God has employed their writing in readers' lives. This, in turn, encourages them (as readers desire) to keep writing.

For Janette Oke, fan mail prompted her to continue the story of Marty and Clark in the "Love Comes Softly" series. Initially, she had no thoughts of writing a series, but after receiving numerous letters asking "What happens next?" and "Where do we go from here?" she ended up with an eight-volume series. And in at least one instance, a reader more than a publisher constrained the work of Shari Macdonald. A fan letter prompted her to temporarily alter her writing style. She described receiving and responding to her most memorable letter: "I got a letter from a woman, she was an older women, who was just incensed that I had not made any reference to Jesus Christ in my book. I had made various references to God, but my assumption was really that I was speaking to a Christian audience." Shari described her reaction as "sort of 'Oh my gosh, I need to do that' and [in her next book] really put in a very, very overt message that I was actually kind of uncomfortable with, because I felt it was too in-your-face. I didn't feel like it was my style." [50] Given the shared interpretive strategies and communal sense of authors and readers, evangelical romance novels not only contain writers' spiritual struggles and imaginative storylines, but they also reflect authors' interactions with readers.

While readers' letters validate authors' literary callings, they also prompt other overtures that affirm the bonds of this female interpretive community. As part of their ministry, some authors write back, as we saw with the exchange between Gemma and Irene Brand. Janette Oke also spoke of answering her letters. She stated, "Sometimes these people just share their hearts, because I am not a threat, I'm not going to see them in church on Sunday, so they're very open to that. So that's the other side of the ministry—the letter contact." Other authors reply through "Dear Reader" letters at the end of novels. In this space, authors express their gratitude to readers and add a personal note. Marta Perry, for example, asked readers about their relationship with God and explained how she found the opening verse for *The Doctor Next Door*. Another author responded to fan mail with prayer. After writing *The Forgiving Hour*, with its plot about marital infidelity, Robin Lee Hatcher found herself deluged with letters and e-mails. She learned to have a box of tissues ready whenever she opened another four-to-five-page letter. Overwhelmed by readers' responses and her responsibility, Hatcher established a prayer basket. "All the letters that tell me anything personal, any kind of personal stories, go into this prayer basket and I pray over it every Friday. And I tell the Lord, 'You know a lot of these may already be solved and taken care of—it doesn't matter, I just am . . . I'll pray for them until I die.'" [51]

While my consultants share a vision of the genre as ministry and voice a connection with each other, these bonds are flexible and fluid. They are subject to readers' spiritual needs and their literary desires. According to literacy scholars David Barton and Roz Ivanic, "There are times in people's lives when they need to write more and times they need to write less." [52] So, too, it seems, there are times when women need to read more and times when they need to read less. When asked to describe their reading patterns, some women used the word "sporadic." They may read many novels over a relatively short period of time and then not read any for a while. They do not always need or want the resources, spiritual or otherwise, offered by the genre. At any given time, they may read to claim leisure time, remember religious beliefs, experience divine presence, or all three. Their fictional devotion, as seen in the previous chapters, depends upon a variety of factors—amount of leisure time, interpretation of romantic elements, and level of spiritual commitment. Given this, they do not always read evangelical romances in the same way or for the same reason. Readers' ability to choose when and how to read the novels gives this devotion the advantage of adaptability. Rather than a religious requirement or a mandatory exercise, readers participate in this fictional devotion when they desire.

In addition, the plot of a given novel will enhance or detract from the bonds of this interpretive community. As we have seen, readers constantly assess authors' plots in terms of fluffy and gritty, unreal and real. For some, if the story relates to their particular experience in a meaningful way, they will narrate their spiritual growth and perhaps write a letter to an author. However, as time moves on, this sense of connection may fade, the letters may stop, and the reader-author bond may change. Or perhaps, the author's next novel will renew their relationship. At the same time, one reader's inspiring novel may be another's disappointing read. In this case, readers may question the author's writing style or her religious commitment. An author failing to respond to a request or writing a disappointing novel may lead women to sever their connection by reading other authors or not reading at all. Some women wrote to criticize Shari MacDonald for her lack of Christian content and it seems likely that others discontinued reading her altogether. This community of women reading and writing constantly adapts and reconfigures itself.[53]

In reflecting on their fictional devotion, both the authors and readers I interviewed framed their stories in terms of evangelical women struggling to maintain their religious commitment. Whether writing their struggles into the novels, narrating their views to an interviewer, or penning their thoughts in a letter, they grapple with the meaning of a ministry for, by, and about women. Through their connection with evangelical romances, these women voice the everyday dilemmas of their faith. Authors spin their spiritual narratives into romantic fiction, allowing readers to discover stories like their own, of women—authors and heroines—trying to live out faith amidst the multiple strands of daily life. Popular culture, according to Michel de Certeau, is the "art of making do," a way in which "people have to make do with what they have. In these combatants' stratagems, there is a certain art of placing one's blows, a pleasure in getting around the rules of a constraining space."[54] Amidst the constraints on women's leadership in evangelicalism, which leaves only informal avenues of ministry open to authors and masculine idioms in the Sunday sermons of readers, my consultants' fictional devotion becomes an instrument for the articulation of their spiritual concerns. For these women, evangelical romances resonate with multiple rhythms of their lives.

However, this view of the evangelical romance novel as more than just a hobby or entertainment sometimes meets with disbelief and scorn (attitudes that perhaps keeps some would-be readers away). Many simply do not believe the claim. For example, when I asked Diana if anyone criticized her reading, she rolled her eyes and responded, "Well, my children pick on me about it. My daughter is into Jane Austen and *Emma* is her favorite. She thinks that is what I should be reading." Gail encountered a similar attitude: "Oh yeah, a guy I dated, it was just fluff to him."[55] For Heidi the criticism came from two fronts—her children and her minister. Her children laughed at her, though they still gave her one of the novels as a gift. Heidi also worried, "I think my preacher might [criticize her romance reading]. I think he thinks it's silly." Similarly, Lila's former pastor "made fun of

us for reading 'mindless sappy novels,' he called them."[56] These criticisms reveal not only literary judgments about romance novels but
also doubts about their capacity to prompt spiritual change. People
like Lila's former minister, it seems, distrust women's devotion to
the genre as well as God's ability or willingness to use it for religious
purposes. This suspicion may also reveal gender strains within evangelicalism, concerns about the effects of women ministering to other
women.

Despite criticism, these women use evangelical romance novels
to gain leisure time, establish female community, narrate spiritual
struggles, and create a women's ministry. However, the question remains: Does reading evangelical romance novels prompt spiritual
change and if so, how? If readers view these narratives as a vehicle
through which one can transform everyday religious life, then what
factors emerge as the driving force behind such transformation? It is
to these questions that we turn, in the following chapters.

My struggle with the Old Order prayer veiling has come to a blissful end. Reverently, I now wear the formal Mennonite covering in obedience to God and to my husband. Such a blessing and delight it is to follow my dear Lord Jesus in this simple act of faith.

Daniel took me as his bride, before God and the many witnesses—mostly Mennonites—who assembled at the Hickory Hollow meetinghouse. I had no idea until much later, after most everyone had gone home, that Mamma had been present for the wedding service, too.

I had returned to the church sanctuary to locate an extra bulletin for our wedding scrapbook. High in the balcony Rebecca stood, looking as radiant as any bride's mother should. "Stay right there," I called to her, rushing around to the stairs.

We kissed and hugged like the long-lost friends we were.

"Katie," she said, touching my white dress, "you're as perty as a picture."

"I can't believe you came, but I'm ever so glad you did!"

She smiled and her hazel eyes lit up like heaven, the way they always used to, back before my shunning. "I wouldn't have missed seein' ya joined with your Daniel . . . not for the world."

"My search is over, Mamma. All the scraps and pieces of my life are a God-ordered design . . . like one of your beautiful quilts. I was looking for fancy things and found a personal relationship with the Lord Jesus. I was

yearning for my roots and found a portion
of heaven on earth." I patted the small white
Bible I'd carried under my wedding roses. "It's
all right here, Mamma. I just didn't know it."

So, the Lord willing, I'll grow very old with
Dan by my side. He'll serenade me on his
guitar while I sow straight rows of tomatoes
and a few rutabagas. I'll sing and play for him,
too, after his long days of blueprint making.
Above all, we'll share the love of Jesus in song
wherever he leads us.[1]

In this closing scene of *The Reckoning*, author
Beverly Lewis concludes her three-volume series with the marriage of
heroine Katie to her childhood sweetheart Dan. The novels feature the
journey of Katie, who was raised with the Old Order Amish in Hickory
Hollow, Pennsylvania, to find herself, faith, and love. After discovering a fancy silk baby dress in her "plain" Amish attic, she embarks on a
journey into her past. This trip eventually leads to the discovery of her
adoption. Filled with details about Lancaster County and the Amish
way of life, the novels chronicle Katie's search for religious truth, biological identity, and marital love. As she finds her wealthy heritage
and birth name (Katherine Mayfield) in the "English" world, Katie
also discovers evangelical Christianity. In the course of her journey,
she realizes, as she tells Mamma, that "following the Ordnung isn't
what matters," but rather, "being a follower of Jesus is what counts." [2]
In the end, she donates her inherited estate to a hospice, marries her
first love, Daniel Fisher, and hopes to live a "plain" life serving the
Lord.

Beverly Lewis, a favorite with the readers that I interviewed, inter-
weaves historical details, romantic elements, and religious differences in her trilogy entitled "The Heritage of Lancaster County." In
Lewis's Lancaster, readers find a combination that works, both religiously and recreationally. Balancing struggle and success, tragedy
and triumph, Lewis offers readers a series that explores religious

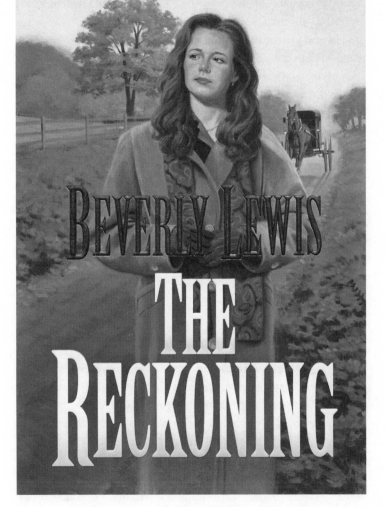

THE HERITAGE OF LANCASTER COUNTY · 3

IT IS THE LIFE SHE'S ALWAYS DREAMED OF, YET HER AMISH
ROOTS ARE CALLING HER HOME.

BEVERLY LEWIS

THE RECKONING

Cover of *The Reckoning* (1998), by Beverly Lewis. Reprinted by
permission of Bethany House, a division of Baker Publishing Group.

growth and romantic love. Evangelical romances like Lewis's become a ministry through which spiritual change occurs, in part, by establishing a two-fold relationship between reader and heroine: identification and inspiration. It is a relationship predicated on the reader's desire for spiritual sustenance and growth or, at times, her sense of pain and inadequacy. In these women's everyday lives, often the reality of faith fades and the sense of God erodes. However, heroines such as Katie, if successful, help readers recapture the certainty of evangelical faith that prompts them to then gain spiritual encouragement, practice evangelical beliefs, and endure religious struggles. In this way, evangelical romance reading does more than provide fun time, strengthen family ties, and bring together church friends. It also offers fictional counterparts who face understandable problems and who model solutions. Through this relationship configured by identification and inspiration, readers move from a fictional story to their real lives with renewed faith. Their escapist desires and happy endings lead them back to their own struggles equipped with renewed evangelical energy, which for them represents the ultimate source of power and change. The sentimentality of these love stories leads to the reality of religious hope.

Helpful Heroines: Identification and Inspiration

For readers, the ministerial effectiveness of a novel depends upon its ability to sweep them away, to transport them from their daily lives to fictional worlds. For fiction readers generally, getting lost in a text, or swept away, is common. Theorist John Fiske describes the phenomenon this way: "It occurs in the body of the reader at the moment of reading when text and reader erotically lose their separate identities and become a new, momentarily produced body that is theirs and theirs alone, that defies meaning or discipline." [3] One can see this movement in Jenna's comment. A married mother of three, she becomes part of the story when she reads and begins to love the heroes: "I fall in love with every one of them!" However, being swept away depends upon the criterion of identification, a sense of likeness established between reader and heroine. For my consultants, this resemblance emerges on a variety of levels.

Almost all of the women I interviewed identified with the heroine of the story based, in part, on their shared gender. In general, the stories emphasize the heroine and her perspective; she becomes the reader's way into the fictional drama. As one woman told me, "I think I identify more with the women, certainly, but I am one." Another responded, "I think I identified more with the woman and what they were going through, you know, if they were falling in love or whatever."[4] Reading about the heroines' lives, often based on the real life struggles of female authors, my consultants describe being swept away into evangelical worlds where the power of faith and the strength of love prevail. However, identification, like their escape itself, is never total or all-encompassing. Identification in fiction reading entails imaginative mobility and manipulation. In the story, readers can shift from character to character and move from insider to outsider. For example, Gwen described as well as qualified her identification: "Well, I guess the heroine, but I think it depends on the story."[5] Speaking of her tendency to identify with the heroines, Lila also qualified her claim: "Sometimes I identify with the man, if the woman is being an idiot." Other women placed themselves more on the sidelines, while some moved back and forth. For example, Jackie explained, "I think I'm more of a spectator. I get into it, but I'm not a character in there or involved per se." For many readers, their level and type of identification depends upon the plot and characters. However, in one way or another (as heroine, hero, or spectator), the women locate themselves within the story. They want, like Christian-school-teacher Janet, "to become part of that story," to establish a relationship with the characters in which, as one reader told me, "It almost becomes real to you, you think of them as real characters."[6] As readers establish similarities between themselves and the heroines, religious inspiration becomes a possibility.

Too much realism or a lack thereof, as discussed in Chapter Three, proved an obstacle to readers' identification with some stories and heroines. However, the women I interviewed, aware of their reading desires, carefully chose their novels and more often than not found compelling stories. For example, at the same time that African American reader Tamara criticized the white images of beauty in the novels, she also spoke of how she overcame this obstacle: "Even though you haven't actually gone through what they have, you identify with the determination and the things that they have to go through."[7] The heroine's resemblance to Tamara's sense of herself as determined and enduring, it seems, trumped their physical and racial differences.

Readers identify with heroines on various levels, such as age, setting, or struggle. For example, a plot where the hero and heroine met through the internet drew Betty into the story since she met her husband that way. Being captured by the plot also happened while reading an evangelical romance that featured international adoption, something Betty experienced. For her, novels that depict familiar situations offer the comfort of literary connection: "Sometimes when you are going through some things that are out of the mainstream, it is kind of neat when someone else experiences it too." Another woman, in her forties, was delighted to find characters her age, while Charlotte related to a heroine's pregnancy because she was also pregnant at the time, and Shari connected with a protagonist dealing with domestic abuse since she volunteers at a women's shelter.[8] For these women, heroines who are like them provide a sense of belonging and companionship. Fictional women validate readers' experiences and affirm that they are not alone.

Familiarity with a particular setting also enhances readers' affinity for a heroine and a novel. It also often prompts women to write and share their own stories with authors. For example, Dorothy wrote to author Peggy Stoks about the setting of her novella, *The Sound of the Water*, "I fell in love with Washington while there and have longed to return. Your novella allowed me to do that and brought back many pleasant memories." In Dorothy's case, through reading she could imaginatively revisit the missed terrain. Readers claimed a tie to characters, as well as authors, through settings they both knew and loved. Despite fictional elements in the stories, readers could identify with the locales, situate themselves in a familiar geography, and enjoy a story "close to home."[9]

More than similar situations and familiar settings, shared religious commitments established the resemblance between heroines and my consultants. Whether a novel features the heroine's coming to faith or her growing in faith, the women I interviewed enjoyed reading about women like them, heroines committed (eventually) to God, marriage, and family. For example, speaking about why she enjoyed the novels, Jackie, a Moravian, remarked, "I like a book where I can connect with the people." She went on to mention specifically the bond of faith. Novels, to her, are more engaging "if you've got characters who have a similar background as you, not being a Christian and then becoming a Christian, meeting people who are Christians or whatever the situation is, or they are living the same type of life that you are." Madeline put it more simply: "It's nice to know that there are other people out there that believe in God."[10] The resemblance between heroine and reader, then, provides a way into the story and also offers a fictional community of faith.

The heroine's esteem for and role in her family also draws readers into the worlds of heroines like Katie Mayfield. As Sally Gallagher writes, family "has become a central metaphor for evangelical identity." Whether through language of male headship, the practice of home schooling, or endorsement of traditional gender roles, evangelicals see beliefs about family as a way to differentiate themselves from the world and to provide a heritage of faith for their children. Gallagher examines the tensions between the rhetoric and the reality of evangelical families, including how men claim spiritual headship but women often enact it. Despite evangelical beliefs that uphold male spiritual leadership in the home, "it is not unusual," Gallagher writes, "for women to say that they, not their husbands, usually take the lead in spiritual matters."[11] Evangelical romance novels explore this disjuncture through narrative. They offer temporarily flawed heroines who play pivotal roles in the spiritual lives of their families. For the women I interviewed who parented, or wanted to parent, Christian families, reading of heroines occupying similar roles supplied another literary connection and a sense of affirmation. For example, sixty-seven-year-old Rose, a divorced mother of one, preferred "to read about the females who have a lot of strength—they are not weak. I like to read about the ones who have a lot of strength and those who are strong in their family leadership."[12] Rose wanted heroines who, like her, provided strong models of Christianity amidst the tensions of family life. Often taking responsibility for the spiritual beliefs of their families, my consultants discovered evangelical romance heroines who did the same.

In addition, family provided a way for readers to stay involved with beloved heroines. Through the common "series" format of the novels, readers follow the continuing stories of favorite characters. For example, Marty and Clark's love story does not end with *Love Comes Softly*; it continues in subsequent volumes as readers learn about their relationship as they age and guide their children through the intricacies of Christian and romantic life. In addition, through the series readers also gain assurance of a parent's power to pass faith on to her children. The novels often show, as one reader described it, "how the history of faith crosses generations," and women enjoy reading about these "generations of faith": faithful parents raising faithful Christian children. For example, Nancy confided, "I really like the storyline when you begin with the early years and continue on when the children grow and mature and as they go into their own families and get children and grandchildren." She also expressed her enjoyment of reading about heroines who are strong Christian examples to their families, such as those "who can influence their daughters." Nancy also admired "the patience that some of the mothers have."[13] Similarly, Betty likes Angela Hunt's work because it features strong heroines in each generation who "stepped out and did something extraordinary." She enjoys reading about women who aren't "wimpy" and that are everything "God needs them to be."[14] Readers enter narratives through identification with heroines based on their shared gender identity, evangelical piety, and family leadership. These resemblances, in turn, inspire consultants to enact religious change.

Their devotion *to* fiction became a devotion *through* which they discover a way to maintain the vitality of their faith.

Numerous endeavors in evangelicalism focus on women's spiritual growth, from self-help books to inspirational tours, from Bible studies to women's mission groups. However, unlike these efforts, evangelical romances use entertaining narratives, rather than personal testimonies or textual study. For readers, stories not sermons, plots not preaching, provide an accessible avenue through which they can maintain evangelical faith in everyday life. Rather than (or in addition to) telling friends or family about your spiritual struggles or listening to an inspirational speaker who has it all figured out, readers can turn to heroines, who resemble them and provide a sense of community while also remaining distant. Unlike Christian family, friends, or teachers, these fictional women do not confront, judge, or patronize the reader. Heroines such as Katie, Missie, Mandy, and Garvin share readers' difficulties and demonstrate, through example and not exhortation, the solution to problems and the possibilities of faith. Through this complicated relationship characterized by both proximity and distance, reader identification becomes religious inspiration. The characters, according to Gail, "set a higher standard for the way I live my life and the way I handle situations." These fictional narratives peopled with women of faith move readers from escapism to engagement and from despair to hope.[15]

Evidence of this emerged when women discussed their ideal heroine. I asked, "What kind of women do you like to read about in the novels?" Typical replies were: "Intelligent, strong, brave"; "Women who are strong."[16] Tamara expressed such preferences for her ideal heroine: "I guess someone that is not shallow and airheaded, someone with determination and has goals, someone that I can relate to me." Readers believe heroines should demonstrate how to deal with situations in a Christian manner. For example, heroine Emily Evans, from Janette Oke's "Women of the West" series, inspired readers by remaining faithful to her missionary calling. "She stood fast to her convictions," Gwen told me; for divinity student Mary, the character provided an example of a strong woman who was actively working and serving in God's kingdom. Readers also found the heroine of Francine Rivers's "Mark of the Lion" series, inspirational. Diana described her this way because "she never gave up. She wouldn't let anyone take away what God had given her." Lila echoed Diana's admiration: "Even though she was tempted in so many ways—she wasn't perfect—but she was just a real encouragement to me to stand firm. Also, you have to be well-grounded in God if you are going to survive, and you have to go back and pray."[17] For readers, a heroine's strength most often referred to her evangelical faith—her ability to endure and grow in her religious beliefs. Tamara, pondering my question, preferred a heroine that "is a strong character, someone that is open to change," and Tina shared, "I like how the characters make it through adversity and the challenges of the world and then are open to the changes that God has in store, to remind me that I need some of those changes in my life."[18] In these fictional worlds, heroines embody a spiritual certainty and strength that illuminates readers' own spiritual complacency or inadequacy even as it inspired them to change. Depending on how readers assess their faith, the changes wrought in readers' lives through evangelical romance reading range widely from the apprehension of spiritual ideas to the revisiting of familiar evangelical practices.

Everyday Encouragement: Religious Change through Reading

Through heroines and plots, some women reported gaining small realizations that helped foster everyday piety. Diana, for example, found that reading made her "think a little deeper" about her relationships. Similarly, Kate responded, "Sometimes they'll just say something and I'll think, 'Well, you know, I've never thought of that before, but in my own Christian life that could be true also.'" She continued, "Maybe one of the characters will say something to the other . . . you know, light bulb going off."[19] Sally also spoke of these "light bulb" moments: "Sometimes you think, 'Am I handling this the way that I should be?' and you know how you question yourself at times, and sometimes the answer is in there and it shows you 'Yes, you are handling something correctly' or 'No you're not.'"[20] Offering insight, assurance, and guidance, the novels integrate themselves into the fabric of readers' religious lives.

When my consultants described the relationship between fictional narratives and their faith commitments, they often spoke of how heroines encouraged them to persevere in their evangelical beliefs. The literary and ministerial effectiveness of evangelical romance depends upon its utility—its ability to transport readers through a fictional story to faith's reality by establishing an emotional connection between reader and heroine. While many want to frame reason and emotion in opposition, for these women their evangelical identity rests upon feeling their faith, and not solely upon their understanding of its logic and coherence. On a daily basis these women confront the fragility of their faith. They know on a rational level what they believe and why, but at times the mundane routine of life dims the vitality of their evangelical emotions, and at other moments a crisis causes some to question the efficacy of their beliefs. Through their literary connection with the heroine, then, my consultants move from a space of isolation and a place of struggle to a sense of belonging and a feeling of faith. The historical definition of emotion, given by the *Oxford English Dictionary*, illuminates this shift. In the past, "emotion" meant a moving out, a migration from one place to another. It denoted a journey. The challenge, as media scholars Elihu Katz and David Foulkes remind us, remains discovering where this fictional journey leads.[21] Applying this idea of motion to the realm of feeling and sentiment reveals ways my consultants' fictional devotion works on a religious level. It moves them from religious uncertainty to Christian confidence, from spiritual neglect to evangelical attention. Whatever the challenge, big or small, these women often turn to evangelical romance not only to escape painful moments and to indulge in happy endings, but to rediscover the applicability of their beliefs amidst the challenges of everyday life. Individual spiritual change achieved through an emotional process configured by identification and inspiration, for them, represents the greatest answer to their questions, the ultimate solution to their problems, including doubts, bitterness, and loneliness.

For example, to women who lacked confidence in their evangelical commitment, reading about characters that endured persecution and remained faithful to God caused them to ponder their own Christian loyalty. It prompted them to examine their beliefs and inspired them to continuing fidelity. Cathy confided, "I always wondered if I was questioned about my faith, would I be a weenie or not?" Jenna, enmeshed in family and friendship networks, had similar thoughts as she read how heroine Katie Mayfield's adoptive Amish community shunned her because of her evangelical faith. Jenna, who talks with her mother at least once a day, wondered if she could endure that type of isolation. "I don't know if I could stand it," she confided. However, even as these women questioned what they would do, the characters' victories inspired them to faithfulness in daily life. As Jenna later remarked, "They just give you a little bit of confidence." Jackie responded similarly: "You just want to strive to be like some of those characters in terms of being strong in your faith and knowing what you believe."[22] In this way, heroines help readers move from spiritual doubts to evangelical assurance.

For others this spiritual encouragement took different forms. Some found it in a novella by Peggy Stoks, *The Beauty of the Season*. The narrative chronicles heroine Bell's search for love and acceptance as she battles her feelings of inadequacy that result from a port-wine birthmark on her face. Bell's happy ending—finding peace with God and a loving spouse—elicited readers' emotions and religious growth. A woman with facial deformities told Peggy Stoks how the story "spoke to her about her worth, beauty, and dignity in God's eyes." Another letter conveyed Tanya's story. Suffering from acne, she wrote, "my face has been the ruin of my life." Unsupported by her parents and teased, like the heroine Bell, Tanya struggled with self-esteem. Through *The Beauty of the Season*, she found hope in God. He had sent her a wonderful husband and showed her that "others make fun of things because they don't or won't try and understand them."[23] Similarly, another woman, dealing with acne after the birth of her children, related to Bell's story. For her, the narrative elicited gratitude for her loving husband and encouraged her to trust in the

Lord alone.[24] In all three women's accounts, Stoks's story—featuring a flawed and faithful heroine—offered a message of religious hope and self-worth. It offered these women the assurance that they did not suffer alone and that their lives had value. In contrast to those who failed them—false friends and faulty parents—God's presence, power, and love became real through Bell's story.

As I interviewed Mindy, she defined spiritual encouragement in a slightly different way. Witty, friendly, and eager to talk about the novels, Mindy automatically connected her evangelical romance reading and her spiritual life. She, like others, identified with the heroines and spiritual lessons of the novels. Preferring flawed characters that she could relate to, this vivacious young woman with reddish brown hair spoke of the novels as reinforcing and helping her faith: "Sometimes there is a Christian who is saved, but they backslide or something. But God brings them back to where they should be, and that encourages me." More specifically, she found the plot of Lori Wick's novel, *The Princess*, inspirational. I asked Mindy what was so admirable about the story's heroine, and she reflected on the example of religious strength: "She had to go through a lot of hard things. She married him because it was God's will for her and he had a first wife and had to get over her to fall in love with her and then she lost her baby in a car accident. She just went through a whole lot of different things and she just continued to pray and trusted God that everything was going to work out." After Mindy recounted this tale of faith's perseverance in the face of multiple tragedies, I asked, "So, that inspired you?" Mindy promptly responded, "Yes, it did," and then elaborated on the link between fictional heroines and her own spiritual life: "Sometimes," she said, "the character is learning something, God is trying to teach them something and it just happens to be something that I need to learn. It's a reinforcement." Throughout Mindy's description of evangelical romances, she highlighted the power of these fictional heroines to offer her religious guidance and spiritual hope. When faith falters or begins to fade, amidst the nature of daily life or the reality of a specific problem, readers such as Mindy use evangelical romances to remember and relearn their faith. Evoking the emotions of assurance and encouragement, heroines help these women realize a sense of evangelical community, fictional and real.[25]

For some women, encouragement prompts a simple reaching out to God through prayer. Assured of God's care for the heroine's problems, whether related to the minutiae of daily life or to the enormity of world affairs, readers respond with their own petitions. As I talked with Gail in a coffeehouse that is owned and operated by her Vineyard Fellowship congregation, she connected reading and praying: "Something will touch my heart and I'll just kind of stop and pray about it. Not like a major prayer, but like 'Okay, Lord, what are you telling me here, what are you saying in this.'" She went on to share how a prayer in a novel by Linda Chaikin affected her. The heroine, in a dangerous situation, prays to God for help. The way this plea was written, ("Oh God comma help me!" according to Gail) showed a "heart for God" that encouraged her. Catherine also commented on how the portrayal of prayer in the novels nurtured her spiritual life: "Just even to hear how other people pray or when they pray or at what moment. It just reinforces a lot of things. If you're doing it right or you're not the only one who does it that way or shows you a different way."[26] Doubting her praying abilities, Catherine found inspiration and assurance through her reading. Similarly, Lila viewed the novels as strengthening her faith, specifically mentioning prayer: "So many of the books include prayer and Scripture and they believe in their prayers and their prayer life is very, very big." Implicitly critiquing her prayer life, the novels reminded readers like her not of a new or unfamiliar lesson, but to "go back and pray." Others wrote of their difficulties in their letters to authors. After relating her struggle with rebellion against God and the beneficial effects of a novel, Victoria wrote a prayer into her letter, "Oh how I long to simply walk in obedience," before continuing her letter with a discussion of the novel's plot.[27] Others mentioned prayers for specific people because of the spiritual issue highlighted in a heroine's life or reported finding that the novels reminded them to pray about a problem. A few felt that the novels represented an answer to their prayers. Some even prayed for authors to write more novels.[28] It seems, as these women juggle various roles and tasks in their lives, familiar religious practices fade into forgetfulness. In this haze of everyday life, evangelical romance heroines remind readers of their ability to change their spiritual lives and maintain their evangelical commitment.

Actively seeking to keep faith integrally involved in their lives, readers use evangelical romance as a way to evaluate their religious lives. It helps them assess their problems and change their circumstances. Needing more than an evangelical heritage and church attendance to sustain their religious identities, they create effective religious alternatives. Some come to remember God's care while others realize their beauty: the novels teach familiar lessons that prompt readers to remember and reclaim their sense of evangelical faith. The genre's sentimentality—its happy endings and emotional revelry—results not only in temporary denial and escapism, but also in a message of hope that gives readers the religious tools with which to address "real-life concerns, personal or social."[29] Many of the changes enacted by my consultants as a result of their reading occur through emotional and spiritual transformations on an individual level. At times, this pattern may result in a type of hyper-individualism and spiritual ghettoization that precludes one's ability (or desire) to assess situations on a macro-structural level or to gain another perspective on one's life. While these concerns are certainly merited, the individualistic tendency characterizes not only my consultants, but also evangelicalism as a whole. To condemn this view establishes an "us" and "them" relationship between scholar and subject that normalizes the practices of the former while problematizing those of the latter. The scholarly role then becomes one of a prophet lamenting the subjects' sins, demanding their repentance, and showing the right path—a dynamic that the field of religious studies seeks to avoid. Rather, the task, I suggest, is one of understanding how and why a particular religious group constructs this type of relationship between themselves and their God as well as between themselves and the perceived world. Evangelical romances provide a glimpse into the building of this religious identity. Behind stereotypes of evangelicals as arrogantly certain of their faith and condemnations of their piety as hopelessly sentimental, the complicated and contested religious lives of these women become visible. The fluidity of their faith, the hard work of being evangelical, emerges.

For Mindy and others like her, the biggest struggle they discussed revolved around one demographic feature—singleness—and one religious ideal—patience. Dreaming of marriage and families, but living without them, reading evangelical romance inspired an acknowledgment of God's control over their romantic lives, the realization of patience. These women felt encouraged when heroines cultivated patience, a faithfulness that God ultimately rewarded with a spouse. Through reading, they were reminded of evangelical lessons in following God's plan and waiting on God's timing. Heroine Emily Evans provided readers with a model of patience and a reason to hope. Choosing the single life and full-time Christian service over marriage to a man without a missionary calling, Emily ultimately finds love. In the last chapter, entitled "Partners in Service," hero Shad reveals how Emily's Christian service inspired him to answer his own call to ministry. The novel ends with the assurance that God does answer prayer —prayers for discovering both one's path in life and one's spouse for life.[30]

Mindy, who jokingly said she identified with the old maid schoolteacher in the novels and who is writing a book with her sister on being single, shared her struggles with the unmarried state and the hope evangelical romance provides. Reading helps her "wait for God's will," rather than try to work things out herself. Others echoed Mindy's story and shared her hope. In a letter to author Irene Brand, Monica wrote, "I've learned to let God bring the right man into my life . . . to be patient also and realize that He knows what's best for me."[31] Bess learned a similar lesson. A recent college graduate, she told Shari MacDonald of her search for Mr. Right and the sadness she faced as her friends got engaged or married. "I find an incredible sense of loneliness sometimes," Bess confided, but went on to write, "Thank you for writing good clean romances that portray believable characters who uncover believable problems and circumstances. It makes these lonely times of mine brighten a little and helps me to dream of my future. God has a plan for me and I will endure to find what is down that road." Narrating a newfound sense of God's involvement in their lives, these women prayed for patience.[32]

In addition, the novels taught these women to let God guide them to the "right guy." Placing their confidence in the power of God's planning (evidence of God's love for them), they felt assured that their desires would be met. For example, Madeline believed "Christianity leads you to the love of your life," and helps you realize that "it's not just your mom and your brother, grandparents, husband—there is love that is everlasting." According to Mindy, "These books are making sure you find the right person" by showing the importance of friendship, not just sexual attraction, in a heterosexual relationship. And through reading, Bess trusted in God's plan for her future and gained encouragement, as did Jocelyn. A widow, Jocelyn viewed romance as part of God's plan and found hope through reading evangelical romance. "There's a part of me," she confided, "when I read these books, [that says] that's the type of relationship I want right there."[33] Madeline, Mindy, and other single readers, like the heroines of the novels, all expressed their reliance on God's timing in their romantic lives. The novels reassure readers about God's plan, that "when they least expected it God was preparing a way." Guided by God and a good novel, these single women felt confident of finding a Christian romance. Some married readers, like Victoria, confirmed this, as they saw their marriages as evidence of God's involvement: "God has sent me a wonderful husband."[34] In the meantime, women like Mindy and Janet displayed their acquired proficiency in patience by telling me that it was "better to be single and wish you were married than married and wish you were single."[35]

While Mindy found patience a difficult spiritual attribute to cultivate, others described grappling with forgiveness and seeking help in evangelical romance and its heroines. Having been wronged by some family members (she did not mention how), Kimberly refused to speak with them for several years until she read one of Terry Blackstock's novels. Its message moved Kimberly from pain to forgiveness. She wrote, "I figured if Lynda can forgive Keith, then I could forgive my family." Kimberly was not alone. Jocelyn narrated a similar struggle. She grappled with forgiveness after the murder of her husband in 1992 and eventually found spiritual help in evangelical romances. Knowing "in her heart" she did not forgive those responsible, she sought guidance. The genre and its female-oriented stories helped her with this issue in a way that her Pentecostal church could not. "I am very active in my church. For example, I hear constantly and know things of forgiveness. However, with fiction it has been able to really sink in where just going and sitting in the pew or saying that I'm practicing what I'm preaching did not get me to that point, but with this fiction I can get over different hurdles." [36] Fictional heroines and narratives, as seen in Jocelyn's statement, work for these women in ways that other evangelical endeavors do not. Through their complicated blending of seemingly disparate binaries—inspiration and identification, entertainment and edification, women and ministry, tragedy and triumph—they make the emotions and beliefs of evangelicalism real in women's lives.

While reading enabled Jocelyn to forgive, others found such a path more complicated. My consultants referred to the struggles of forgiveness most often in relation to Robin Lee Hatcher's *The Forgiving Hour*, briefly discussed in Chapter Four. Romance causes the problems experienced by Claire, the protagonist. Divorced because of her ex-husband's infidelity, Claire finds it difficult to reconcile her evangelical belief in forgiveness with the reality of her son's engagement to her ex-husband's former mistress. Claire eventually forgives her future daughter-in-law and her former spouse, but the practice of forgiveness remained difficult for some readers. Facing dilemmas like Claire's, they wrote Hatcher with their stories of pain and betrayal. For example, in a neatly typed letter on plain white paper, Gabrielle wrote of her confusion and hurt: "I am 35 years old. I have two daughters, one 32 months, one 12 months. I dated my husband for five years before we were married. Our ten year anniversary was December 9th. My husband left us on June 28th. He is having an affair with a woman who is married and has a seven year old son. He has had two affairs during the course of our marriage that I was completely unaware of."

Gabrielle wrote about her continuing struggle to forgive. Unwilling to consent to a divorce and in the face of continued infidelity, she wrote, "I have tried to forgive him, but dealing with the pain is most of the time overwhelming to me."[37] Gabrielle closed her letter by seeking advice from Hatcher. For Gabrielle and others like her, Hatcher's novel addressed both the reality of infidelity and the difficulty of faith. When faced with a crisis, some turn to evangelical romance and discover that they are not alone. While perhaps not able to forgive, these women forge bonds with authors and characters who share in their grief and offer guidance—a community characterized by distance, fictional and real, but also by its understanding of readers' lives. Even as they struggle to make sense of their evangelical beliefs amidst crisis, these women articulate their pain and seek to recover the feeling of faith.

Others reported more success than Gabrielle, but still wrote of the difficulty posed by forgiveness. For example, Stacy had forgiven her husband for his infidelity prior to reading the novel, but forgiving the "other woman," her sister-in-law, remained a problem. Seeing the novel as God-given helped her forgive this woman and released them both from, in her words, the "prison of unforgiveness." Forgiveness also troubled Judith. In prison "as a result of mistakes made involving my ex-husband," she took responsibility for her actions, but found it difficult to deal with her husband's decision to divorce her and "seek love elsewhere." She wrote to Hatcher, "Your message regarding the importance of forgiveness spoke so eloquently to my problems right now."[38] Struggling with betrayal and grief, women found in *The Forgiving Hour* an author (and heroine) who had experienced a similar pain and a story that suggested a difficult spiritual path. Faced with the disparity between their evangelical beliefs and their everyday lives, these women found an acknowledgement of their grief through their fictional devotion. Sometimes, in interviews or in their letters to authors, they chronicle their ability to recover their sense of faith and their ability to forgive. At other times, for those unable to forgive, knowing that others, whether authors or heroines, endured similar pain offered the promise of hope, a hope that eventually they would regain their evangelical equilibrium.

In addition, women whose parents had experienced the effects of infidelity wrote about the power of Hatcher's novel. These women wrote about how the novel helped their mothers, who still struggled with forgiveness years later. Elena gave the novel to her mother, who responded by taking "a hard look at herself" and forgiving her ex-spouse. In another case, the novel helped Tracy better understand her mother's perspective. While she did not agree with her mother's continuing "unforgiveness," she hoped that her mother would come to forgive and let go of the bitterness that affected her whole family.[39] For these women, evangelical romance offered a familiar message of forgiveness, but one that occurred in a plot that related to their experiences. Rather than an abstract sermon on the necessity of forgiveness, Hatcher's combination of this religious message with a relevant plot provided readers with a vital spiritual resource. While not an easy lesson to learn and still impossible for some, it enabled many of these readers to persevere in living their religion. They knew—from attending church, hearing sermons, being a Christian—that forgiveness constitutes a vital component of evangelicalism. In their view, just as God forgave their sins, they needed to forgive to grow in their relationship with God and others. However, despite this knowledge, inspirational heroines and romantic fiction helped women realize this in a new way. "A story," writes J. Hillis Miller, "is a way of doing things with words. It makes something happen in the real world."[40] For these women, evangelical romances make something happen. Through identification and inspiration, women discover a way to align their evangelical beliefs with their everyday emotions and actions. The genre acknowledges the reality of their problems and offers the hope of spiritual solutions. Most often, as I interviewed readers, they emphasized the effectiveness of their fictional devotion, the ways that it helped them improve and sustain their faith. However, as evidenced in their narrations on forgiveness, sometimes the desired spiritual growth remains elusive.

Even as readers explicitly enumerated their religious triumphs, they occasionally implied or voiced spiritual tensions produced by their fictional devotion. For some, reading evangelical romance led to inadvertent competition and disappointing comparisons. In at least two ways, romantic fiction and evangelical faith could work at cross purposes: evangelical romance heroes competed with real-life husbands and reading the novels often took precedence over Bible reading. As we have seen, most often the readers I interviewed identified with the heroines of these love stories. Given that the novels center on the heroine and often tell the story from her point of view, the character of the hero at times seems less developed, but that does not mean he remains unimportant to readers.

The heroes of evangelical romance leave no room for doubting their masculinity. The heroes' physical stature and good looks reinforce their virility and attractiveness to heroines (and presumably readers). With black hair, "startling gray eyes," and standing over six feet tall, Marshall Riggs overshadows other men in Lori Wick's *Whatever Tomorrow Brings*. His occupation further enhances his manhood. In this historical tale, situated in the nineteenth-century West, Marshall Riggs owns the town mercantile, an occupation that requires both brains and brawn. For example, supplies have to be loaded and unloaded for the store, a task that impressed Rigg's heroine. "Both men were stripped to the waist and Kate saw in an instant why Rigg's shoulders and arms looked powerful enough to lift a draft horse. Kaitlin watched as he hefted enormous crates without visible effort, sometimes swinging one onto his shoulder and carrying another under his arm." Even with all this activity, "he was not even breathing hard."[41] Other heroes resemble Marshall Riggs—handsome and strong—and in these ways do not seem so different from the men peopling the pages of secular romance novels.

However, religion sets these heroes apart from their secular counterparts. The novels seamlessly weave together the masculinity of these heroes with evangelical Christianity. Through their religious lives, these heroes achieve balance and wholeness—a reconciliation of work and home, strength and tenderness, masculine and feminine. For example, in Marshall Riggs's case, Christianity simultaneously tempers his masculinity and enhances his attractiveness to both the heroine and the reader. He is unafraid of marriage and commitment: "He [Rigg] wished his own wife was shopping somewhere in the store. But Rigg didn't have a wife. He believed that if he was to have a wife, God would provide one. But the fact that God was in control did not change his desires, the deepest of which was to have a family." Marriage and commitment do not scare away the evangelical hero. In contrast to secular heroes, who often resist commitment and deride marriage, evangelical heroes are confident enough in their masculinity to reveal their sensitive side and their domestic desires. In those novels featuring a married couple this domestic side emerges even more strongly. Heroes willingly cook, do dishes, move furniture, and even clean. Hero Sean Donovan offers, "Why don't you let me finish breakfast?" much to the surprise of his wife.[42] In general, evangelical heroes make life easier for their (present or soon-to-be) wives by listening, nurturing, and praying. The novels portray this domestic side as a natural outgrowth of their Christian commitment and concern for their wives. Firmly committed to being an active participant in the home, the evangelical hero naturally also takes seriously his responsibilities as a parent. When parenting constitutes part of the plot, the hero cultivates a relationship with either his father or his son characterized by respect, fairness, and involvement. Not an absent father or a workaholic dad, these heroes exhibit good looks, good faith, and good parenting.

This message reinforces present gender and familial prescriptions in evangelicalism. In their study "Symbolic Traditionalism and Pragmatic Egalitarianism," Sally Gallagher and Christian Smith examine how evangelicals use the concept of "male headship" in evangelical family life. Describing the multiple ways evangelicals negotiate gender, they question what women gain from this symbolic belief in gender hierarchy. "Emotional intimacy and greater economic security" is their answer: "It preserves men's pride and effectively obligates men to greater participation in the emotional, nurturing work that is central to our ideals of companionship marriage, as well as solidifying men's responsibility for the economic well-being of a house-hold."[43] The novels uphold these ideals. In evangelical romance, with its domestic heroes and inspiring heroines, the themes of marital partnership, as well as male involvement in the home, frequently arise. Through the novels, authors hope to minister to readers' romantic lives.

These idealistic portrayals of romantic heroes elicited various reactions from my consultants. Single women, as we have seen, often gained the hope of finding a hero and the promise of romance through reading, but married women responded in various ways. Some married readers discovered that the genre helped them in their romantic relationships. Betty found this to be true, as she explained: "I think that is one good thing about reading fiction. It helps you relate to one another." Lila expressed a similar sentiment. For her, evangelical romance served as "a real reminder of what I have and what a blessing and a rare thing that is." She explained how reading encourages her to work on her own marriage and to express her gratitude. "I'm so thankful that I'm married to who I'm married, and it makes me want to go remind him."[44] Similarly, a member of Mona's Book Club confided, "If things get a little slow in the marriage, by reading these books, I can tell you now, my husband's happy." And Fiona stated that some evangelical romances make her "feel more loving."[45] For these women, then, fictional heroes help keep the romantic spark alive with real husbands. Through their fictional devotion, their spiritual lives and marital relationships improved.

Others, however, found that in a comparison between husband and hero their husbands did not measure up. This led some married women to criticize the novels, rather than their spouses. Melody, for example, when she first started reading evangelical romance, liked "the beautiful men, the perfect husbands" featured in the novels, but that changed over time. Now, she prefers more realistic portrayals. She remarked, "I reject this idea of husbands that are what most husbands aren't," and went on to defend both marriage and her position: "I don't mean to come across as a cynic, but you know, I think marriage is great, but it's not storybook." Readers wanted portrayals of men that "could really be," "rugged but real." [46] With realistic heroes and heroines, women could identify and learn about their own relationships. They want to learn how to work through problems, to read about "women struggling with their faith and struggling with not a pie-in-the-sky marriage, but a real marriage." [47] As we have seen throughout this study, readers insist on realistic portrayals that will help them in their day-to-day lives.

Reflecting on this hero-husband relationship, other married women criticized their husbands, rather than the heroes. These women expressed disappointment with their own spouses in light of their reading. For Cathy the difference between hero and husband left her wanting more. "Sometimes," she said, "I wish my husband was like some of the men in those books." As we discussed this, Cathy initially labeled the novels unrealistic, but as she continued to think about it, she remembered specific examples of real-life men resembling the heroes — husbands buying flowers and planning weekends away. Cathy reluctantly concluded, "I guess it happens in real life, just not mine!" Jean related a similar sentiment. With her husband "obsessed with checkers on the computer," she has plenty of time to read and reflect on the disparity between husband and hero. The heroes, in Jean's view, "always sound like they do everything for the girl because of their love, but also because of their love for God." Like Cathy, she determined that "there are people out there like that, but my husband's not like that." [48] For these women, more than others I interviewed, their fictional devotion helps them escape disappointing spouses, but does not result in the religio-romantic improvements that they may desire. Rather, it seems to reinforce their dissatisfaction with their partners. However, at the same time, reading may also increase their reliance on God, a relationship that may help mitigate the pain of a disappointing spouse.

At times, heroes compete with husbands, but even more common is the contest between Bible and evangelical romance reading. When scholars attempt to define evangelicalism, the authority of the Bible inevitably constitutes one of the hallmarks of this religious movement. Its authority is important for both men and women; as Crystal Manning writes in *God Gave Us the Right*, "Evangelical women see their acceptance of Scripture as a given as what distinguishes them from liberal Protestants and secular Americans."[49] However, just as the rhetoric of subcultural distinction belies the permeable boundaries between evangelical and secular, we must recognize that believing in the authority of the Bible does not mean that these women are reading their Bibles.

For many of the women I interviewed, evangelical romance becomes their window into the Bible. Many did not frame the biblical and romance narratives as competitors; instead, their comments reveal how they access the Bible through the genre. Reading evangelical romance prompts thinking about, features verses from, and applies principles of the Bible, but often it replaces actual study of the Bible. With a focus on women's spiritual struggles as well as entertaining plots that connect readers to other women, romantic fiction works religiously in a way that biblical narratives do not. Reading stories that apply biblical principles and passages to everyday situations, as more than one reader told me, "makes you think." For example, readers "learned a lot about the Bible" from Francine Rivers's work. Tamara added that Rivers "sort of takes everyday situations that actually happen and she deals with it from a biblical standpoint and it sort of encourages me to be able to go on." She went on to say that the novels give her "food for thought in Scripture."[50] At times, this "food for thought" prompts some women to explore spiritual issues by going back to their Bibles. "Sometimes," as one reader explained, "it feeds into wanting to do more study about something."[51] However, more often than not, it seems evangelical romance reading supplants Bible reading. Reading the novels prompted one woman, healing from an injury, to set some spiritual and physical goals during her recovery. On a numbered list that included exercising and crocheting (to keep her creative juices flowing), Bible reading occupied first place. However, implicitly, Ann's new priorities reveal that prior to her injury, Bible reading ranked further down the list.[52] For her and others, evangelical romance became the lens that filtered and focused their approach to the Bible.

While these women did not view reading romances and the Bible as conflicting, others recognized that their Bible reading took second place, a realization that elicited mixed feelings. Jenna expressed this ambivalence: "Sometimes I feel bad because I'm reading them and not my Bible. But, I think a lot of times it helps. They always list Scripture in them and if anything has God's word in it, it is going to be beneficial to me."[53] Others shared Jenna's feelings. "I don't want to take it as a replacement for reading my Bible," Jackie told me, but she went on to say that "you can learn some things." Cathy contrasted her reading with Bible study. Though she was glad that no one would quiz her on her evangelical romance reading like they do in studies of Scripture, she decided, "I think they are good spiritually to learn from."[54] These women know what they ideally should be doing—reading their Bibles—but at the same time, they keep reading evangelical romance and justify it by emphasizing how much the narratives teach them about the Bible. Filtering the Bible through love stories centered on women's religious lives, the power of evangelical romantic fiction at times outweighs that of the biblical narrative.

Some, however, wish for a passion for Bible reading that equals their love of novel reading. One letter writer felt she could not balance the two. In a letter dated October 15, 1999, Patty shared her struggle for the proper balance between Bible reading and novel reading, telling of how God used the novels themselves to illuminate this struggle. A Christian for two years, Patty labeled her novel reading idolatrous since it had supplanted her Bible reading and decided to give it up. "I have to believe that it was all in God's plan that your writing would reconfirm both the conviction and the action I need to take as a result of that conviction. So though I truly enjoy reading your books, you will be losing me as one of your supporters until I can learn to prioritize my time and put God #1 in my life where He rightfully belongs." She closed with a blessing for the author, that God would continue to use her, and requested prayer to sustain her Bible-reading resolve.[55]

Alongside Patty's struggles and Jenna's ambivalence emerged yet other responses. These included discussions of how novel reading prompted a focus on the Bible to gratitude for the biblical passages used in the novels. Caroline, an inmate, wrote how much the novels, "especially the verses and reading from the Bible," meant to her and shared with author Irene Brand that she read her Bible every morning and attended prison ministries. She even ended her letter with a biblical passage that she had read that day, Psalm 91:4: "He will cover you with his pinions, and under his wings you will find refuge." For others, the Bible verses highlighted at the beginnings of chapters or as part of the plot touched a chord in readers and heightened their sense of providence. Carol, for example, confided, "I felt this verse was for me right now." Women described feeling touched or moved by the relevance of verses to their present circumstances.[56] For many of the women I interviewed, evangelical romance made the Bible real in a different and perhaps more meaningful way. It touched their emotions and sparked their faith. In contrast to the Bible, it seems, readers find that evangelical romances reflect their concerns, or to paraphrase John Fiske, they relate to their everyday lives in a practical, direct way.[57]

Why are these narratives so powerful for readers, in a religious sense and otherwise? In part, their power rests on eliciting sentiment or emotion. For my consultants, the heroine's combination of resemblance and inspiration engages them on an emotional level. Through the genre, they discover women, heroines and authors, like themselves—not seemingly perfect and unrealistic church ladies, but rather women who struggle with life but also persevere in their faith. Kevin Hetherington, in *Expressions of Identity*, states, "People want to belong, they want to have some way of showing their empathy with like-minded people, they want a form of solidarity based on shared ethical and aesthetic values." Through evangelical romance women find this solidarity with female friends, family, authors, and characters. Through their fictional devotion they find a community of faith that recognizes the difficulties of being an evangelical woman. This resemblance, in turn, fuels spiritual inspiration. Offering emotional encouragement and solidarity, fiction helps these women find their way religiously as they face challenges to their evangelical beliefs.[58] Evangelical romance narratives affirm that these women, struggling or not, belong to the evangelical community of faith. Anthropologist Anthony Cohen writes that belonging "suggests that one is an integral piece of the marvelously complicated fabric which constitutes the community; that one is a recipient of its proudly distinctive and consciously preserved culture."[59] For readers, this sense of belonging affirms their place within evangelicalism, even as it bolsters their evangelical identity—their sense that as evangelicals they have "something in common, whether it be real or imagined, trivial or important, strong or weak."[60] One woman described it this way: "Whatever I'm doing in my life, it is comforting to see someone in a book that also either dealt with it or argued with it in the storyline. It is just comforting to me that God is with me and someone else is going through a similar experience. And it just comforts me to know that I'm not alone, and it opens up to me a big wide world— that a lot of people are experiencing things that are hard."[61] Just as heroine Katie found that "all the pieces of my life are a God-ordered design," readers also discover their place in the fabric of evangelicalism. These women's devotion *to* evangelical romance became a devotion *through* which they sustain their faith, in large part by identifying with and being inspired by heroines. However, as the next chapter demonstrates, identification and inspiration lead not only to spiritual change and evangelical commitment, but also to a sense of divine immanence and intimacy. This sacred love story also fuels readers' fictional devotion.

She thought she had been saved by his love for her, and in part she had been. It had cleansed her, never casting blame. But that had been only the beginning. It was loving him in return that had brought her up out of the darkness. *What can I give him more than that? I would give him anything?*

"Amanda," Michael said, holding her tenderly. "Tirzah . . ."

Sarah, came the still, soft voice, and she knew the one gift she had to offer. Herself. Angel drew back from Michael and looked up at him. "Sarah, Michael. My name is Sarah. I don't know the rest of it. Only that much, Sarah."

Michael blinked. His whole body flooded with joy. The name fit her so well. A wanderer in foreign lands, a barren woman filled with doubt. Yet Sarah of old had become a symbol of trust in God and ultimately the mother of a nation. Sarah. A benediction. Sarah. A barren woman who conceived a son. His beautiful, cherished wife who would someday give him a child.

Michael laughed with her and pulled her into his arms to kiss her. He felt her arms around him as she kissed him back. She was home for good this time. Not even death would part them.

When they drew breath, Michael swung her around and lifted her above him joyously. She threw back her head and spread her arms wide to embrace the sky, tears of celebration streaming down her cheeks.

Michael had once read to her how God had

cast a man and woman out of Paradise. Yet,
for all their human faults and failures, God
had shown them the way back in.
Love the Lord your God, and love one
another. Love one another as he loves. Love
with strength and purpose and passion and
no matter what comes against you. Don't
weaken. Stand against the darkness, and love.
That's the way back into Eden. That's the way
back to life.[1]

So ends *Redeeming Love*, a novel that many au-
thors and readers call the "ultimate romance," as it celebrates the
power of unconditional love. Francine Rivers overlays the love story
between Angel and Michael with a larger love story: the unconditional
love of God for all people. Set in the nineteenth-century West, Rivers's
novel is modeled on the biblical book of Hosea. It chronicles the loneliness and love experienced by the heroine Angel, a woman sold into
prostitution as a child, and Michael Hosea, the moral man who loves
her. After being beaten by a brothel bouncer, Angel marries Michael.
But plagued by her abusive past, she refuses to believe in herself, God,
or Michael's love. Just as the biblical Gomer fleas Hosea, she leaves
Michael and only after her conversion to evangelical Christianity—
when she accepts Jesus Christ as her savior and recognizes her worth
as a child of God—does she return to him. As they reunite, in the scene
above, Angel reveals herself as a child of God by offering Michael her
given name: Sarah. The novel ends with an epilogue that assures readers of the Christian dynasty founded by Michael and Sarah, including
four children and sixty-eight years of marriage. But their story does
not end there.

The story of *Redeeming Love* is one that resonates with readers'
lives. With a plot featuring a fallen woman and unfailing forgiveness,
it fulfills all of their expectations for fiction: identification, inspiration, entertainment, and edification. Like the heroines and novels
mentioned in the previous chapter, *Redeeming Love* helps readers re-

gain evangelical emotions and enact spiritual change. The previous chapter examined how my consultants use evangelical romances as a means to articulate their faith, acknowledge their struggles, and —often—improve their spirituality. Through their fictional devotion they gain a sense of evangelical community and Christian belonging. However, more importantly, *Redeeming Love* and other evangelical romances also help readers realize and remember a romancing God. Gaining this divine intimacy and immanence occurs in part through identification with the heroine, but also through the genre's portrayal of romance. These depictions, in turn, evoke a larger sacred historical narrative that situates my consultants at the center of evangelicalism and God's love. God is the ultimate lover who pursues them and will always be there for them. For these readers, then, Christianity itself becomes a love story as the novels narrate the power of God's love, not the force of his judgment.

Redeeming Love: A Case Study

For many of my consultants, *Redeeming Love* was the novel that provided the most accessible means to voice their views about the romancing God. The history of this novel's publication and reception illustrates many of the strands woven throughout this study, even as the novel's plot highlights the theme of God's unconditional love. As this novel travels through the "communication circuit," from author to publisher to readers, dimensions of women's fictional devotion with its emphasis on God's love are evident at every stage.[2]

For Francine Rivers, *Redeeming Love* signaled a change in her own spiritual journey. It marked her shift from non-Christian to Christian publishers and her move from secular to evangelical romance. She originally published the novel in 1991 with Bantam Books not as a Christian romance but as a historical romance.[3] However, in 1997, Multnomah reissued the novel as an evangelical romance. The volume had the same title, author, and characters—Angel and Michael —but it was not the same book. The copyright page states that the novel "is the *redeemed* version of *Redeeming Love*, published by Bantam Books in 1991," and Rivers acknowledges the help of her editor "in redeeming it for the Christian reader."[4] Rivers's rewrite was prompted by her conversion experience. The process became, in her words, "a form of worship," a way for her to explore her experience of and gratitude for God's love.[5] Designed to communicate this love, much of the new story mirrored the original version, but with important changes. The second version was published by a Christian press for a largely Christian audience, with a didactic intent. At the end of the book Rivers writes that she "wants to bring the truth to those trapped in lies and darkness, to tell them that God is there, He is real, and He loves them—no matter what."[6] Again, Rivers stresses God's love, a love that leads her to redeem more than the lives of her heroine and hero. "Shit" becomes "dung," and "whores" become "soiled doves." Graphic sexual language is transformed into suggestive métaphor, and the vague voice of God becomes a clear message of salvation through Jesus Christ.[7] In the original, Angel dreams of being cleansed by God and learns to recognize her self-worth, but the redeemed Angel proclaims her belief in Jesus Christ as the son of God at a Sunday morning church service.[8] To Rivers, *Redeeming Love* reflects changes in her spiritual life and her commitment to women's ministry, offering a more explicit message of salvation and of God's love for humanity.

However, even as Rivers sought to "offer light to those in darkness," the redemption of this novel raised some concerns for her publisher. As discussed previously, evangelicals zealously monitor the content of fictional depictions to ensure that they uphold Christian beliefs. Due to the fear of participating in sin through the portrayal of evil, this retelling of the book of Hosea raised some concerns. In the frontispiece, the president of Multnomah Books, Donald C. Jacobson, cautioned the reader, "Scripture deals openly and frankly with Gomer's marital infidelity and prostitution. How much 'detail' then, should Francine include to bring that impact into a fresh setting? As you can see in her author's note on pages 465–468 she was concerned that you her readers would understand why she must deal so directly with these issues. We believe that you will understand—when you have

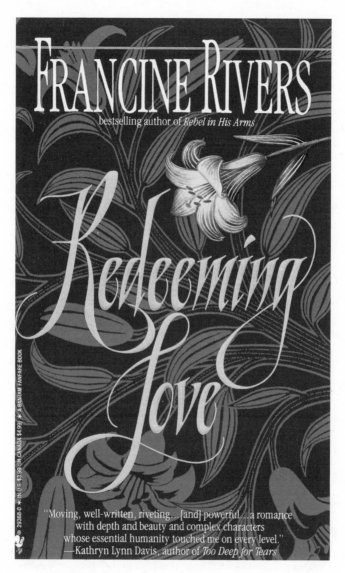

FRANCINE RIVERS

bestselling author of *Rebel in His Arms*

Redeeming Love

"Moving, well-written, riveting...[and] powerful...a romance
with depth and beauty and complex characters
whose essential humanity touched me on every level."
—Kathryn Lynn Davis, author of *Too Deep for Tears*

29368-0 ★ IN U.S. $3.99 (IN CANADA $4.99) ★ A BANTAM FANFARE BOOK

Cover of *Redeeming Love* (1991), by Francine Rivers. Reprinted
by permission of Bantam Books, a division of Random House, Inc.

Cover of *Redeeming Love* (1997), by Francine Rivers.
Reprinted by permission of Multnomah Publishers.

read the whole book. But until you have, please exercise discretion with younger readers."[9] Jacobson attempts to warn readers and guide them through the novel, but as a publisher he is willing to risk the perils of Rivers's in-depth portrayals because of the book's message of God's love. Compared with many other evangelical romances authors, Rivers addresses more sensitive subjects—abuse, prostitution, and adultery—but for her and her publisher, portraying the depths of human sin highlights the reaches of God's love.

For readers, and at least one author, this message proved powerful. Author Robin Lee Hatcher, who had a successful career writing secular romance and served as a president of Romance Writers of America, described how *Redeeming Love* proved pivotal in her writing career. The American Booksellers Association (ABA) was the arena in which she honed her writing talent, but her "heart was being drawn to Christian fiction from the moment I read *Redeeming Love* in 1991." She added, "A book of Francine Rivers's grabs me by the collar and says you need to think about this issue." However, doubting her ability to write for God, Hatcher did not immediately follow Rivers's example. Rather, "God had to change my thinking and help me see that we're all imperfect." Eventually, inspired by Rivers, she crossed over into the Christian market with *The Forgiving Hour*. For Hatcher, *Redeeming Love* prompted recognition of her potential as a writer and revealed the power of evangelical romance.[10]

However, more than author reactions and publisher explanations, readers' own responses to *Redeeming Love* reveal how they used it to articulate a view of God as the great romancer, offering unconditional love. Tamara displayed this perspective as she explained the power of the novel in her spiritual life: "I loved the way she brought it to contemporary terms. I cried while I was reading because it just revealed the love of the Father to me for us. No matter what we do or what can happen, his love can buy us back and he wants us no matter what." Tamara emphasized the unconditional and unrelenting love of God for her and all humanity. The power of *Redeeming Love* and other evangelical romances rests on their ability to make the divine present. In his analysis of popular devotional art, David Morgan writes, "The power of visual piety consists in enhancing the immanence of the spiritual referent through the image."[11] So, too, does the power of fictional devotion revolve around its ability to make God real and his love felt. Instead of an angry judge or a distant relative, God emerges in the novels as a pivotal figure who would never stop loving these women. Tamara continued her description by explaining, like the novel does, how heterosexual love mirrors divine love: "A lot of people don't realize that God is not against romance. In fact, I know that God created sex. I know he did and he wants us to enjoy it, but within a loving relationship. And the way the Father woos us is romantic and before I got engaged to my husband, he was my first love, the Lord. And he still is my first love. That is who I spent most of my time sitting there [with] saying 'I love you, I love you.' Even though I still do that, then I have my husband that I have to tell, too. The love of the Father is romantic." Interweaving strands of heterosexual and divine love, Tamara's romance with God remains primary. For her, evangelical romances reveal this love in a powerful way that elicits tears and provides certainty. Jackie's response echoed Tamara's: "*Redeeming Love*, that was just such a powerful book, comparing the story of Hosea, obviously, a marriage parallel to God and his love for us and his willingness to continuously take us back. I just love Hosea and I like Angel, whatever their names all were." Later she added, "You know the story [of Hosea], but it doesn't really hit you as loud in the Bible as it does in the book." Here we see once again how evangelical romances become filters for interpreting and understanding the Bible. For Tamara, Jackie, and others, the novel's message of unconditional love brought them closer to a romancing God in a way that the biblical book of Hosea did not. Interestingly, even those who disliked the "meat" of Rivers's novel approved of the message. The abuse and evil in the novel almost made Laura physically ill, but she stated that nevertheless, "I think the concept was correct, you know, the unconditional love." Gwen also questioned her enjoyment of the book but "liked the way it ended."[12] Through *Redeeming Love*, as well as through other evangelical romances, these women found a relationship with a present, personal, providential, and loving God.

Heidi, a forty-six-year-old schoolteacher and married mother of two from Danville, Virginia, also emphasized the power of this title in her life. I asked her about her favorite evangelical romance. "I loved the Francine Rivers one. Michael, the main character, he just loved, he loved the way that God would have loved. In the way that you wish you could love everybody. It was like God told him to do something and he did it. And he stuck by it no matter—even though it didn't look promising or that she was going to end up being able to love him after all." In addition to learning about God and better understanding his love, Heidi was prompted by the novel to appreciate her husband more. Though "he'd always been there" for her, she had taken this for granted. Reading this novel, she remarked, "does help [their marital relationship]." However, for Heidi's sister, *Redeeming Love* "put her in a total depression, because her husband didn't measure up." As Heidi explained, "It really affected her, but in a wrong way. And I've heard other people say that, 'Oh, to have been loved that way.' And I thought, you know, we are. Christ loves us that way. Not in that sex . . . but he loves us in that 'I'm going to keep coming back after you' kind of way." [13] For these women—married or single, with Michael-like husbands or not—evangelical romances like *Redeeming Love* assure them of God's never-ending romance and unconditional love.

Redeeming Love helped many readers discover the "keep coming back after you" kind of love that evangelical Christianity's God has for everyone. For example, Lila, a forty-year-old white Baptist who is married with two children and actively involved in her independent Baptist church, shared a transformative moment. Reading inspirational romances, especially *Redeeming Love*, afforded Lila, who has suffered from an anxiety disorder for the past eight years, a vehicle for realizing the divine romance. Although she grew up within evangelicalism, Lila told how through this story she experienced and learned about God's love in a new way: "I think it really impacted me, how much he loves them [the protagonists] and gave them so many opportunities, and he stuck by them with his commitment and that had a big impact on me as far as accepting the fact of how much he loves me and that he has unconditional love. I think that was the first time I *knew* it. I had heard it, but it just really hit me in that book." For Lila and other readers, fictional devotion transforms hearing into knowing, doubt into certainty, and a vague sense of God into a clear daily reality. Crying as she read the book, Lila felt reassured that God would not forsake her no matter what, that "no matter where I go, no matter what happens, he is going to be there."[14] For Lila, who had heard these words before, the novel helped her envision and encounter a God who romances her with his love and care. To maintain their faith, women like Lila and Tamara needed to hear this message and claim its power more than once. As the certainty of God's presence slips away at different times in their lives, evangelical romances provide these women with a way to relearn and regain this intimacy. Through the power of these narratives—evangelical romance and divine romance—my consultants fortify their faith and claim their place as God's beloved.[15]

Realizing the Romancing God

Amidst the ups and downs of everyday life, whether caused by disappointing husbands or eroding beliefs, the romantic vision of God offers the possibility of an intimate relationship that will not disappoint. Through these novels, authors and readers define their relationships with God in terms of romance. In plots about love, authors demonstrate how a heterosexual relationship between a man and a woman depends upon a prior and continuing relationship with a personal God. To convey this vision, authors emphasize God's desire for a relationship with humanity—the way he romances humanity through his presence, guidance, and most especially his unconditional love. It is, to quote Robin Lee Hatcher, "that love that allows you to give up your life for another. It's that 1 Corinthians 13 kind of love that we seek."[16] For example, in *A Gathering of Memories*, after learning of her father's death, Mandy's new faith in God's love and care provides her with solace. She tells her brother, "There were years of hurting before I understood how much God cares for me, and I'm hurting right now, but Levi, I have hope, something I never had before I trusted in God. Pa is dead and I can't change that, but I do know that God still loves us and always will." Despite her past and present pain, Mandy empha-sizes the certainty of God's comfort. Similarly, her hero Ross Beckett "fell asleep trusting that God was in control and that His infinite love for both him and Amanda would guide and shield them in the days to come."[17] Authors write and women read about this romancing God in the lives of characters like Mandy and Ross. This God has a plan for their lives, and love provides its foundation.

Just as identification and inspiration prompt spiritual change, images of marriage, in fiction and in life, help readers and authors grasp the notion of a romancing God. For these women, marriage re-flects, albeit dimly, the greater unconditional love of God for human-ity. Peggy Stoks explained it this way: "God pursuing his people, de-siring their greatest good, is infinite love. The marriage covenant of husband and wife is an image of the love relationship between Christ the bridegroom and his bride, the Church. Romantic love between a man and a woman is a reflection of the love of the creator for his cre-ated." Likewise, single reader Mary stated, "The image of a marriage relationship is also representative of God's love for the world." She went on to tell me how evangelical romances convey that message.[18] Author Terry Blackstock confided, "I think, in many ways, [marriage is] a picture of how God loves us. Until I had a wonderful, godly hus-band who nurtured me and cared for me, I had a hard time seeing God as that [romancer]." Still single and "waiting for Mr. Right," Gail placed marriage amidst a list of God's other good gifts to humanity, including colors, smells, and chocolate. In her view, "If we treat [ro-mance] appropriately we are able to enjoy what God gave us. I think that is the Father's heart for us. It's about Christ and the Church. The picture God gave us for his love for us is marriage."[19] Gwen took this similarity a little further, claiming that heterosexual love was "just the same as our relationship with God." And Dana compared the growth of her relationship with God to the growth of a hetero-sexual relationship. In her view, the two relationships go through similar phases: infatuation, getting to know one another, spending time together, and growing in love for each other. Reflecting on her thirty years of marriage, Barb remarked, "It's such an analogy for the way that [God] loves us."[20] For my consultants, these comparisons both reflect and shape their evangelical romance reading. Entering a fictional world featuring an idealized relationship between hero and heroine becomes more than a simple boy-meets-girl tale. These seemingly simple love stories become chronicles of the romance between readers and God.

Through their depictions of marriage and love, evangelical romances elicit the sense of God's romance with readers—his immanence and intimate involvement in their lives. For example, one letter-writer named Karen, going through hard times, discovered a renewed sense of God's care through evangelical romance. She needed this assurance because she was having the toughest year of her life. Her letter to Irene Brand lists a litany of events that would tax anyone's emotional resources: her father died unexpectedly, her husband was laid off, her mother temporarily moved away to care for a dying aunt (who was only 59 years old), and two days before she wrote the letter her husband's grandmother died. A Christian since the age of seven, Karen found her faith shaken by these crises, but reading restored her perspective: "It is good to remember that God does care about everyday problems." She closed with thanksgiving to Brand for the enjoyment she received and the encouragement she gained from her works.[21] The novels helped her recognize God's presence in her life and that she was not alone.

For my consultants, evangelical romance novels succeed in supplying the sacred romance, the assurance that God actively desires to participate in their lives and loves them no matter what. For example, I talked with Diana, a fifty-four-year-old white woman, as we sat on the sofa in her living room decorated with Christmas objects, family photos, and a television set. When we talked about the most satisfying aspect of reading evangelical romance, her response emphasized a sense of divine presence. For Diana, "the message you get, that God is involved" gave hope and reassurance. So intertwined were romance and God that she later said, "It is amazing that they can have the same love story as a worldly novel." Similarly, Jill wrote, "That faith and God's love is so intermingled throughout the story is a real blessing and encouragement!"[22] Teenage Carly wrote how she "knows God more" because of her reading, and a Baptist reader explained how she learned that God's love endures even in moments when she does something wrong.[23]

Reading the right romance at the right time further affirmed these women's faith in God's care for their lives. It provided evidence of the romancing God. Clarissa wrote to Shari MacDonald that "it is no accident I picked this book to read today." Others used the language of attraction. Janice felt "drawn" to *The Forgiving Hour* as she surveyed the shelves of her town library, and some expressed amazement at how God could use novels to help them at exactly the right time.[24] One reader in particular responded to Robin Lee Hatcher's italicized presentation of God's voice. Writing to applaud this approach, Ruth told of her attempts to listen more carefully to God, and like the author, felt sure that "He always speaks to us, if we will listen." Another wrote to Peggy Stoks, "I loved the way Elmore talked with God, and how Betsy learned that God can speak to you. We can commune with Christ, and know what He wants from our lives."[25] Reading the novels heightened readers' sense of God's presence and love amidst the busyness and forgetfulness of their lives.[26] This was especially important for Denise, who in a letter to Robin Lee Hatcher explained, "It was awesome to remember He loves me so much. I need to be reminded every other minute."[27] Always forgetting and ever seeking, these women used reading to keep experiencing God's love.

Some women realized this unfailing love in more dramatic ways, including dedication of one's life to evangelical Christianity. This experience came up when I asked authors about their most memorable fan mail. Authors often referred to letters that spoke of salvation and conversion. A letter from a fifteen-year-old girl who realized through evangelical romance reading that "Jesus could do more for her than Satan ever could" stayed with Robin Jones Gunn. Gunn also remembered another that told her "when Christy got on her knees and gave her life to Christ, I got on my knees and prayed right along with her and I gave my life to the Lord because I realized I never had."[28] However, because all the women I interviewed espoused Christianity prior to reading evangelical romance, none spoke of such a transformative event. One particular letter, however, illuminated the parameters of this moment.

For Lynda, an evangelical romance dramatically changed her life. Undated and only about half-a-page long (two paragraphs) on plain paper, the neatly printed letter from Lynda, a woman from Charlotte, North Carolina, expressed gratitude and recounted her spiritual experience. Gillian, the heroine of Shari MacDonald's novel *Stardust*, helped prompt in Lynda a realization and subsequent actions. Gillian's struggles with loneliness, distrust, and worthlessness echoed Lynda's own feelings of inadequacy. She described her struggle and eventual triumph to the author: "When Gillian accepted Christ in the story, her fears of being unlovable and unforgivable, even to God, and her feelings of unworthiness, completely broke me down. I could relate to Gillian so well, because I'd been carrying the same burdens. Yet her turning it all over to God and accepting God's love was so simple that I put the book down and turned my life (and all of my unworthiness) over to God *again*." Twice in one short paragraph Lynda mentions love—her fear of being unlovable and the difficulty of accepting God's love. However, for her, *Stardust* communicated God's love in a way, it seems, that other evangelical sources could not. By becoming aware of God's love, Lynda could release her "burdens" and regain her value as a child of God. Her letter also includes a key word: "again." Here, Lynda reveals her prior relationship with God and her inability to sustain it. While the letter does not make it clear whether this event is a rededication or a conversion, it provides a glimpse into the power of evangelical romance narratives in readers' lives. In chronicling heterosexual and divine romance, these narratives provide an immanent deity, as well as female community and religious guidance. Lynda closed her letter, as she opened it, with gratitude. Thankful for Shari and her work, and asking God's blessing for her, Lynda emphasized how the novel showed her that God "cares for us and is ever present guiding us lovingly through life."[29] My consultants, using romance and love interchangeably, repeatedly emphasized how through reading they reconciled their beliefs and experiences, their knowledge and emotions, their evangelical identity and daily living.

Amidst the banality of daily life, these women lose their sense of God's love and struggle to maintain their faith. Through their fictional devotion, they reclaim a romance with God. Using the image of marriage, readers and authors cast themselves as the beloved and God as the lover in their spiritual lives. One woman told me simply, "The Lord woos us." Similarly, Valerie stated that God "romances us. Think of all the books in the Bible that talk about that. The Song of Solomon, the description between a man and a woman and their love for each other. That is in the Bible. He gave that to us and there are all different stories of love relationships and romances that should be there between ourselves and our Father." Valerie defines the evangelical's romantic relationship with God by moving from marital love to divine love. Beth echoed this: "God is truly our ultimate love and he loves us more than anyone ever could." [30] Emphasizing the depths of God's love, compared with the shallow nature of human love, Beth and other readers wanted to feel the power of that passion. For soon-to-be sixteen-year-old Glenda, that kind of relationship with God was one of her dreams. After reading Shari MacDonald's *Diamonds* and *Stardust*, she wrote, "Wow. CAN IT REALLY ever be that way? That's my biggest dream [an evangelical romance], next to that I want to be so passionate about God that all else pales in comparison." [31] As these women expressed their desire for intimacy with God and implied their distance from that ideal, they cited evangelical romance as a way to re-establish God's immanence and intimacy.

To rediscover the reality of God's love for them, these women needed to rekindle their passion for God. Often, the two processes worked together as the women read evangelical romance novels. For example, when I asked, "What's Christian about the concept of romance?" Jane collapsed the definitions of romance and love and asked me a question in return: "Well, God is love, right?" She went on to describe how reading the novel *Christy*, by Catherine Marshall, helped her realize this principle: "The whole implication or message that I got from that segment of that story is that God is pure love. To understand God you have to understand pure love and pure love is what gives the energy to make everything thrive." Similarly, Sharise, a member of Mona's Book Club, answered, "God is romance. I mean, he is love. God's the author of it." Betty told me, "Well, geeze, God is love."[32] In portrayals of romantic relationships from an evangelical perspective, these women learned and relearned the lesson of God's unfailing love, his romance with humanity. Not surprisingly, authors answered the question "What's Christian about the concept of romance?" in similar ways. Lori Wick stated, "I think he's a very romantic God." Shari MacDonald answered, "God is the greatest romancer of them all." And Robin Jones Gunn emphatically declared, "God is the relentless lover and we are his first love and he wants us back. He's not going to give up on us. He pursues us."[33] Perceiving God as a romancer because of his unfailing love, women respond to this courtship with increased faith, which in turn romances God and keeps him actively involved in their daily lives. Romancing, then, works both ways. God pursues, women respond in kind, and the relationship flourishes.

This vision of God as romancer is not without precedent in Christianity and evangelicalism specifically. Historically, the romance recorded in the Song of Solomon has been interpreted by many theologians as representing the romance between God and the Church. In addition, one finds the language of God as lover throughout historic Christianity. For example, in the thirteenth century, Mechthild of Magdeburg, member of a Beguine community, recorded her romantic descriptions of the love between God and humanity. In "How the Soul Speaks to God," she writes, "Lord, you are my lover, My longing, My flowing stream," to which God responds, "It is my nature that makes me love you often, For I am love itself. It is my longing that makes me love you intensely, For I yearn to be loved from the heart. It is my eternity that makes me love you long, For I have no end."[34] In evangelicalism, one sees this strain not only in romance novels, but also in other forms of literature and in public events. In 1997, Brent Curtis and John Eldredge published *The Sacred Romance: Draw-*

ing Closer to the Heart of God. Echoing several themes embodied in evangelical romance novels, Curtis and Eldredge define the Christian life as "a love affair of the heart," cite the importance of stories for realizing this romance, and depict God as "the ageless romancer." In a chapter bearing this phrase as a title, they open with a quote from Simon Tugwell: "So long as we imagine it is we who have to look for God, we must often lose heart. But it is the other way about—He is looking for us." [35] This theological perspective emphasizes hope and perseverance in one's faith through a reimagining of God, just as the novels do. Other evangelical authors and speakers have also built on this theme. A survey of the "Christmas Catalog" published by Christian Book Distributors, a popular mail-order company featuring an array of evangelical literature and products, reveals others focusing on this theme. In a section entitled "Just for Her," women can purchase the *Boundless Love: Conference in a Box—Video Curriculum*, featuring popular speakers Barbara Johnson, Luci Swindoll, and Sheila Walsh, and the *Falling in Love with Jesus Workbook* by Dee Brestin and Kathy Troccoli. There are also numerous "best-selling" titles that range from Elizabeth George's *Life Management for Busy Women* to Kay Arthur's *Lord, Give Me a Heart for You*. [36] Evangelical romance novels, then, are not alone in their reenvisioning and revisiting of God as romancer.

However, the evangelical romance genre predates many of these efforts, and my consultants did not mention these titles or speakers as sources for their interpretations or their insights. While this theme reflects a common theological strand in contemporary evangelicalism, the women I interviewed recounted discovering the power of this romancing God through their reading of evangelical romance novels. While some evangelical self-help and theology books emphasize God's "boundless love," the novels convey this message through stories to which these women respond. Through their reading they realize the presence of this romancing God who pursues and woos them. The novels affirm God's presence and participation in these women's lives, as well as his love for them. This assurance initiates, for readers, a larger love story—a sacred romance. As these women describe their desire for God's love, their longing to claim the feeling of that love, they reveal the fragility of this sense of the divine in everyday life. Their religious struggles with familiar evangelical practices, including prayer, forgiveness, and Bible reading, pale in comparison with their inability to sustain an experience of God's love and to love him in return. Often the religious commitment of my subjects revolves around their ability to feel in touch with God. As R. Marie Griffith writes, "Since the revivals led by George Whitefield and John Wesley, the evangelical tradition has accentuated an experiential piety of ardent feeling and devotion, in which realization of God's love and power ignites the passions of saint and sinner alike."[37] For the women I interviewed, evangelical romances enable this realization of God's love and help them transform the complacency of everyday life into the vitality of evangelical living.

The Story of God's Love

In addition to portrayals of marriage, the novels' depictions of history also establish a relationship between reader and text that reinforces the message of a romancing God. While I situate evangelical romance novels in the social and cultural history of late-nineteenth- and twentieth-century evangelicalism, my consultants place evangelical romances within a larger religio-historical narrative. While some novels feature contemporary settings, many of the most popular titles set their heroines in the past. In these historical portrayals, the women I interviewed not only found solidarity with heroines and authors but also discovered the sense of God's romancing. This sense emerged as they discerned not only the individual but the historical nature of his providential planning. For those who are struggling to understand their historical role as evangelical women, these novels offer a glimpse into a past controlled by a loving, involved God.

Over and over again, these conservative Protestant women told me about their love of learning history in an entertaining manner. Most would not be the first to pick up a history book, but through the novels they explore the events of long ago. Despite individual preferences for different time periods and types of stories, almost all readers seemed to view the novels as historically accurate and enjoy learning about the past through them. Tina told me, "I really enjoy the history that I learn when I read a book, [especially] Irish history—and I also enjoyed the Russian series." For her, "The books are not just full of stories, they are full of information." [38] While some tend to select "exotic" settings to read about, including England, Ireland, and Russia, others enjoy a variety. As one reader told me, "I have so many favorites. I love World War II, I like the Holocaust books. I love Janette Oke as well." When asked why, she replied, "I love history." [39] Family trees, maps, and diagrams of the protagonists' travels and terrain further enhance readers' ties to the past.

Whether or not evangelical romances accurately depict the past, while an interesting question, is not the point here. Some authors do extensive research, others do not, but readers view the novels as historically accurate regardless. This unquestioning acceptance reveals readers' desire to learn about a Christian past as they seek to make sense of their contemporary role as evangelical women. The historical settings of the novels enable readers to imaginatively visit various locales, to learn about historical events, and to discover their place in history—as women and as evangelicals. The novels depict a past where God and conservative Protestant women (and men) dominate. For my consultants, reading about evangelical heroines who influenced world history affirms their importance and God's providential control.

Consider, for example, representations of the "Old West," the backdrop of many evangelical romances. For some readers the lure of the nineteenth-century trans-Mississippi West proves to be particularly strong. Women enjoy "pioneer stories" that portray the West as a promised land. For example, in both *Sweetbriar* and *Love's Long Journey* the landscape of the West (in contrast with the civilized and crowded East) is depicted as a vast terrain that provides characters with a wide open space to house their dreams and hone their honor. For the protagonists, the West promises possibilities. Wanting to start over and to own his own land, hero Dan Winslow decided "at some point between Manassas and Gettysburg, that if he lived through the war he would become a cowboy."[40] Such dreams were not easily achieved, but evangelical Christianity provides the pioneers with courage and hope. For example, after almost plunging over a waterfall, heroine Louisa Boren clutches her sister-in-law's hand and whispers a verse from the Bible: "Though the waters roar and be troubled we will not fear." Similarly, for Missie LaHaye, the heroine of *Love's Long Journey*, a flooded river becomes both an enemy and an ally. The river claims a fellow member of the wagon train, but at the same time it separates pioneers from the threat of "almost naked" Indians: "Missie shivered as she wondered what could have happened if the swollen river had not been between them. Maybe this was one fulfillment of God's promise, 'Yea, I will help thee.'"[41] The landscape may present obstacles, whether raging waters or Indian warriors, but God's promises enable these evangelical pioneers, these prairie women, to overcome them.

Once settled in the land, these heroines face the challenge of appreciating it. At first, Missie struggles with life in the West. The vast landscape of the Western prairie intensifies her loneliness as she endeavors physically and spiritually to build a new life for herself and her family in a sod hut. She misses her parents, doubts her husband, and questions God. However, as she reconciles with God, her doubts dissipate and the stark landscape is transformed into a scene of beauty. Composing a letter to her parents at the end of the novel, Missie writes, "You know how Willie boasted of his land when he came back? Well, it's even prettier than that. I didn't see it that way at first, but I love it now. The air is so crisp and clean, you can almost serve it on a platter. And the distant mountains change their dress as regularly as a high-fashion city lady. It's so beautiful."[42] However, Missie's realization of the West's beauty and her acceptance of her new life there depend upon her recognition of God's love and faithfulness. Only with God can the beauty of the land be appreciated, and only with God can she live there. In both *Sweetbriar* and *Love's Long Journey*, acceptance of the West as a land of dreams cannot be separated from fidelity to the God of evangelical Christianity.

While the heroes and heroines of the novels encounter troubles in the Western terrain, with God's help they ultimately triumph. The novels' happy endings assure readers of the characters' victories over adversity, their creation of Christian families, and their founding of a Christian America through their civilizing of the West. The historical narrative in these works is defined by God's romance with humanity as evidenced in his planning, power, and participation. Cathy conveyed the pleasure in experiencing this history most concisely. Amidst the country decor of her living room, this fifty-three-year-old woman eagerly told me about her favorite evangelical romances that feature the nineteenth-century West. "I'll tell you why I like them the best if you're going to ask me that! I like them because you learn the history behind them, and I like to learn history like that. I'm assuming they have their facts correct." Later she remarked, "I've learned a lot through Janette Oke and a lot of history." Cathy was not alone in her enjoyment of the historical dimension of the novels. Valerie said, "I enjoy history. I particularly like the romances that go back in time." And Nancy told me, "I like all the history and I like the courtships and to learn about different religions and I also like it when there is a lot of description about the setting." [43] Cathy and other readers like her enjoy reading about a Christian past and learning historical facts. Through reading, they not only encounter heroines like themselves but also a larger lineage of faith—a history peopled by evangelicals and guided by God.

For readers, this idealized Western landscape spills over into their contemporary environs. Reading this genre allows them to think about topics that they do not have the time or inclination to explore through other avenues. Even more importantly, it becomes a way for them to imagine and define their role in history as evangelical women. More than historical details of specific people and places, part of the genre's appeal to its readers comes from learning or imagining that women like them, with moral and religious values like theirs, comprised an important part of historical events. Through these narratives, evangelical readers can claim a central place for themselves in the past and in the present, in the United States and in the world. As anthropologist Zdzislaw Mach notes, "A symbolic concept of the group's land, whether actual or potential or past, serves as an idea of the proper place in the world where the group belongs."[44] For these readers, the novels' portrayals of women, families, and history demonstrates that as evangelical women, as women beloved by God, they occupy a central place within Christianity and the United States, in the past and today. The novels affirm that their lives and religious beliefs matter.

Further, this historical knowledge contributes to how readers assess and respond to current events. Gail shared, "The Thoene's have written several series on the Ireland/England situation and just learning about the history, I mean, I'm not going to read history books, it's just not going to happen and I won't retain it. But I've learned so much [through evangelical romance] about how that all started and what it was all about." She concluded her discussion by acknowledging the effects of learning this history: "It's a mind expander. It's a heart expander, if you let it." And Tina agreed. Reading about history in the novels "gives you a heart for gaining knowledge." These two women learned, like Madeline, "a lot about the history of Christianity." Gaining a sense of Christian history, a history in which women played an active role, affects readers' lives. Stories of the past become a resource for the present. For example, some women read Beverly Lewis's trilogy on the Amish, in part, because their town was becoming home to an increasing number of Amish. Diana enjoyed the books, "probably because of the Amish coming here and we don't know a lot about them, so it gives you a lot of information about what they believe and their culture. It made all of those people a little more real."[45] For these women, Lewis's fictional Hickory Hollow offered them romance but also provided them with knowledge that they enjoyed and used to understand the world around them.

The novels' portrayals of the past provide readers with a history where God's control remains constant, evangelicals emerge triumphant, and America is Christian. Imagining a past where God takes center stage assures readers of his continuing central role in the present. As one woman told me when asked what was most satisfying about reading these novels, "In all of the novels, no matter what, God is still supreme in all of them. He is glorified throughout."[46] To know not only that others struggle and believe as they do but that the everyday living out of one's faith matters to God and to God's plan for the world evokes powerful emotions in readers: hope, perseverance, and love. Through their fictional devotion, these women learn that the passage of time, as well as the details of their lives, ultimately belong to God. They recognize God's involvement in history and in their everyday lives. "The Lord will get you where he wants you," past, present, or future, according to Evelyn, because "his love is never changing."[47] While these narratives help readers validate the historical (and hence contemporary) importance of evangelical women and men, for my consultants the genre's power also derives from its evocation of a sacred story characterized by God's historical involvement and romantic inclinations, a story that begins at the start of their sacred history as recorded in the Bible.

One might expect, in this regard, a kind of evangelical "me and Jesus" rhetoric from these women. Given the evangelical desire to infuse all of life with religious meaning, one might realistically imagine that Jesus provides an accessible image of divine love. From WWJD bracelets to Warner Sallman's *Head of Christ*, evangelicalism emphasizes the salvific power of the life, death, and resurrection of Jesus, as well as how he experienced the sufferings of humanity while remaining without sin. Surprisingly, however, my consultants rarely invoked Jesus as friend, lover, or savior. Instead, in this sacred romance, they focused on God—the creator God of Genesis, the God who seeks a relationship with humanity through his covenant with Israel and his love for the church.[48]

This blending of the Bible, romance, and history became apparent as I asked my consultants, "What is Christian about romance?" In response, they placed the novels' historical renderings within a larger evangelical narrative of biblical history. For them, the evangelical romance begins in sacred history. They constructed a narrative of romance rooted in Genesis, in God and his creation. From the same biblical passages that evangelical aestheticians like Frank Gabelein and

Leland Ryken cite as the source for a Christian view of the arts, readers claimed the foundation for the concept of romance and that of the romance between God and humanity. Speaking of romance, they told me: "God invented it," "God ordained it," and "God created it." [49] Romance, in their view, is Christian. These women claim the goodness of romance and the importance of love in evangelicalism. This view, in turn, becomes a way for readers to interpret the biblical narrative and their relationship with God.

This love story, according to my consultants, begins with Adam and Eve. Repeatedly referring to this duo, my consultants place romance at the creation of the world. Romance, defined in terms of heterosexual courtship and love, represents part of God's design for the world. According to Diana, it is "the way God set it up," and many others agreed. Valerie provided this vision of the beginning of the world: "He [God] is the one that saw Adam in the garden and saw that he was alone and it was not good. He is the one that created Eve. He could have created another person who looked just like Adam. He is the one that created love. The one that created the attraction between a man and a woman." Offering a similar interpretation, Betty explained, "I think it goes right back to the beginning that he created male and female in his image and that men and women were meant to complement one another." And Kate responded similarly, "Well, God created romance. He created Adam and Eve. They were the first lovers." [50] Through this interpretation, my consultants claimed romance for evangelicalism and rejected "worldly" alternatives—divorce, promiscuity, and homosexuality, as well as social constructions of sexuality. By claiming the sanctity of romance and heterosexual marriage, they upheld the genre of evangelical romance, the beliefs of their subculture, and their emphasis on God's love.

In addition, for evangelical women who distinguish themselves, at least rhetorically, from the world through their commitment to the "traditional" definitions of marriage and family, this biblical interpretation supports their claims and validates their choices. If a vital part of God's plan for the world includes romance, marriage, and family, then my consultants can see themselves playing an important role in that plan; through their roles as wives and mothers, they occupy a central place in Christian history and God's design. As Evelyn told me, "That is why God sent his son, so that we could have love, that is what a family is all about."[51] While being careful to state that not all are called to marry and while firmly rejecting homosexuality, these women located marriage and family in the power of God's planning and providence. Charlotte said "God created marriage" and went on to argue, "It is his plan for families to be around." Similarly, Janet stated, "God created marriage, God created the home, church, and the government."[52] These women viewed heterosexuality as a God-given essential aspect of humanity, because "the first thing he did was he made man and then he made woman so they could be together."[53] From this perspective, Adam and Eve represent the first romance, the first marriage, the first family. Weaving together Christianity and romance, these women foregrounded God's plan for families and, accordingly, the importance of being Christian wives and mothers.

Authors echoed this interpretation of romantic history. For example, Irene Brand cited specific passages from Genesis to illustrate the point: "In the beginning God created them, male and female. . . . The Lord said, it is not good that man should be alone; I will make him a helpmeet for him."[54] Reinforcing the relationship between God, gender, and heterosexuality, authors, like readers, view evangelical romance as a retelling of this creation story. Author Lyn Coleman and reader Sharise explained the origins of romance in strikingly similar language. Sharise told me, "You can't have anything [romance] without him," while Coleman stated, "God created love and romance. Without him there would be none." Robin Lee Hatcher echoed this view of God's plan: "God made us to long for relationship and he also made us to be couples. He made man and woman to be a part of each other so whether we are Christian or not, we are seeking that person that God made for us."[55] Romance, love, and sexuality, then, do not reflect the sins of the Fall, but rather the glories of Creation. Often using romance and love interchangeably, my consultants view these emotions and feelings as a characteristic of how God interacts with humanity and as an important part of history.

While many interpret the creation story in Genesis in terms of romance, they also read other biblical passages as evidence for "the scriptural theme of unfailing love"—their theology of romance.[56] Here, as also seen in the previous chapter, these women use evangelical romance as a lens through which to picture the Bible; accordingly, they express a vision of the Bible as a love story. Frequently these women claimed the love between Hosea and Gomer, and even more the love of God for Israel, as evidence of this biblical and evangelical romance, a theme most thoroughly explored in *Redeeming Love*. However, readers also cited numerous other examples of biblical romance: Adam and Eve, Ruth and Boaz, Jesus and the Church, as well as the lover and beloved in the Song of Solomon. Laura told me, "Think of all the books in the Bible that talk about that [a romancing God]. The Song of Solomon, the description between a man and woman and their love for each other. That is in the Bible. He gave that to us and there are all different stories of love relationships and romances that should be there between ourselves and our Father."[57] Similarly, Mindy stated simply, "It [romance] is God-created and that is very biblical," while Nancy explained, "I think that God intends for there to be romance in life, love between a man and a woman. He has indicated that in the Old Testament."[58] Others, like Mary, emphasized romance throughout the Bible: "There is certainly imagery in the biblical narrative of loving relationships or romantic relationships, even references to Christ and the Church being Christ's bride."[59] For readers, not only is romance an inherently Christian category, but the Bible itself embodies the theme. In this view, love instead of hate, romance instead of indifference, and forgiveness instead of judgment become the guiding themes of Christianity.

Authors, perhaps because they must often justify and answer questions about the romance genre, were quick to cite this biblical evidence in their discussions with me. In addition to the passages in Genesis, Irene Brand cited Jesus's attendance at the wedding at Cana as the Bible's "blessing of marriage," along with "touching love scenes" also found in the Bible. Brand also referred me to two verses in particular: "Whosoever findeth a wife findeth a good thing, and obtaineth the favor of the Lord" and "What therefore God hath joined together, let not man put asunder" (Proverbs 18:22 and Matthew 22:30). As examples of romance stories in Scripture, she listed the love between Isaac and Rebekah, between Jacob and Rachel, and the Song of Solomon. She ended her evidence with the New Testament example of Christ's love for the Church, an example also invoked by other authors.[60] Terry Blackstock, for instance, stated, "The Bible tells husbands to love their wives as Christ loved the Church and laid down his life for her. That's powerful love, and it's not something humans came up with. God gave that to us for a reason, and I think that kind of love should always point to Christ." Similarly, Lyn Coleman declared that the Bible "compares us to being the bride and his son as being the bridegroom and one day we will sit with him at the wedding feast."[61] Marshalling both Old and New Testament passages, authors and readers alike interpret the Bible as a love story and weave romance into the very fabric of Christianity.

Author Robin Jones Gunn articulated this perspective most clearly as she related the following story. When asked in a radio interview how she could call herself a Christian and write romance novels, she replied,

"I think it's because when I was young, as a teenager, I read a love story that changed my life. In the first few chapters everything falls apart and you think they're never going to get back together again. And then, about three quarters of the way through, he does everything he can to prove his love to her and she still won't come to him and be his bride. But then in the last chapter he comes riding in on a white horse and he takes her away to be with him forever." And the interviewer said, "Hmmpf, how could that change your life? It sounds like a formula romance novel." I said, "Really? I was talking about the Bible—white horse and everything."[62]

In this view, God's romance of humanity, not his judgment or his holiness, becomes the hallmark of Christianity. For Gunn and other evangelical romance readers and writers, the divine romance animates the creation of the world and its ultimate re-creation in Revelation, it fuels relationships with humanity and with God, and it situates women within historical events and within the divine plan. While not mentioning white horses, author Carole Gift Page also envisioned Christianity as a love story. "I love writing romances about people of faith, because it gives me a chance to explore the ideal romance, not just two people deeply in love, but God's boundless love for his people who've strayed from his side." For these women, the Bible narrates the story of God's relentless love for humanity, a fact that not only validates their importance to the divine, but also helps them realize it in a new way.[63]

Through their fictional devotion, these women re-envision their relationships with Christianity and God. The novels portray a history where evangelical women play pivotal roles. While upholding "traditional" gender ideals, the novels highlight the importance of these women and their contributions as Christians, wives, and mothers. More than that, the genre evokes a larger sacred narrative the places romance, marriage, and family at the foundation of the world. As these women juggle multiple demands, the message that their choices represent part of God's plan confirms their central place in Christian history and in God's creation. These narratives transform history from a series of random events into a carefully ordered design that demonstrates God's romance with humanity. Women's fictional devotion, then, both shapes and reflects this narrative of a God who loves unconditionally.

He gathered her in his arms. The door closed with his kick. Darkness fell as he blew out the candles.

"Louisa?" he asked, lowering her into the warm bed.

"Yes, David?"

"Do you love me?"

She laughed. "You know that I do."

"Even though I've been a fool?"

"Even though you've been a fool." He thought he heard her laugh again. "David?"

"Yes?"

"What about the horses? You've left them out in the cold."

"The horses! I've gone and left them out in the cold, standing in the road!" He reached for his boots and jacket. "Just a minute, Liza, I'll be right back!"

Cold air swept in twice—once when he left, and once when he returned. The blanket was warm on top of them, the colored squares and patches hidden in the night. And on the door, still swinging from the jolt of David's boot, hung three hats: a baby hood, a sunbonnet, and a cap.[1]

With the hats still swinging, *Sweetbriar Bride*, the sequel to *Sweetbriar*, ends. This evangelical romance chronicles the continuing love story of David and Louisa Denny. It narrates their struggles with being married, becoming parents, and building Seattle. At times doubting David's love and almost miscarrying, Louisa takes solace in her faith. When asked why she remained certain her child would live, she responds, "Psalm 121." When her life is in jeopardy during childbirth, the doctor urges David to talk to her because "lots of people are brought back from the very brink of death because they hear the voice of someone they love." Holding Liza, "the words came," and David reclaims his faltering faith and his wife's life as he quotes Louisa's Psalm. "I will lift up mine eyes unto the hills, from whence cometh my help. My help cometh from the Lord, which made heaven and earth. He will not suffer thy foot to be moved; he that keepeth thee will not slumber. Behold, he that keepeth Israel shall neither slumber nor sleep. The Lord is thy keeper; the Lord is thy shade upon thy right hand. The sun shall not smite thee by day, nor the moon by night. The Lord shall preserve thee from all evil; he shall preserve thy soul. The Lord shall preserve thy going out and thy coming in from this time forth and even forevermore." David's recitation of these biblical words is efficacious, as Louisa and their baby daughter Emily survive. Having overcome doubts about their love and their faith, the family ends up happily tucked away in their Christian home.[2]

Ending and Beginning: The Cycle of Fictional Devotion

For readers, the novels' endings represent a moment they have awaited but also dreaded. Jenna described it this way: "I can't wait to get to the end, but when I'm done, I'm like, 'Those people are gone out of my life.'" When I asked what was least satisfying about reading a Christian romance, many women replied, "When it ends." They spoke of a sense of loss upon finishing a good book and of their desire to know "what happened" to the characters. Diana said, "If I'm really in love with a character, it takes me a long time to let them go, because I will often think about them and wonder what happened."[3] Similarly,

Mary told me that "when you are done with the books there is a sense of loss." Others put it more simply: "I hate when it's over."[4]

However, for most of the women I interviewed, the story is never really over. The ending of one novel means the beginning of another. They read new books, await upcoming sequels, and revisit familiar favorites. They return to the formula of evangelical romance over and over again. In part, this cyclical reading pattern reflects their desire to maintain connections with beloved characters. When asked what they would change about the novels, many replied, "I want more novels!" and "Maybe that they would continue it a bit more or make it into a series."[5] Mindy wished that Janette Oke's "Love Comes Softly" series, already containing eight volumes about Marty and Clark, their children, and their grandchildren, "would go on and on." It may be "excruciating" to wait for the next volume, but these women want more.[6] Readers' letters voice similar wishes: "I hope there is more to come in this series," and "I was thrilled to know you'd follow up with Olivia's friends Romy and Elena."[7] Even when authors fail to keep up with readers' demands for sequels, my consultants reread their favorites to recapture the connections they provided. Mary, who spoke of her sense of loss when finishing a novel, explained that "I think this is the reason that I reread things." For other readers, the books are so enjoyable that they keep returning to them: "I read them over and over again. I can't seem to part with them." Jackie remarked with some surprise about a particular book, "I've read it twice and I don't read books over again and I will read it again. I have it at home now." Others shared with authors, "I've read it more than once."[8]

However, the cyclical nature of these women's reading reflects more than a desire to retain bonds with fictional characters. They return repeatedly to the genre as they try to keep the spark alive in their own romances with evangelicalism—a relationship that necessitates constant care and attention. As we have seen throughout, fictional devotion emerges at sites of negotiation and disjuncture, such as the need for leisure time, the frustration with gender roles, or the problem of complacent faith. However, even as women struggle with everyday evangelical living, they choose a reading practice that affirms and bolsters their religious identity. As a result, their cyclical reading practice helps keep them within the circle or subculture of evangelicalism. "To use a literary metaphor," David Morgan writes, "a world is a story that is told and retold in order to fortify its spell of enchantment."[9] My consultants read and reread these novels to sustain their evangelical worlds. Tamara described the need for and power of the enchantment cast by evangelical romance novels: "You want to read another one. I just always want to read another one. Plus it leaves you with an outlook—sometimes I get hope and encouragement. I know that sounds corny, from a novel, but you do, you get hope and encouragement." As the feeling of faith fades, evangelical romance novels "remind you of what you have and encourage you to persevere. That is what the secular novels don't do very often."[10] Amidst the doubts and dilemmas that characterize daily life, these fictional worlds reaffirm religious identities, validate women's experience, and make the love of a transcendent deity an immanent reality. This devotion reminds readers of a love story that has no end. As a part of this tale, no matter what their failures or their flaws, women can rest assured that God's romance— his unconditional love for them—remains constant. It is a message these women need to hear again and again. Denise's remark bears repeating: "It was awesome to remember he loves me so much. *I need to be reminded every other minute.*"[11] Even as the novels end, readers' relationships with God and the evangelical subculture begin anew.

The cyclical nature of these women's reading practice and the circumscribed character of their religious commitment cause some critics unease. Viewing the novels as escapist and evangelicalism as oppressive, they want these women to break out of their reading cycle and evangelical circle. For these critics, my consultants' desire to remain within these boundaries seems unfathomable. However, by examining how these women characterize their own reading practices, we see that maintaining religious belief matters more to them than modern literary standards, contemporary feminist concerns, and male-dominated theological aesthetics. Staying within the circle, within the evangelical subculture, and cultivating a relationship with God is precisely the point. To expect them to escape, then, from either romance reading or evangelical faith, is to disregard the priority of their religious world. However, at the same time, these women's explanations also reveal the difficulty of maintaining this "spell of enchantment." Their evangelical world is fragile. As a result, repetitive evangelical romance reading becomes a way to achieve and sustain the vitality of their faith.

Unlike stereotypical depictions of evangelicals as triumphantly devout or arrogantly steadfast, these women's stories reveal a more complicated and cyclical picture of evangelical religious life. Buffeted by the waves of daily living, their faith ebbs and their certainty erodes. Growing up in Christian homes and attending church more than once a week is not enough. However, rather than abandon their faith, they seek ways to shore up their religious identities. Evangelical romances, then, become a means to reverse, or at least endure, the direction of these corrosive currents. Ministering through stories rather than sermons, heroines rather than biblical patriarchs, and pleasure reading rather than Bible study, evangelical romances speak to these women's religious lives in powerful ways. Jackie preferred *Redeeming Love* to Hosea, Jocelyn was prompted to forgive by evangelical romance rather than a Sunday sermon, and Lila claimed God's love through reading these novels despite having heard the same message in church.[12] Amidst sometimes choppy and ever-changing evangelical waters, my consultants' fictional devotion helps them preserve their faith. Their cyclical reading reveals the fluidity that characterizes these women's religious identities and their everyday evangelicalism.

Toward an Evangelical Aesthetic

Evangelical women, and much of the evangelical subculture and its products, prize religious beliefs and artistic achievements that differentiate them from other forms of American Protestantism. As scholars seek to map the landscape of American religion and situate evangelicalism within that terrain, it seems that moving toward a better understanding of this evangelical aesthetic would enrich our scholarly geographies. Sociologist Andrew Greeley writes of the

"Catholic imagination," the idea "that Catholics are more likely to imagine God as present in the world and the world as revelatory instead of bleak. Much that is thought to be distinctively Catholic results from this distinctive style."[13] Similarly, it seems that evangelicals exhibit a distinct imagination. Their ideas of what constitutes truth and beauty, as well as how those concepts are expressed and experienced, differ from those of others, whether academician or aesthetician. Many participants in and products of the evangelical subculture endorse an alternate aesthetic ideal that cannot be separated from their religious commitments. If popular culture is the "art of making do," as Michel de Certeau writes, then evangelicals have mastered it by creating an artistic vision that is, seemingly, uniquely their own. From George Whitefield's magazines to Oral Roberts's televangelism to Lori Wick's romances, evangelicals have exhibited a distinct sense of religious and artistic life. In this religio-aesthetic world, mediocrity, predictability, utility, and sentimentality reign. What many would call creative flaws are labeled by evangelicals as artistic achievement and theological truth.

In part, this aesthetic and its popularity rest on the concept of mediocrity, defined historically as the mean between two extremes. Using the historical rather than the pejorative meaning illuminates facets of the evangelical imagination. Based on compromise, the ideal of mediocrity or, put another way, the in-between, resonates with evangelicals on multiple levels. It reflects their theological beliefs about being in, but not of, the world—to use Christian Smith's phrase, of "engaging with distinction." Evangelical popular culture is predicated on reconciling and mediating this tension. It affords evangelicals opportunities to consume products which resemble yet remain distinct from their secular counterparts. Whether as rock music, greeting cards, or romance novels, these various popular culture forms offer evangelicals ways to participate in the wider culture and simultaneously separate themselves from it. Accordingly, what some would label substandard art becomes in the evangelical imagination a vital resource for the maintenance of religious identity.

In addition, even as mediocre products help evangelicals negotiate their relationship with the perceived wider culture, these popular culture endeavors also mitigate other tensions in evangelical life by bringing together seemingly disparate subjects. Evangelical romance novels occupy this in-between position, which reconciles women and ministry, faith and fun, escapism and engagement, as well as ordinary life and divine presence. Other forms of evangelical popular culture, such as contemporary Christian music and Christian film, rest on similar combinations. They join concepts that are often viewed in terms of opposition—rock music and evangelical lyrics, cinematic license and Christian beliefs—and through these mixtures reflect and shape the evangelical imagination. By incorporating unexamined or controversial topics like leisure, gender, and sexuality, these products offer ordinary evangelicals a means to reflect upon and refine their own theological thinking amidst the routine of daily life.

The popularity of evangelical romance, then, rests on its ability to meet diverse needs, mitigate multiple tensions, and sustain evangelical faith. As John Fiske writes, "If the cultural resource does not offer points of pertinence through which the experience of everyday life can be made to resonate with it, then it will not be popular. As everyday life is lived and experienced fluidly, through shifting social allegiances, these points of pertinence must be multiple, open to social rather than textual determinations, and transient."[14] At any given moment, these women find various and adaptable points of pertinence in evangelical romance. The genre affords enough malleability that it meets a variety of needs and expectations. At times women can read for escape, while on other occasions they can read for edification.

This flexibility does not seem limited to evangelical romance novels. Other evangelical endeavors, including children's videos and wall art, function similarly. A framed print featuring a mother holding her infant while they both gaze out the window with a verse from Jeremiah centered underneath the image, "For I know the plans I have for you . . . to give you a future and a hope," can meet multiple desires, including artistic beauty, theological hope, and domestic adornment.[15] These products supply entertainment and edification, artistic achievement and religious utilitarianism. They serve multiple functions and, like evangelical romance, provide a way for evangelicals to bring together their ideas of truth and beauty, religion and art, evangelical and world. For evangelicals trying to find the relevance and sustain the efficacy of their faith during the ups and downs of everyday life, the mediocrity of this popular culture becomes a spiritual asset rather than, as some would say, an artistic liability.

While mediocrity occupies center stage in this religio-aesthetic world, predictability also plays a vital role. Using a predictable form or formula connects the evangelical present with its historical past. Contemporary products evoke earlier incarnations that enhance the objects' salience. Janette Oke's novels bring to mind Grace Livingston Hill's, and the "Left Behind" films resonate with *A Thief in the Night*, an earlier rapture movie endeavor. This repetition of forms provides evangelicals with a sense of religious and cultural stability. It affirms their sense that they are maintaining the historic evangelical faith amidst the innovations of contemporary secular culture. Scholar David Morgan argues that the repeated use of a devotional form "generates a stability or baseline against which to measure one's well-being."[16] Applying this theory more broadly suggests that evangelical popular culture's reliance on repetition of forms and predictable formulas functions as a diagnostic tool. It becomes a standard against which artists and art forms are judged. Those violating this aesthetic ideal, as we saw earlier with some authors and with musician Amy Grant, find themselves facing criticism of their faith and their work. This is not to say that evangelical popular culture is a static entity or outside the effects of history, but rather to illuminate how and why evangelicals prize predictability as an ideal.

For many evangelicals, the predictability embodied in these popular culture products reminds them that past lessons learned must be lived out in daily life. Evangelical romance novels prompt readers to recapture the feeling of faith, reestablish a sense of community, and revisit a variety of practices and beliefs, including prayer, forgiveness, and patience. Other products, such as "Veggie Tale" videos and mugs emblazoned with Galatians 5:22–23 ("Love, Joy, Peace, Patience, Kindness, Goodness"), repeat similar themes. This popular culture teaches the basics of evangelical theology: the reality of God's love, the centrality of Jesus's salvific role, the necessity of conversion, and the importance of evangelism. Even as the ordinariness of life mitigates the vitality of faith, these products affirm that the rules that govern one's relationship with God do not change. My consultants enjoyed reading novels featuring a heroine's conversion, a lesson they had heard before, because it highlighted the importance of this event, reminded them of their own experiences, and spurred them to self-reflection and evangelical attention. The "Evangecube Keychain," it seems, fulfills a similar function. This Rubik's-like cube features images of Jesus's life, death, and resurrection, which emphasize the importance of salvation. Attached to one's keys, it does not offer a radical theology or a new idea, but rather serves as both a reminder of God and a tool for evangelism.[17] On a trying day, this simple reminder can help its owner to negotiate the complexities of faith or prompt sharing the gospel with a friend. For many evangelicals, repetition rather than innovation and predictability rather than novelty characterize their everyday religio-aesthetic world.

Closely related to the aesthetic ideal of predictability is that of utility. To the dismay of some espousing modernist aesthetics, evangelicals reject notions of art for art's sake. Rather, in the view of many evangelicals, all of life—art and popular culture included—revolves around initiating and nurturing a relationship with God. Ordinary products, then, serve extraordinary ends. As we have seen throughout this study, my consultants believe that God works through evangelical romance novels and influences the course of their daily lives. This utility is not limited to the genre. The range of evangelical popular culture articulates the presence and participation of God in everyday life, from the emphasis on divine light in Thomas Kinkade paintings to the making of a cross necklace from nails. These creations infuse the mundane with the transcendent and become vehicles for the divine. While artistic skill and technical excellence represent an artist's stewardship of her abilities, this by itself is not enough to make readers experience God or to prompt necklace wearers to repent. For evangelicals, divine power or use of a product fuels the apprehension of familiar lessons. Utility, then, reinforces predictability, and like this ideal, assures readers of God's power and participation in daily life. The utilitarian aesthetic reflects a theological conviction about how God works in the world. The God that animates popular culture actively seeks a relationship with humanity and uses a variety of means at his disposal to achieve it.

These beliefs about God also shape the sentimental aesthetic exhibited in much of evangelical popular culture. If God is immanent and involved in daily life, then such involvement reflects his unconditional love for humanity. Evangelical romances, perhaps more than other evangelical forms, articulate this vision of a romancing God. By focusing on love, both human and divine, these narratives help readers appreciate God's care and with that knowledge comes the promise of Romans 8:28: "And we know that in all things God works for the good of those who love him." As one faces a crisis of faith, the demands of parenting, or the need for leisure, the novels assure readers that they are not alone, that they can endure these struggles, and that God loves them during these hard times. A romancing God and a fictional happy ending, then, reinforce the theological belief that everything will work out in the end. A reader may not understand why a problem arises or a crisis occurs, but reading evangelical romance confirms the sense of God's love and his plan for life, which for these evangelical women promises hope and an eventual real-life happy ending. Their sentimentality, then, is not a denial of evil's reality, but rather an emphasis on the power of faith. Like Greeley's Catholics who focus on revelation instead of bleakness, evangelicals highlight hope over despair, immanence over distance, love over hate, and goodness over evil. Other forms of evangelical popular culture also exhibit this sentimentality. Christian music lyrics often emphasize the trials, but eventual triumph, of one's faith. Devotional aids, self-help books, and theological treatises acknowledge the difficulties of evangelical living but instruct readers about how to overcome problems and to grow spiritually.

Evangelical artistic endeavors celebrate the presence of God and the power of belief. For many evangelicals, the sentimental choice is one of faith, not immorality or naiveté. Rather than lamenting their choice of ideals, we need to move toward a better understanding of this evangelical aesthetic. Instead of dismissing or stereotyping those who read evangelical romance, we, as scholars and citizens, need to examine the impulse that drives them do so. Understanding this religio-aesthetic world, which lauds the very concepts that many disdain—mediocrity, predictability, utility, and sentimentality—forces us to re-examine our own scholarly imaginations. By tackling that which seems most unpalatable or unfathomable we can challenge old presuppositions, advance new paradigms, and tell more nuanced stories.

For my consultants, the writing and reading of evangelical romance novels represents a devotional practice. It helps them sustain their religious identities amidst religious crisis and complacency. The genre offers these women a powerful religious idiom for articulating everyday evangelicalism because these stories speak to their lives. The narratives acknowledge readers' various struggles, and at the same time move evangelical women to the center of the evangelical story. Their concerns and capabilities as Christian women, wives, and mothers are validated. Further, the sacred historical narrative invoked by evangelical romances sacralizes these roles as it locates them in the biblical creation and God's design for the world. Women's fictional devotion reveals a theological aesthetic that celebrates God's romance of humanity. For these women, realizing and keeping this romance alive represents the ultimate happy ending, one that will never end. "In the long ago we came to these shores, finding a goodly land," states the heroine Louisa Boren Denny. She continues, "We have planted, builded, cultivated, nurtured all the beginnings of civilization. We have made homes and reared our children. Soon we shall go on to find that *better country*. Press on, I say, for the great majority, our friends and companions of the long ago, are waiting for us over there."[18] In the religio-aesthetic world of evangelical romance, these women, like Louisa Boren Denny, can rest assured that the divine romance present in this life is but a pale reflection of eternal life with God.

NOTES

Prologue

1 Wilbee, *Sweetbriar*, 135–36.
2 Ibid., 7, 105, cover.
3 See Mussell, "Romantic Fiction," 317. See also Cawelti, "The Concept of Formula in the Study of Popular Literature," 381–90.
4 Boyle, *One Night of Passion*.
5 Radway, *Reading the Romance*, 134–35, 46–85, 119–56 (especially 140–50). See also Mussell, "Romantic Fiction," 317–23; Modleski, *Loving with a Vengeance*, 35–49.
6 Baer, *Shadows Along the Ice*, 150.
7 Krentz, *Dangerous Men and Adventurous Women*, 11; Ramsdell, "Romance 2000," 86; Linden and Rees, "I'm Hungry. But not for Food."
8 Harrison, "Spinning Spiritual Tales that Sell," S6; Beals, "Quality Religious Fiction is the Target at Crossway Books," 65–67; Keylock, "Evangelical Protestants Take Over Center Field," 32–33. For a geographical breakdown of romance readers in the United States, see "Romancing the Novel."
9 Roof, *Spiritual Marketplace*, 11.
10 For more on this approach, see Lofland and Lofland, *Analyzing Social Settings*; Maxwell, *Qualitative Research Design*, 69–73; and Marshall and Rossman, *Designing Qualitative Research*, 55–58. Unlike other methods, this approach yields readers in ways not constrained by institutional affiliation, site-specific criteria, or other participant criteria.
11 After the interviews, I asked readers to fill out a survey to elicit demographic and reading data. The race, age, marital status, income, and educational levels of those who completed the survey follow. Race: 41 white/Caucasian, 2 white/Hispanic, 5 African American/black. Age: 7 (20–29), 9 (30–39), 17 (40–49), 6 (50–59), 3 (60–69), 1 (70–79). Marital

Status: 33 married, 8 single, 2 divorced, 2 widowed. Income: 1 ($10,000–$14,999), 5 ($15,000–$24,999), 11 ($25,000–$49,999), 11 ($50,000–$74,999), 4 ($75,000–$99,999), 3 ($100,000–$124,999), 3 ($125,000 or more). Education: 1 (some high school), 4 (completed high school), 2 (some college), 21 (completed college), 8 (some postgraduate), 6 (completed M.A.). States: 32 (N.C.), 5 (N.Y.), 4 (Pa.), 3 (Minn.), 1 (Md.), 1 (Ill.), 1 (Fla.), 1 (Mass.).

12 Smith, *American Evangelicalism*, 32–33; McDannell, *Material Christianity*, 256.

13 Ellingsen, *The Evangelical Movement*, 47; Marsden, *Evangelicalism and Modern America*, ix–x; Balmer, *Mine Eyes Have Seen the Glory*, especially 278–79. For more, see also Davison Hunter, *American Evangelicalism*, and Dayton and Johnston, *The Variety of American Evangelicalism*.

14 Griffith, *God's Daughters*, 11–12.

15 Morgan, *Visual Piety*, 21–22.

16 Ibid., 9–10.

17 Miller, "Narrative," 70; Fiske, *Understanding Popular Culture*, 161.

18 Smith, *American Evangelicalism*, 118–19.

19 Roof, *Spiritual Marketplace*, 33.

Chapter One

1 Hill, *The Finding of Jasper Holt*, 167–69.

2 Munce, *The Grace Livingston Hill Story*, 98–100, 106, 168–72. While an example of Christian hagiography, Munce's work remains one of the only biographical treatments of Hill.

3 Ibid., 170. Packer, "Leisure and Life-Style," 360. For this evangelical interpretation of Matthew 25:14–30, see Gaebelein, *The Christian, the Arts, and Truth*, 62.

4 Schultze, *American Evangelicals and the Mass Media*, 13, 25; Sweet, *Communication and Change in American Religious History*, 12–15; Nord, "Systematic Benevolence," 239–69; Moore, *Selling God*, 12–39.

5 Ryken, "Literature in Christian Perspective," 220.

6 Flint, *The Woman Reader*, 4, 10–11, 22–25, 30–35; see also McDannell, *Material Christianity*, 8, 82–83.

7 Moore, *Selling God*, 20–25, 99, 116–17. For more on the relationship between conservative Protestants and fiction, see Newell, "Early Evangelical Fiction," and Reynolds, *Faith in Fiction*.

8 Tompkins, *Sensational Designs*, 149; Kelly, *Private Woman, Public Stage*, ix; Baym, *Women's Fiction*, 11. See also Papshvily, *All the Happy Endings*,

Cowie, "The Vogue of the Domestic Novel," and Welter, "The Cult of True Womanhood."

9   Stowe, *Uncle Tom's Cabin*; Stowe, *The Minister's Wooing*; Warner, *The Wide, Wide World*.

10 Mussell, *Fantasy and Reconciliation*, 3–11; Thurston, *The Romance Revolution*, 34–35; Baym, *Women's Fiction*, 12; Modleski, *Loving with a Vengeance*, 15–24.

11 Hill, *The Finding of Jasper Holt*, 3–4, 76.

12 Marsden, *Fundamentalism and American Culture*, 4; DeBerg, *Ungodly Women*, 97, 23, 128; Bendroth, *Fundamentalism and Gender*, 6, 32, 40. See also McDannell, *Material Christianity*, 68.

13 Carpenter, *Revive Us Again*, 3–28; Lundin, "Offspring of an Odd Union," 143–44.

14 McDannell, *Material Christianity*, 162–64.

15 Nerdrum, *On Kitsch*, 10–12; McDannell, *Material Christianity*, 162–66, 193, 196; "Grace Livingston Hill," <http://users.tellurian.net/bksleuth/GLHInfo.html>, July 17, 2000; Munce, *The Grace Livingston Hill Story*, 168–69.

16 Smith, *American Evangelicalism*, 10, 1–19; Carpenter, *Revive Us Again*, 201; Carpenter, "From Fundamentalism to the New Evangelical Coalition," 3–16.

17 Carpenter, "Contemporary Evangelicalism and Mammon," 403. See also Jorstad, *Popular Religion in America*, 1–49.

18 Ostling, "Evangelical Publishing and Broadcasting," 46–55. Some sources date the foundation of CBA to 1949.

19 Bethany House, <http://www.bethanyhouse.com>, March 30, 2002; Zondervan, <http://www.zondervan.com>, March 30, 2002.

20 "Shop Talk," 577–78; Pilkington, "Backlist Best Bets among the Books for Protestants," 986–89; Luccock, "Religion in the Bookstore," 990–93; "Religious and Inspirational Novels Continue to be Popular," 764–65.

21 For more on religious book sales in the 1950s and 1960s, see "Religious Book Publishers Expect Another Year of High Sales," 755–56; "The Market is Still Increasing for Religious Books and Bibles," 879–82; "News and Trends of the Week" (*Publishers Weekly* 171), 41–42; "News and Trends of the Week" (*Publishers Weekly* 173), 37–38; "Currents," 175: 43–44; "Currents," 181: 51–52; "Currents," 187: 53–55; "Currents," 191: 39–41; and "Currents," 193: 37–38.

22 Marshall, *A Man Called Peter*, and *Christy*; "Best Sellers," 193: 98, 138.

23 For more on the emergence of evangelical popular culture, see Jorstad, *Popular Religion in America*, 21–49, 135–52. Jorstad attributes the growth

of evangelical popular culture to four factors — "high technology," "evangelical history," "parachurch preference," and "mass media evangelizing," 3–7. Interview with Carol Gift Page.

24 "Religious Best Sellers" (*Publisher's Weekly* 213), 88–90. For more on other best sellers in the 1970s, see "The Best Sellers," 213: 54–58. According to their Web site, Bethany House "developed over forty years ago out of Bethany Fellowship International's ministry training and sending missionaries around the world." <http://www.bethanyhouse.com>, March 30, 2002. Dr. Kenneth N. Taylor established Tyndale House Publishers, Inc., in 1962. <http://www.tyndale.com/tyndalestory.asp>, March 30, 2002.

25 Simora, *The Bowker Annual 25th Edition*, 476; Julia Moore, *The Bowker Annual 30th Edition*, 498; Hamilton, "More Money, More Ministry," 122.

26 Ferré, "Searching for the Great Commission," 99–117; McDannell, *Material Christianity*, 261, 222–69; Hamilton, "More Money, More Ministry," 104–38.

27 Radway, *Reading the Romance*, 33–34. Woodiwiss, *The Flame and the Flower*.

28 Interview with Janette Oke; Oke, *Love Comes Softly*, Preface, vii.

29 Interview with Janette Oke. For more on Oke, consult Logan, *Janette Oke*, and Hensley, "Janette Oke," 32–35.

30 Griffin, "Fiction for the Faithful," 27–29. Interview with Janette Oke. See also Jorstad, *Popular Religion in America*, 141–43. Jorstad, "Pressers on and Holders Fast," 181–87; Harrison, "Spinning Spiritual Tales that Sell," S6–S14.

31 Beals, "Quality Religious Fiction is the Target at Crossway Books," 65–67; "Spring Religious Titles," 49–63; "New Books for Adults," 55–68.

32 "Serenade/Serenata," 54–55; "Serenade/Saga," 62–63. See also Meehan, "Zondervan's Mission and Marketing Goals Translate into Retail Expansion," 90–93.

33 Tyndale House Publishers, <http://www.tyndale.com>, June 17, 2000, and HeartQuest Books, <http://www.heartquest-romance.com>, June 21, 2000.

34 Ferré, "Searching for the Great Commission," 114; McDannell, *Material Christianity*, 256; Hamilton, "More Money, More Ministry," 130.

35 "Religious Bestsellers" (*Publishers Weekly* 231), 43, and "Best-Selling Christian Books," 39. Bogart, *The Bowker Annual 42nd Edition*, 513; Bogart, *The Bowker Annual 45th Edition*, 515.

36 Barr, *The Bowker Annual 40th Edition*, 600. In comparison, in 1996, *Drums*

of *Change* sold 258,444 copies, Jonathan Harr's *A Civil Action* sold 269,600 copies, and Ann Rice's *Memnoch the Devil* sold 240,270. Bogart, *The Bowker Annual 41st Edition*, 632; Bogart, *The Bowker Annual 42nd Edition*, 608–11.

37 Bogart, *The Bowker Annual 43rd Edition*, 622–26; Bogart, *The Bowker Annual 44th Edition*, 639–42; Bogart, *The Bowker Annual 45th Edition*, 636–43; "Voice of the Industry," <http://www.cbaonline.org/voice/a_fiction .html>, May 11, 2001. Given the popularity of these authors, I open each chapter with an extended quote from one of their novels.

38 Andraski, "Seasonal Escapes," 36–37; Rabey, "No Longer Left Behind," 26–33. Rivers's "Hooked on Romance" was one of the few articles treating romance novel reading, 38–41. See Langberg, "He's Lost that Lovin' Feeling," 15–16; Dillow and Pintus, "Five Questions Women Ask About Sex," 28–34.

39 Interview with Carole Gift Page; Interview with Janette Oke; Interview with Robin Jones Gunn.

40 Ryken, "In the Beginning, God Created," 57.

41 Gaebelein, "The Aesthetic Problem," 5; Gaebelein, *The Christian, the Arts, and Truth*, 72.

42 Ryken, "In the Beginning, God Created," 62; Gaebelein, *The Christian, the Arts, and Truth*, 99, 225, 228; Ryken, "The Creative Arts," 114–16.

43 Gaebelein, "The Aesthetic Problem," 6; Gaebelein, *The Christian, the Arts, and Truth*, 62, 65.

44 Schaeffer, *Addicted to Mediocrity*, 23, 44; Gaebelein, "The Aesthetic Problem," 4–5.

45 Ryken, "The Creative Arts," 129; Schaeffer, *Addicted to Mediocrity*, 47, 110; Lundin, "Offspring of an Odd Union," 144.

46 Gaebelein, "The Aesthetic Problem," 3–4; Gaebelein, *The Christian, the Arts, and Truth*, 77.

47 Solomon, "On Kitsch and Sentimentality," 1–14.

48 Mussell, *Fantasy and Reconciliation*, 164, 172–73, and especially chapters six and seven. Modleski, "The Disappearing Act," 435–48, and *Loving with a Vengeance*, 38.

49 Radway, *Reading the Romance*, 215–17.

50 Jorstad, *Popular Religion in America*, 143.

51 Baym, *Women's Fiction*, 43–44; Munce, *The Grace Livingston Hill Story*, 168–69.

52 Krentz, *Dangerous Men and Adventurous Women*, 1.

53 Emerson and Smith, *Divided by Faith*.

Chapter Two

1 Oke, *Love's Long Journey*, 163–64.

2 Ibid., 168.

3 Interview with Nancy.

4 Interview with Debbie; Interview with Jenna; Letter from Lisa to Peggy Stoks, no date.

5 Interview with Betty; Interview with Evelyn; Interview with Jane; Interview with Rose; Interview with Madeline; Interview with Baptist Women's Group; Henderson, "Broadening an Understanding of Women, Gender, and Leisure," 1–7. Barbara Sicherman also discovered this sense of getting lost in a book in her study of nineteenth-century reading. See "Sense and Sensibility," 206–11.

6 Interview with Charlotte.

7 Morgan, *Visual Piety*, 14.

8 Radway found a similar emphasis on escape in her interviews with secular romance readers. See *Reading the Romance*, 86–92. Richard Hoggart also suggests that people have long viewed art as escape. See his discussion in *The Uses of Literacy*, 196. Interview with Charlotte; Interview with Heidi.

9 Interview with Gail; Interview with Mindy and Janet.

10 Interview with Evelyn; Interview with Cathy.

11 Letter from Lillian to Peggy Stoks, no date; Letter from Paige to Shari MacDonald, no date.

12 Letter from Megan to Peggy Stoks, April 4, 2001; Letter from Christy to Irene Brand, August 23, 2000; Letter from Lindsay to Irene Brand, September 1, 2000. Reading and letter writing offered these women "travel" opportunities similar to those explored by Robert A. Orsi in his study of women, illness, and pilgrimage. See his articles, "The Cult of the Saints and the Reimagination of the Space and Time of Sickness in Twentieth-Century American Catholicism," 63–67, and "The Center Out There, In Here, and Everywhere Else," 213–32.

13 Interview with Valerie; Interview with Betty; Interview with Diana; Interview with Jane; Interview with Ellen; Interview with Mindy and Janet; Interview with Nancy; Interview with Lila; Interview with Madeline; Interview with Baptist Women's Group.

14 Interview with Valerie; Interview with Mindy and Janet. Many others also mentioned sharing this devotion with their mothers, including Kate, Laura, Melody, Judy, Jane, Ellen, and Jenna. This theme also emerged in

multiple letters: Letter from Megan to Peggy Stoks, April 4, 2001; Letter from Eleanor to Shari MacDonald, January 30 1999; Letter from Louise to Terry Blackstock, December 23, 2000; Letter from Ruth to Robin Lee Hatcher, no date; Letter from Susannah to Robin Lee Hatcher, March 15, 2000; and Letter from Joyce to Irene Brand, September 3, 2000.

15 Interview with Fiona; Interview with Rita; Interview with Kate and Eva. Other Grace Livingston Hill readers include Jocelyn, Jackie, Jenna, Lila, Betty, and the Baptist Women's Group.

16 Interview with Laura; Interview with Gail.

17 Interview with Evelyn.

18 Interview with Lila; Interview with Mary.

19 Interview with Nora; Interview with Betty; Interview with Baptist Women's Group; Interview with Tamara.

20 For more information on these publishers, see Steeple Hill, <http://www.steeplehill.com>, Waterbrook Press, <http://www.randomhouse.com/waterbrook/>, and Zondervan, <http://www.zondervan.com/>.

21 Letter from MaryAnn to Irene Brand, no date; Letter from Audrey to Irene Brand, September 2, 2000; Letter from Helen to Irene Brand, September 28, 2000.

22 Interview with Carole Gift Page. Interview with Irene Brand.

23 Interview with Sharon Ewell Foster; Interview with Victoria Christopher Murray.

24 Walkworthy Press, <http://www.walkworthypress.net>, April 12, 2001.

25 Interview with Roxanne; Interview with Baptist Women's Group; Interview with Betty; Interview with Jackie.

26 Packer, "Leisure and Life-Style," 356.

27 Marsden, *Fundamentalism and American Culture*, 43–55, and Dayton and Johnston, *The Variety of American Evangelicalism*, 5–21.

28 Shaw, "Gender, Leisure, and Constraint," 8–15.

29 Katz and Foulkes, "On the Use of the Mass Media as 'Escape,'" 377–88.

30 Gallagher, *Evangelical Identity and Gendered Family Life*, 150, 134. See also Gallagher and Smith, "Symbolic Traditionalism and Pragmatic Egalitarianism," 211–33.

31 Interview with Jane; Interview with Lila.

32 Interview with Gail.

33 Interview with Baptist Women's Group; Interview with Mary; Interview with Mindy and Janet.

34 Interview with Evelyn; Interview with Betty; Interview with Jane; Letter from Sarah to Peggy Stoks, November 16, 2000.

35 Interview with Nancy.

36 Letter from Marie to Peggy Stoks, July 26, 1999 (emphasis added); Letter from Elizabeth to Peggy Stoks, January 3, 2001 (emphasis added).

37 Letter from Jeannette to Peggy Stoks, no date; Interview with Valerie; Interview with Jane; Interview with Rose; Interview with Diana; Interview with Mindy and Janet.

38 Letter from Jill to Robin Lee Hatcher, August 24, 2000; Letter from Amanda to Terry Blackstock, June 8, 2000; Letter from Gemma to Irene Brand, no date.

39 Letter from Edith to Robin Lee Hatcher, no date; Letter from Denise to Robin Lee Hatcher, no date; Letter from Melissa to Irene Brand, February 9, 2000; Letter from Amy to Terry Blackstock, December 30, 2000; Letter from Victoria to Peggy Stoks, May 3, 2000.

40 Seiter et al., eds., *Remote Control*, 1.

41 Murray Smith, "Film Spectatorship and the Institution of Fiction," 113–27.

42 Tuan, *Escapism*, xi; Pearlin, "Social and Personal Stress and Escape Television Viewing," 255–59.

43 Katz and Foulkes, "On the Use of the Mass Media as 'Escape,'" 377–88.

44 Wellman, *Networks in the Global Village*, 83, 89–90, 109.

45 Hetherington, *Expressions of Identity*, 17.

46 Interview with Nancy; Interview with Jackie. Janice Radway discovered a similar community of readers that likewise was not based around a book club. *Reading the Romance*, 46–50.

47 Interview with Gwen; Interview with Gail; Interview with Betty.

48 Hetherington states, "Identity is not only achieved through identification with groups of individuals who share a common outlook but also through recognisable performative repertoires that are expressive and embodied." *Expressions of Identity*, 17–18.

49 Field notes, Raleigh, North Carolina, September 26, 2000.

50 Granovetter, "The Strength of Weak Ties," 1373, and Wellman and Berkowitz, *Social Structures*, 483–84.

51 Fiske, *Understanding Popular Culture*, 32. Hetherington adds that "we need to see this process of identity formation as a performative process that has a distinct spatiality." *Expressions of Identity*, 102.

52 Interview with Nora. Evangelical romance readers working at local Christian bookstores occupied a role like that of church librarians. They provided information, books, and points of connection for readers. Rita explained, "I know my fiction customers when they walk in the door. I can say so and so has a new book out and here it is." Brooke, also a sales asso-

ciate and avid reader, played a similar recommender role for her fiction customers. Interview with Rita; Interview with Brooke. See also Radway, *Reading the Romance*, 46–55. In Peter Willmott's analysis of friendship, he finds that women (more than men) serve as "social secretaries" in their friendship and kin networks. They provide information, schedule meetings, and keep in touch. See *Friendship Networks and Social Support*, 30, 41.

53 Interview with Cathy; Interview with Nancy; Interview with Jenna.

54 Interview with Mindy and Janet; Interview with Evelyn; Interview with Gwen; Interview with Mary.

55 Interview with Diana; Interview with Jean; Interview with Kate and Eva; Letter from Lindsay to Irene Brand, September 1, 2000. Also, Letter from Marge to Shari MacDonald, August 2, 2000; Letter from Sarah to Peggy Stoks, November 16, 2000; Letter from Tracy to Robin Lee Hatcher, August 10, 2000; Letter from Lily to Shari MacDonald, September 9, 1999.

56 Interview with Theresa; Interview with Melody.

57 Wellman and Berkowitz, *Social Structures*, 221–23, especially Harrison C. White's assessment of market networks in chapter 9, and Willmott's analysis of relationships in *Friendship Networks and Social Support*, especially 20–27.

58 McHenry, *Forgotten Readers*, 3, 18, 298–314; Interview with Mona.

59 Interview with Mona's Book Club.

60 Morgan, *Visual Piety*, 23.

Chapter Three

1 Ewell Foster, *Ain't No River*, 65.

2 Smith, *American Evangelicalism*, 121.

3 Interview with Melody; Interview with Gail; Letter from Lindsey to Irene Brand, September 1, 2000.

4 Interview with Mona's Book Club; Interview with Lila; Letter from Eleanor to Shari MacDonald, January 30, 1999.

5 Interview with Lila; Interview with Cathy; Interview with Charlotte; Interview with Jane; Interview with Valerie; Interview with Evelyn; Interview with Nora; Interview with Baptist Women's Group; Interview with Mona's Book Club; Interview with Diana; Interview with Heidi.

6 Wick, *A Gathering of Memories*, 245–46; Banks, *The Lone Rider Takes a Bride*, 46–49.

7 Interview with Diana; Interview with Mary; Interview with Nancy; Inter-

view with Jackie; Interview with Jean; Interview with Mindy and Janet; Interview with Nora; Interview with Roxanne.

8 Interview with Nancy; Interview with Mindy and Janet; Interview with Baptist Women's Group; Interview with Valerie; Interview with Cathy.

9 Interview with Baptist Women's Group.

10 Interview with Diana; Interview with Cathy; Interview with Charlotte; Letter from Marie to Peggy Stoks, July 26, 1999.

11 Bethany House, "Author Guidelines," November 3, 1999; Barbour Books, "Heartsong Presents Guidelines for Authors," March 30, 2002; Multnomah Publishers, "Palisades Pure Romances: Writers' Guidelines," May 12, 2000; "Heartquest Books," June 21, 2000.

12 Interview with Peggy Stoks; Interview with Irene Brand; Interview with Lori Wick; Oke, *The Calling of Emily Evans*, 217–22. Interview with Madeline; Interview with Lila.

13 Interview with Betty; Interview with Sally.

14 Rivers, *Redeeming Love* (1997), 317. Interview with Gail; Interview with Jocelyn; Interview with Baptist Women's Group.

15 Interview with Lila; Interview with Kelly.

16 Baer, *Shadows Along the Ice*, 139.

17 Brand, *Where Morning Dawns*, 171.

18 Snitow, "Mass Market Romance," 141–61; Light, "Returning to Manderley," 7–25.

19 Balmer, *Mine Eyes Have Seen the Glory*, 279.

20 Tracie J. Peterson, *My Valentine*, 122–23, 128–30, 169–70.

21 Interview with Lyn Coleman.

22 Wick, *Whatever Tomorrow Brings*.

23 McCourtney, *Betrayed*, 63, 224, 236, 284.

24 Oke, *Love Comes Softly* and "The Canadian West" Series, which includes *When Calls the Heart, When Comes the Spring, When Breaks the Dawn*, and *When Hope Springs New*.

25 Interview with Valerie; Interview with Baptist Women's Group; Interview with Nora.

26 Interview with Jackie; Interview with Lila; Interview with Nora; Interview with Charlotte; Interview with Madeline; Interview with Nancy.

27 Interview with Tamara.

28 Interview with Madeline.

29 Interview with Mindy and Janet; Interview with Baptist Women's Group; Interview with Madeline; Interview with Nora; Interview with Jackie.

30 Interview with Jenna; Interview with Cathy; Interview with Rose; Inter-

view with Mindy and Janet; Interview with Laura; Interview with Gwen. Radway, *Reading the Romance*, details the features of the "failed romance" in the secular market, 157–85. Interview with Lila; Interview with Betty; Interview with Gail; Interview with Valerie; Interview with Baptist Women's Group.

31 Morgan, *Visual Piety*, 32.

32 Interview with Jackie; Interview with Betty.

33 Interview with Baptist Women's Group; Interview with Lila.

34 Interview with Lila; Interview with Tamara; Interview with Betty.

35 Interview with Gwen; Interview with Lila; Interview with Baptist Women's Group.

36 Interview with Mary.

37 Interview with Jackie.

38 Interview with Shari MacDonald; MacDonald, "Home for the Heart," in *Restoration and Romance*, 99–179.

39 Letter from Cheryl to Shari MacDonald, August 1, 2000; Letter from Tara to Shari MacDonald, February 17, 1999; Letter from Meg to Shari MacDonald, January 10, 1998; Interview with Shari MacDonald, July 12, 2000.

40 Interview with Baptist Women's Group; Interview with Madeline.

41 Romanowski, "Behind the Eyes," 44–46; Collum, "The Cross and the Crossover," 50–51; Zoba, "Take a Little Time Out," 86.

42 Smith, *American Evangelicalism*, 118–19; de Certeau, *The Practice of Everyday Life*, xiv, 30–39.

43 Ryken, "The Creative Arts," 125.

44 Howard, "On Evil in Art," 112. See also Leitch, "Reality in Modern Literature," 194.

45 Frank, "The Christian and the Arts," 24–25.

46 Hein, "A Biblical View of the Novel," 341, 343.

47 Barbour Books, "Heartsong Presents Guidelines for Authors," March 30, 2002, and Multnomah Publishers, "Palisades Pure Romances: Writers' Guidelines," May 12, 2000.

48 Hensley, "Janette Oke," 32–35; Interview with Lori Wick; Interview with Shari MacDonald.

49 Solomon, "On Kitsch and Sentimentality," 4.

50 Solomon, "On Kitsch and Sentimentality," 3; Brown, *Good Taste, Bad Taste, and Christian Taste*, 143–44; Orsi, *Thank You, St. Jude*, 194–95, 197.

51 Phillips, *Dream A Little Dream*, especially page 106.

52 Brown, *Good Taste, Bad Taste, and Christian Taste*, 141.

53 Solomon, "On Kitsch and Sentimentality," 12.

54 Noll and Niemczyk, "Evangelicals and the Self-Consciously Reformed," 217–18.

55 Smith, *American Evangelicalism*, 192–93 and 37–42.

Chapter Four

1 Wick, *A Gathering of Memories*, 139.
2 Ibid., 140.
3 Interview with Laura; Interview with Jocelyn.
4 For more on this perception, see McDannell, *Material Christianity*, 8.
5 Fiske, *Understanding Popular Culture*, 37.
6 De Certeau, *The Practice of Everyday Life*, 18; Fiske, *Understanding Popular Culture*, 32–43.
7 Eugene H. Peterson, *The Message*, 41. Field notes, New Orleans Convention Center, New Orleans, Louisiana, July 10, 2000.
8 Interview with Janette Oke.
9 Morgan, *Visual Piety*, 33 (emphasis added).
10 Manning, *God Gave Us the Right*, 31, 97.
11 Brekus, *Strangers and Pilgrims*.
12 Interview with Robin Jones Gunn.
13 Interview with Tracie Peterson; Interview with Debra White Smith; Interview with Robin Lee Hatcher; Interview with Doris Elaine Fell.
14 Interview with Peggy Stoks.
15 Interview with Lori Wick; Interview with Shari MacDonald.
16 Bethany House, "Author Guidelines," November 3, 1999; Barbour Books, "Heartsong Presents Guidelines for Authors," March 30, 2002; Multnomah Publishers, "Palisades Pure Romances: Writers' Guidelines," May 12, 2000.
17 Brasher, *Godly Women*, 85, 116; Interview with Lori Wick; Interview with Robin Lee Hatcher; Interview with Irene Brand; Interview with Terry Blackstock; Interview with Sharon Ewell Foster; Interview with Lyn Coleman; Interview with Victoria Christopher Murray; Interview with Shari MacDonald; Interview with Doris Elaine Fell; Interview with Carole Gift Page; Interview with Maureen Pratt; Interview with Tracie Peterson.
18 Interview with Robin Lee Hatcher; Hatcher, *The Forgiving Hour*, 393.
19 Interview with Shari MacDonald; Interview with Terry Blackstock.
20 Interview with Maureen Pratt.
21 Interview with Robin Lee Hatcher; Interview with Lyn Coleman; Interview with Victoria Christopher Murray; Interview with Tracie Peterson; Interview with Sharon Foster.

22 Radway, "Reading is Not Eating," 7–29. Also, for overviews of reader-response theory, see Suleiman and Crosman, *The Reader in the Text*, Freund, *The Return of the Reader*, and Tompkins, *Reader Response Criticism*.

23 Letter from Elsie to Robin Lee Hatcher, no date; Letter from Tracy to Robin Lee Hatcher, August 10, 2000; Letter from Victoria to Peggy Stoks, May 3, 2000; Letter from Elsie to Robin Lee Hatcher, no date; Letter from Tabitha to Shari MacDonald, no date; Letter from Helen to Irene Brand, September 28, 2000; Letter from Roberta to Shari Macdonald, February 18, 1998; Letter from Jill to Robin Lee Hatcher, August 24, 2000.

24 Letter from Mabel to Terry Blackstock, November 24, 2000; Letter from Christine to Terry Blackstock, January 22, 2001.

25 Nerdrum, *On Kitsch*, 17, 11.

26 Schaeffer, *Addicted to Mediocrity*, 23.

27 Mach, *Symbols, Conflict, and Identity*, 5; Richard Jenkins, *Social Identity*, 4, 109.

28 Interview with Lila; Interview with Baptist Women's Group; Letter from Rachel to Robin Lee Hatcher, no date; Letter from Susannah to Robin Lee Hatcher, March 18, 2000.

29 Fiske, *Understanding Popular Culture*, 11; Richard Jenkins, *Social Identity* 25, 109; Hetherington, *Expressions of Identity*, 17–18.

30 Interview with Laura; Interview with Jean.

31 Fish, *Is There a Text in this Class?*, 170–71. See also his article "Literature in the Reader: Affective Stylistics," 70–100.

32 Cohen, *Belonging*, 5. See also Bourdieu, *Outline of a Theory of Practice*, 95; Eagleton, *Literary Theory*, 74–75; Fiske, *Understanding Popular Culture*, 137; Morris and McClurg Mueller, *Frontiers in Social Movement Theory*, 114; Hoggart, *The Uses of Literacy*, 174.

33 Interview with Lila.

34 Kenyon, *800 Years of Women's Letters*, ix–x. Barton and Ivanic, *Writing in the Community*, viii, 3, 10–11. According to scholars, reading and writing "takes on a social meaning" and can be seen as "constitutive of identity and personhood." Maybin, *Language and Literacy in Social Practice*, 140; Barton and Hall, *Letter Writing as a Social Practice*, 11, 19.

35 Letter from Marie to Peggy Stoks, February 12, 1999; Letter from Elena to Robin Lee Hatcher, September 13, 2000; Letter from Jeannette to Peggy Stoks, no date; Letter from Susan to Peggy Stoks, February 1, 2001; Letter from Lydia to Irene Brand, August 29, 2000; Letter from Karen to Irene Brand, August 30, 2000; Letter from Tara to Shari MacDonald, Feb-

ruary 17, 1999; Letter from Rebecca to Shari MacDonald, December 12, 1999; Letter from Jeanne to Terry Blackstock, January 4, 2000.

36 Letter from Amy to Terry Blackstock, December 7, 2000; Letter from Monica to Irene Brand, September 20, 2000; Letter from Pamela to Robin Lee Hatcher, September 3, 2000; Letter from Eleanor to Shari MacDonald, January 30, 1999; Letter from Kimberly to Terry Blackstock, January 22, 2001; Letter from Tanya to Peggy Stoks, July 13, 2000; Letter from Christy to Irene Brand, August 23, 2000.

37 This pattern follows general letter style: salutation, securing of goodwill, narrative, petition, and conclusion. See Barton and Hall, *Letter Writing as a Social Practice*, 6.

38 Letter from Marsha to Shari MacDonald, January 24, 2000, and Letter from Pamela to Robin Lee Hatcher, September 3, 2000; Letter from Stephanie to Shari MacDonald, no date, and Letter from Nicole to Shari MacDonald, no date.

39 Letter from Danielle to Shari MacDonald, January 20, 1998.

40 Letter from Loretta to Irene Brand, February 27, 2000; Letter from Emily to Peggy Stoks, August 2, no year; Letter from Lily to Shari MacDonald, September 9, 1999; Letter from Sharon to Shari MacDonald, December 6, 1999.

41 Letter from Grace to Robin Lee Hatcher, no date; Letter from Carol to Terry Blackstock, July 14, no year; Letter from Ann to Irene Brand, no date; Letter from Jill to Robin Lee Hatcher, August 24, 2000.

42 Letter from Carrie to Peggy Stoks, September 29, 2000; Letter from Bonnie to Shari MacDonald, April 7, 1999; Letter from Courtney to Irene Brand, September 7, 2000; Letter from Shirley to Shari MacDonald, April 26, 2000; Letter from Alyssa to Shari MacDonald, November 1, 2000; Letter from Gemma to Irene Brand, no date; Letter from Elena to Robin Lee Hatcher, September 13, 2000.

43 Letter from Carly to Shari MacDonald, no date.

44 Letter from Jennifer to Shari MacDonald, January 11, 1999; Letter from Phoebe to Shari MacDonald; Letter from Roberta to Shari MacDonald, February 28, 1998.

45 Letter from Danielle to Shari MacDonald, January 20, 1998. I include the stationery description because "a writer's choices are not neutral . . . as much as any other items that people own and use in their lives, it [writing equipment] can represent who one is, what one believes, where one belongs, and how one wants to be perceived by others." Barton and Hall, *Letter Writing as a Social Practice*, 87.

46 Letter from Caroline to Irene Brand, November 2, 2000. For more on prison and letter writing, see Janet Maybin, "Death Row Penfriends: Some Effects of Letter Writing on Identity and Relationships," especially page 171. Of inmates writing letters, Maybin states, "Through these dialogues they felt that they had reclaimed or reconstructed parts of themselves which had been lost or destroyed."

47 Letter from Pamela to Robin Lee Hatcher, September 3, 2000; Letter from Gemma to Irene Brand, no date.

48 Interview with Jocelyn.

49 Interview with Tracie Peterson; Interview with Peggy Stoks; Interview with Shari MacDonald; Interview with Diana Crawford; Interview with Terry Blackstock.

50 Interview with Janette Oke; Interview with Shari MacDonald. For more on fan mail's influence on artists, see Price, "McCready Stays True to Her Voice," Rosen, "Special Delivery," and Henry Jenkins' discussion of *Beauty and the Beast* in *Textual Poachers*, 120–51.

51 Interview with Janette Oke; Perry, "Dear Reader," in *The Doctor Next Door*, 255; Cheryl Wolverton, "Dear Reader," in *For Love of Mitch*, 253; Interview with Robin Lee Hatcher.

52 Barton and Ivanic, *Writing in the Community*, 11.

53 Wellman, *Networks in the Global Village*, 83–87; Willmott, *Friendship Networks and Social Support*, 88–89.

54 De Certeau, *The Practice of Everyday Life*, 18.

55 Interview with Diana; Interview with Gail; Interview with Tamara; Interview with Madeline.

56 Interview with Heidi; Interview with Lila.

Chapter Five

1 Lewis, *The Reckoning*, 279–81.

2 Ibid., 280.

3 Fiske, *Understanding Popular Culture*, 50–51; de Certeau, *The Practice of Everyday Life*, xxi.

4 Interview with Jenna; Interview with Betty; Interview with Mary.

5 Interview with Gwen; Interview with Charlotte. For more on the complexities of identification, see Krentz, *Dangerous Men and Adventurous Women*, 31–52.

6 Interview with Lila; Interview with Jackie; Interview with Evelyn; Interview with Mindy and Janet.

7 Interview with Tamara.

8 Interview with Betty; Interview with Baptist Women's Group; Interview with Charlotte; Interview with Shari.

9 Letter from Dorothy to Peggy Stoks, February 12, 1999; Letter from Hilarie to Peggy Stoks, no date; Letter from Lillian to Peggy Stoks, no date; Letter from MaryAnn to Irene Brand, no date.

10 Interview with Jackie; Interview with Madeline.

11 Gallagher, *Evangelical Identity and Gendered Family Life*, xi, 1–4, 92.

12 Interview with Rose; Interview with Gwen; Interview with Betty; Interview with Nancy; Interview with Mindy and Janet; Interview with Jenna.

13 Interview with Nancy; Interview with Mary.

14 Interview with Betty.

15 Interview with Gail; Interview with Diana; Interview with Cathy; Interview with Lila; Interview with Baptist Women's Group.

16 Interview with Gwen; Interview with Valerie; Interview with Cathy; Interview with Mindy and Janet; Interview with Betty; Interview with Diana; Interview with Ellen; Interview with Mary.

17 Interview with Tamara; Interview with Gwen; Interview with Mary; Interview with Diana; Interview with Lila; Interview with Valerie.

18 Interview with Tamara; Interview with Baptist Women's Group.

19 Interview with Diana; Interview with Kate and Eva.

20 Interview with Sally.

21 Katz and Foulkes, "On the Use of Mass Media as 'Escape,'" 384.

22 Interview with Cathy; Interview with Jenna; Interview with Jackie; Interview with Lila; Interview with Mindy and Janet; Interview with Betty.

23 Interview with Peggy Stoks; Letter from Tanya to Peggy Stoks, July 13, 2000.

24 Letter from Hilarie to Peggy Stoks, no date.

25 Interview with Mindy and Janet.

26 Interview with Gail; Interview with Catherine.

27 Interview with Lila; Letter from Victoria to Peggy Stoks, May 3, 2000.

28 Letter from Tracy to Robin Lee Hatcher, August 10, 2000; Letter from Elise to Robin Lee Hatcher, no date; Letter from Susannah to Robin Lee Hatcher, March 18, 2000.

29 Katz and Foulkes, "On the Use of the Mass Media as 'Escape,'" 384.

30 Oke, *The Calling of Emily Evans*, 217–22.

31 Interview with Mindy and Janet; Letter from Monica to Irene Brand, September 20, 2000; Interview with Gail.

32 Letter from Bess to Shari MacDonald, July 24, 1995; Interview with Ellen; Interview with Gail; Letter from Clarissa to Shari MacDonald, Febru-

ary 15, 1998; Letter from Mabel to Terry Blackstock, November 24, 2000; Interview with Debbie.

33 Interview with Madeline; Interview with Mindy and Janet; Letter from Bess to Shari MacDonald, July 24, 1995; Interview with Jocelyn; Letter from Monica to Irene Brand, September 20, 2000; Letter from Mabel to Terry Blackstock, November 24, 2000.

34 Letter from Victoria to Peggy Stoks, July 13, 2000; Interview with Robin Jones Gunn.

35 Interview with Mindy and Janet.

36 Letter from Kimberly to Terry Blackstock, January 22, 2001; Interview with Jocelyn.

37 Letter from Gabrielle to Robin Lee Hatcher, no date.

38 Letter from Stacy to Robin Lee Hatcher, August 22, 2000; Letter from Judith to Robin Lee Hatcher, September 23, 2000.

39 Letter from Elena to Robin Lee Hatcher, September 13, 2000; Letter from Tracy to Robin Lee Hatcher, August 10, 2000.

40 Miller, "Narrative," 69.

41 Wick, *Whatever Tomorrow Brings*, 183.

42 Ibid., 63–64; Wick, *Sean Donovan*, 98.

43 Gallagher and Smith, "Symbolic Traditionalism and Pragmatic Egalitarianism," 228.

44 Interview with Betty; Interview with Lila; Letter from Hilarie to Peggy Stoks, no date.

45 Interview with Mona's Book Club; Interview with Fiona.

46 Interview with Melody; Interview with Diana; Interview with Barb; Interview with Jane.

47 Interview with Melody; Interview with Lila; Interview with Jackie; Interview with Baptist Women's Group.

48 Interview with Cathy; Interview with Jean.

49 Manning, *God Gave Us the Right*, 112.

50 Interview with Cathy; Interview with Gwen; Interview with Lila; Interview with Jackie; Interview with Tamara.

51 Interview with Betty; Letter from Mabel to Terry Blackstock, November 24, 2000; Letter from Christine to Terry Blackstock, January 22, 2001.

52 Letter from Ann to Irene Brand, no date.

53 Interview with Jenna; Letter from Louise to Terry Blackstock, December 23, 2000.

54 Interview with Jackie; Letter from Helen to Irene Brand, September 28, 2000; Interview with Cathy.

55 Letter from Patty to Terry Blackstock, October 15, 1999.

56 Letter from Caroline to Irene Brand, November 2, 2000; Letter from Carol to Terry Blackstock, July 14, no year; Letter from Janice to Robin Lee Hatcher, August 14, 2000; Letter from Denise to Robin Lee Hatcher, no date.

57 Fiske, *Understanding Popular Culture*, 57, 32–43.

58 Hetherington, *Expressions of Identity*, 63; Morris and McClurg Mueller, *Frontiers in Social Movement Theory*, 104–5, 110; and Richard Jenkins, *Social Identity*, 81.

59 Cohen, *Belonging*, 21.

60 Richard Jenkins, *Social Identity*, 104.

61 Interview with Baptist Women's Group.

Chapter Six

1 Rivers, *Redeeming Love* (1997), 461–62.

2 Darnton, "What is the History of Books?," 31.

3 Francine Rivers, *Redeeming Love* (1991). Other secular historical romances by Rivers include *Rebel in His Arms*, *Outlaw's Embrace*, and *A Fire in the Heart*.

4 Rivers, *Redeeming Love* (1997), copyright/acknowledgments.

5 Rivers, *Redeeming Love* (1997), 467. Rivers also writes, "Everything in *Redeeming Love* was a gift from the Lord: plot, characters, theme. None of it is mine to claim."

6 Ibid., 467.

7 Compare Rivers, *Redeeming Love* (1991), pages 79, 156, 251–52, 357, 373, with Rivers, *Redeeming Love* (1997), pages 94, 178, 285, 399–400, 428.

8 Rivers, *Redeeming Love* (1997), 428.

9 Rivers, *Redeeming Love* (1997), "Publisher's Preface."

10 Interview with Robin Lee Hatcher.

11 Interview with Tamara; Morgan, *Visual Piety*, 43.

12 Interview with Tamara; Interview with Jackie; Interview with Laura; Interview with Gwen.

13 Interview with Heidi.

14 Interview with Lila.

15 Letter from Jill to Robin Lee Hatcher, August 24, 2000.

16 Interview with Robin Lee Hatcher.

17 Wick, *A Gathering of Memories*, 153, 198.

18 Interview with Peggy Stoks; Interview with Mary.

19 Interview with Terry Blackstock; Interview with Gail.

20 Interview with Gwen; Interview with Mona's Book Club; Interview with Barb.

21 Letter from Karen to Irene Brand, August 30, 2000.

22 Interview with Diana; Letter from Jill to Robin Lee Hatcher, August 24, 2000. Also, Letter from Mabel to Shari MacDonald, February 15, 1998.

23 Letter from Carly to Shari MacDonald, no date; Interview with Baptist Women's Group.

24 Letter from Clarissa to Shari MacDonald, February 15, 1998; Letter from Janice to Robin Lee Hatcher, August 14, 2000. Also, Letter from Sheila to Terry Blackstock, December 7, 2000; Letter from Elsie to Robin Lee Hatcher, no date; Interview with Cathy.

25 Letter from Ruth to Robin Lee Hatcher, no date; Letter from Martha to Peggy Stoks, no date.

26 Interview with Gwen; Interview with Baptist Women's Group; Interview with Cathy; Letter from Christine to Terry Blackstock, January 22, 2001; Letter from Carol to Terry Blackstock, July 14, no year.

27 Letter from Denise to Robin Lee Hatcher, no date.

28 Interview with Robin Jones Gunn.

29 Letter from Lynda to Shari MacDonald, no date (emphasis added).

30 Interview with Anonymous African American Author; Interview with Valerie; Interview with Baptist Women's Group; Interview with Evelyn.

31 Letter from Glenda to Shari MacDonald, February 25, 1997.

32 Interview with Jane; Interview with Mona's Book Club; Interview with Betty.

33 Interview with Lori Wick; Interview with Shari MacDonald; Interview with Robin Jones Gunn.

34 Tyson, *Invitation to Christian Spirituality*, 170.

35 Curtis and Eldrege, *The Sacred Romance*, 8, 38, 69.

36 Christian Book Distributors, "CBD Christmas," *CBD Catalog*, A16.

37 Griffith, "Joy Unspeakable and Full of Glory," 219.

38 Interview with Baptist Women's Group.

39 Interview with Mindy and Janet; Interview with Jackie.

40 Morris, *The Valiant Gunman*, 101–5.

41 Wilbee, *Sweetbriar*, 101–2; Oke, *Love's Long Journey*, 67.

42 Oke, *Love's Long Journey*, 206–7.

43 Interview with Cathy; Interview with Valerie; Interview with Nancy.

44 Mach, *Symbols, Conflict, and Identity*, 173, 175, 56–57.

45 Interview with Gail; Interview with Baptist Women's Group; Interview with Madeline; Interview with Jenna; Interview with Diana.

46 Interview with Cathy; Interview with Diana.

47 Interview with Evelyn.

48 Brenda Brasher found a similar emphasis on God, rather than Jesus, in her study of conservative Protestant women. See *Godly Women*, 104–5.

49 Interview with Mindy and Janet; Interview with Baptist Women's Group; Interview with Valerie; Interview with Cathy; Interview with Gail; Interview with Diana; Interview with Charlotte; Interview with Nancy; Interview with Jenna; Interview with Melody; Interview with Barb; Interview with Laura; Interview with Vicki.

50 Interview with Diana; Interview with Betty; Interview with Melody; Interview with Valerie; Interview with Kate and Eva.

51 Interview with Evelyn.

52 Interview with Charlotte; Interview with Mindy and Janet.

53 Interview with Gwen.

54 Interview with Irene Brand. Also, Interview with Debra White Smith; Interview with Lori Wick.

55 Interview with Lyn Coleman; Interview with Mona's Book Club; Interview with Robin Lee Hatcher.

56 Letter from Elizabeth to Peggy Stoks, January 3, 2001.

57 Interview with Laura. Also, Interview with Valerie.

58 Interview with Mindy and Janet; Interview with Nancy.

59 Interview with Mary.

60 Interview with Irene Brand.

61 Interview with Terry Blackstock; Interview with Lyn Coleman; Interview with Debra White Smith.

62 Interview with Robin Jones Gunn.

63 Page, *In Search of Her Own*, 251.

Epilogue

1 Wilbee, *Sweetbriar Bride*, 237–38.

2 Ibid., 127, 161, 231–33.

3 Interview with Jenna; Interview with Diana; Interview with Valerie.

4 Interview with Mary; Interview with Gail.

5 Interview with Jenna; Interview with Diana.

6 Interview with Mindy and Janet; Interview with Valerie; Interview with Tamara.

7 Letter from Amanda to Terry Blackstock, June 8, 2000; Letter from Carrie to Peggy Stoks, September 29, 2000; Letter from Susan to Peggy Stoks, February 1, 2001.

8   Interview with Mary; Letter from Marie to Peggy Stoks, July 26, 1999; Interview with Jackie; Letter from Emma to Robin Lee Hatcher, August 4, 2000; Letter from Shirley to Shari MacDonald, April 26, 2000; Letter from Marge to Shari MacDonald, August 2, 2000; Letter from Kimberly to Terry Blackstock, January 22, 2001.

9   Morgan, *Visual Piety*, 9.

10 Interview with Tamara; Interview with Lila.

11 Letter from Denise to Robin Lee Hatcher, no date (emphasis added).

12 Interview with Jackie; Interview with Jocelyn; Interview with Lila; Interview with Janette Oke.

13 Greeley, *The Catholic Myth*, 4.

14 Fiske, *Understanding Popular Culture*, 25, 129.

15 Family Christian Stores, "Harvest Sale Catalog, October 1–27," 27.

16 Morgan, *Visual Piety*, 204.

17 Family Christian Stores, "Savings Spectacular, February 4–March 2," 3.

18 Wilbee, *Sweetbriar Spring*, 254.

BIBLIOGRAPHY

CONSULTANT INTERVIEWS

Readers

Interview with Heidi, June 11, 2000.

Interview with Shari, June 11, 2000.

Interview with Nora, September 15, 2000.

Interview with Valerie, September 22, 2000.

Interview with Baptist Women's Group, September 26, 2000.

Interview with Rita, August 1, 2000.

Interview with Brooke, August 3, 2000.

Interview with Cathy, October 3, 2000.

Interview with Betty, October 4, 2000.

Interview with Debbie, October 5, 2000.

Interview with Gail, October 14, 2000.

Interview with Nancy, October 19, 2000.

Interview with Rose, November 8, 2000.

Interview with Jenna, November 25, 2000.

Interview with Jackie, November 28, 2000.

Interview with Melody, December 7, 2000.

Interview with Evelyn, December 18, 2000.

Interview with Lila, December 19, 2000.

Interview with Diana, January 2, 2001.

Interview with Jane, January 2, 2001.

Interview with Mary, January 19, 2001.

Interview with Ellen, January 23, 2001.

Interview with Barb, February 16, 2001.

Interview with Tamara, February 16, 2001.

Interview with Gwen, February 23, 2001.

Interview with Charlotte, April 25, 2001.
Interview with Mindy and Janet, May 7, 2001.
Interview with Catherine, May 8, 2001.
Interview with Madeline, May 8, 2001.
Interview with Mona's Book Club, May 11, 2001.
Interview with Fiona, May 14, 2001.
Interview with Judy, May 14, 2001.
Interview with Michelle, May 14, 2001.
Interview with Mona, May 16, 2001.
Interview with Laura, June 22, 2001.
Interview with Vicki, June 25, 2001.
Interview with Jocelyn, July 5, 2001.
Interview with Kate and Eva, July 10, 2001.
Interview with Theresa, July 26, 2001.
Interview with Jean, September 1, 2001.
Interview with Kelly, September 6, 2001.
Interview with Sally, September 6, 2001.
Interview with Roxanne, September 15, 2001.

Authors
Interview with Lisa Tawn Bergren, June 21, 2000.
Interview with Lori Wick, July 10, 2000.
Interview with Robin Lee Hatcher, July 10, 2000.
Interview with Debra White Smith, July 10, 2000.
Interview with Robin Jones Gunn, July 11, 2000.
Interview with Shari MacDonald, July 12, 2000.
Interview with Doris Elaine Fell, July 12, 2000.
Interview with Carole Gift Page, July 12, 2000.
Interview with Traci DePree, July 21, 2000.
Interview with Janette Oke, September 13, 2000.
Interview with Irene Brand, November 2, 2000.
Interview with Tracie Peterson, November 20, 2000.
Interview with Terry Blackstock, January 18, 2001.
Interview with Sharon Ewell Foster, March 25, 2001.
Interview with Peggy Stoks, April 12, 2001.
Interview with Lyn Coleman, April 13, 2001.
Interview with Victoria Christopher Murray, April 22, 2001.
Interview with Dianna Crawford, April 30, 2001.
Interview with Maureen Pratt, June 17, 2001.
Interview with Anonymous African American Author, July 23, 2001.

FAN MAIL

All fan mail cited is unpublished and in the possession of the respective author to whom it was sent.

ADDITIONAL SOURCES

Allen, Richard. "Film Spectatorship: A Reply to Murray Smith." *Journal of Aesthetics and Art Criticism* 56 (Winter 1998): 61–63.

Allen, Robert C. *Speaking of Soap Operas.* Chapel Hill: University of North Carolina Press, 1985.

Andraski, Katie. "Seasonal Escapes." *Christianity Today* 35 (November 25, 1991): 36–37.

Ang, Ien. *Watching Dallas: Soap Operas and the Melodramatic Imagination.* New York: Methuen, 1985.

Baer, Judy. *Shadows Along the Ice.* Grand Rapids: Zondervan, 1985.

Balmer, Randall. *Mine Eyes Have Seen the Glory: A Journey into the Evangelical Subculture in America.* New York: Oxford University Press, 1989.

Banks, Leanne. *The Lone Rider Takes a Bride.* New York: Silhouette Books, 1998.

Barbour Books. "Heartsong Presents Guidelines for Authors." <http://www .barbourbooks.com/index.asp>, March 30, 2002.

Barr, Catherine, ed. *The Bowker Annual 40th Edition.* New Providence, N.J.: R. R. Bowker, 1995.

Barton, David, and Nigel Hall, eds. *Letter Writing as a Social Practice.* Amsterdam and Philadelphia: John Benjamins Publishing Company, 2000.

Barton, David, and Roz Ivanic, eds. *Writing in the Community.* Newbury Park: Sage Publications, 1991.

Baym, Nina. *Women's Fiction: A Guide to Novels by and about Women in America, 1820–1870.* Ithaca: Cornell University Press, 1978.

Beals, Linda. "Quality Religious Fiction is the Target at Crossway Books." *Publishers Weekly* 221 (February 12, 1982): 65–67.

Bendroth, Margaret Lamberts. *Fundamentalism and Gender.* New Haven and London: Yale University Press, 1993.

"Best Sellers." *Publishers Weekly* 193 (January–March 1968): 98, 138.

"The Best Sellers." *Publishers Weekly* 213 (February 20, 1978): 54–58.

"Best-Selling Christian Books." *Publishers Weekly* 235 (March 3, 1989): 39.

Bethany House. <http://www.bethanyhouse.com>.

Bethany House. "Author Guidelines." <http://www.gospelcom.net/bhp/man
.html>, November 3, 1999.

Blodgett, Jan. *Protestant Evangelical Literary Culture and Contemporary
Society*. Westport, Conn.: Greenwood Press, 1997.

Bogart, Dave, ed. *The Bowker Annual 41st Edition*. New Providence, N.J.: R. R.
Bowker, 1996.

———, ed. *The Bowker Annual 42nd Edition*. New Providence, N.J.: R. R.
Bowker, 1997.

———, ed. *The Bowker Annual 43rd Edition*. New Providence, N.J.: R. R.
Bowker, 1998.

———, ed. *The Bowker Annual 44th Edition*. New Providence, N.J.: R. R.
Bowker, 1999.

———, ed. *The Bowker Annual 45th Edition*. New Providence, N.J.: R. R.
Bowker, 2000.

Boissevain, Jeremy. *Friends of Friends: Networks, Manipulators and
Coalitions*. New York: St. Martin's Press, 1974.

Bourdieu, Pierre. *Distinction: A Social Critique of the Judgment of Taste*.
Cambridge: Harvard University Press, 1984.

———. *Outline of a Theory of Practice*. Cambridge: Cambridge University
Press, 1977.

Boyle, Elizabeth. *One Night of Passion*. New York: Avon Books, 2002.

Brand, Irene. *Where Morning Dawns*. Grand Rapids: Zondervan, 1985.

Brasher, Brenda E. *Godly Women: Fundamentalism and Female Power*. New
Brunswick: Rutgers University Press, 1998.

Brekus, Catherine A. *Strangers and Pilgrims: Female Preaching in America,
1740–1845*. Chapel Hill: University of North Carolina Press, 1998.

Brown, Frank Burch. *Good Taste, Bad Taste and Christian Taste: Aesthetics in
Religious Life*. Oxford: Oxford University Press, 2000.

———. *Religious Aesthetics: A Theological Study of Making and Meaning*.
Princeton: Princeton University Press, 1989.

Carpenter, Joel A. "Contemporary Evangelicalism and Mammon: Some
Thoughts." In *More Money, More Ministry*, edited by Larry Eskridge and
Mark A. Noll, 399–405. Grand Rapids: William B. Eerdmans, 2000.

———. "From Fundamentalism to the New Evangelical Coalition." In
Evangelicalism and Modern America, edited by George Marsden, 3–16.
Grand Rapids: William B. Eerdmans, 1984.

———. *Revive Us Again: The Reawakening of American Fundamentalism*.
Oxford: Oxford University Press, 1997.

Cawelti, John G. *Adventure, Mystery, and Romance: Formula Stories as Art and
Popular Culture*. Chicago: University of Chicago Press, 1976.

————. "The Concept of Formula in the Study of Popular Literature." *Journal of Popular Culture* 3 (1969/1970): 381-90.

Christian Book Distrubutors. "CBD Christmas Catalog" (November/ December 2002).

Cohen, Anthony, ed. *Belonging: Identity and Social Organisation in British Rural Cultures*. Manchester: Manchester University Press, 1982.

Collum, Danny. "The Cross and the Crossover." *Sojourners* 14 (December 1985): 50-51.

Cowie, Alexander. "The Vogue of the Domestic Novel." *South Atlantic Quarterly* 41 (1942): 415-24.

"Currents." *Publishers Weekly* 175 (February 9, 1959): 43-44.

"Currents." *Publishers Weekly* 181 (January 29, 1962): 51-52.

"Currents." *Publishers Weekly* 187 (February 8, 1965): 53-55.

"Currents." *Publishers Weekly* 191 (February 27, 1967): 39-41.

"Currents." *Publishers Weekly* 193 (February 19, 1968): 37-38.

Curtis, Brent, and John Eldredge. *The Sacred Romance: Drawing Closer to the Heart of God*. Nashville: Thomas Nelson Publishers, 1997.

Darnton, Robert. "What is the History of Books?" In *Reading in America*, edited by Cathy N. Davidson, 27-52. Baltimore: Johns Hopkins University Press, 1989.

Davison Hunter, James. *American Evangelicalism: Conservative Religion and the Quandary of Modernity*. New Brunswick: Rutgers University Press, 1983.

Dayton, Donald, and Robert K. Johnston, eds. *The Variety of American Evangelicalism*. Downers Grove, Ill.: InterVarsity Press, 1991.

DeBerg, Betty. *Ungodly Women: Gender and the First Wave of American Fundamentalism*. Minneapolis: Fortress Press, 1990.

de Certeau, Michel. *The Practice of Everyday Life*. Berkeley: University of California Press, 1988.

Dillow, Linda, and Lorraine Pintus. "Five Questions Women Ask About Sex." *Today's Christian Woman* 21 (July/August 1999): 28-34.

Eagleton, Terry. *Literary Theory: An Introduction*. Minneapolis: University of Minnesota Press, 1996.

Ellingsen, Mark. *The Evangelical Movement*. Minneapolis: Augsburg, 1988.

Emerson, Michael, and Christian Smith. *Divided by Faith: Evangelical Religion and the Problem of Race in America*. Oxford: Oxford University Press, 2000.

Ewell Foster, Sharon. *Ain't No River*. Sisters, Ore.: Multnomah Publishers, 2001.

Family Christian Stores. "Harvest Sale Catalog, October 1-27" [no year].

———. "Savings Spectacular, February 4–March 2" [no year].

Ferré, John P. "Searching for the Great Commission: Evangelical Book Publishing Since the 1970s." In *American Evangelicals and the Mass Media*, edited by Quentin J. Schultze, 99–117. Grand Rapids: Academie Books, 1990.

Fish, Stanley. *Is There a Text in this Class?* Cambridge: Harvard University Press, 1980.

———. "Literature in the Reader: Affective Stylistics." In *Reader Response Criticism*, edited by Jane P. Tompkins, 70–100. Baltimore: Johns Hopkins University Press, 1980.

Fiske, John. *Understanding Popular Culture*. New York: Routledge, 1996.

Flint, Kate. *The Woman Reader, 1837–1914*. Oxford: Clarendon Press, 1993.

Frank, Rene. "The Christian and the Arts." *Christianity Today* 7 (April 12, 1963): 24–25.

Freund, Elizabeth. *The Return of the Reader*. London: Metheun, 1987.

Gaebelein, Frank E. "The Aesthetic Problem: Some Evangelical Answers." *Christianity Today* 9 (February 26, 1965): 3–6.

———. *The Christian, the Arts, and Truth: Regaining the Vision of Greatness*. Portland: Multnomah Press, 1985.

Gallagher, Sally K. *Evangelical Identity and Gendered Family Life*. New Brunswick: Rutgers University Press, 2003.

Gallagher, Sally K., and Christian Smith. "Symbolic Traditionalism and Pragmatic Egalitarianism: Contemporary Evangelicals, Families, and Gender." *Gender and Society* 13 (April 1999): 211–33.

"Grace Livingston Hill." <http://www.christianbook.com/html/authors>. July 17, 2000.

"Grace Livingston Hill." <http://users.tellurian.net/bksleuth/GLHInfo.html>. July 17, 2000.

Granovetter, Mark S. "The Strength of Weak Ties." *American Journal of Sociology* 78 (1973): 1360–80.

Greeley, Andrew M. *The Catholic Myth*. New York: Collier Books, 1990.

Griffin, William. "Fiction for the Faithful." *Publishers Weekly* 238 (April 19, 1991): 27–29.

Griffith, R. Marie. *God's Daughters: Evangelical Women and the Power of Submission*. Berkeley: University of California Press, 1997.

———. "Joy Unspeakable and Full of Glory." In *An Emotional History of the United States*, edited Peter N. Stearns and Jan Lewis, 218–40. New York: New York University Press, 1998.

Hamilton, Michael S. "More Money, More Ministry: The Financing of American Evangelicalism since 1945." In *More Money, More Ministry*, edited by Larry Eskridge and Mark A. Noll, 104–138. Grand Rapids: William B. Eerdmans, 2000.

Harrison, Nick. "Spinning Spiritual Tales that Sell." *Publishers Weekly* 245 (August 17, 1998): S6–S14.

Hatcher, Robin Lee. *The Forgiving Hour.* Colorado Springs: Waterbrook Press, 1999.

Heartquest Books. <http://www.heartquest-romance.com>, 2000; <http://www.heartquest.com>, 2005.

Hein, Rolland N. "A Biblical View of the Novel." In *The Christian Imagination: Essays on Literature and the Arts,* edited by Leland Ryken, 255–62. Grand Rapids: Baker Book House, 1981.

Hendershot, Heather. *Shaking the World for Jesus: Media and Conservative Evangelical Culture.* Chicago: University of Chicago Press, 2004.

Henderson, Karla A. "Broadening an Understanding of Women, Gender, and Leisure." *Journal of Leisure Research* 26 (Winter 1994): 1–7.

Hensley, Dennis E. "Janette Oke: Fifteen Million Sold—and Counting." *Writer's Digest* 78 (September 1998): 32–35.

Hetherington, Kevin. *Expressions of Identity: Space, Performance, Politics.* London and Thousand Oaks: Sage Publications, 1998.

Hill, Grace Livingston. *The Finding of Jasper Holt.* New York: Bantam Books, 1977. First published 1915 by McBride, Nast & Co.

Hoggart, Richard. *The Uses of Literacy.* London: Chatto and Windus, 1957.

Howard, Thomas. "On Evil in Art." In *The Christian Imagination: Essays on Literature and the Arts,* edited by Leland Ryken, 111–17. Grand Rapids: Baker Book House, 1981.

Jenkins, Henry. *Textual Poachers: Television Fans and Participatory Culture.* New York and London: Routledge, 1992.

Jenkins, Richard. *Social Identity.* London: Routledge, 1996.

Jorstad, Erling. *Popular Religion in America: The Evangelical Voice.* Westport, Conn.: Greenwood Press, 1993.

———. "Pressers On and Holders Fast: Evangelicalism and Popular Culture." *Dialog* 24 (1985): 181–87.

Katz, Elihu, and David Foulkes. "On the Use of the Mass Media as 'Escape': Clarification of a Concept." *Public Opinion Quarterly* 26 (Autumn 1962): 377–88.

Kelly, Mary. *Private Woman, Public Stage.* Oxford: Oxford University Press, 1984.

Kenyon, Olga. *800 Years of Women's Letters.* Boston: Faber and Faber, 1992.

Keylock, Leslie. "Evangelical Protestants Take Over Center Field." *Publishers Weekly* 225 (March 9, 1984): 32–33.

Kilby, Clyde S. "The Artistic Poverty of Evangelicalism." *Eternity* 16 (1965): 16–18.

Knight, Deborah. "Why We Enjoy Condemning Sentimentality: A Meta-Aesthetic Perspective." *Journal of Aesthetics and Art Criticism* 57 (Autumn 1999): 411–20.

Krentz, Jayne Ann. *Dangerous Men and Adventurous Women.* Philadelphia: University of Pennsylvania Press, 1992.

Langberg, Diane Mandt. "He's Lost that Lovin' Feeling." *Today's Christian Woman* 24 (January/February 2002): 15–16.

Leitch, Addison. "Reality in Modern Literature." In *The Christian Imagination: Essays on Literature and the Arts,* edited by Leland Ryken, 193–96. Grand Rapids: Baker Book House, 1981.

Lewis, Beverly. *The Reckoning.* Minneapolis: Bethany House, 1998.

Light, Alison. "Returning to Manderley—Romance Fiction, Female Sexuality and Class." *Feminist Review* 16 (April 1984): 7–25.

Linden, Dana Wechsler, and Matt Rees. "I'm Hungry. But not for Food." *Forbes* 150 (July 6, 1992): 70–75.

Lofland, John, and Lyn H. Lofland. *Analyzing Social Settings: A Guide to Qualitative Observation and Analysis.* Belmont, Calif.: Wadsworth Publishing, 1984.

Logan, Laurel Oke. *Janette Oke: A Heart for the Prairie.* Minneapolis: Bethany House, 1993.

Luccock, Halford. "Religion in the Bookstore: An Old Alliance Stouter than Ever." *Publishers Weekly* 157 (January–February 1950): 990–93.

Lundin, Roger. "Offspring of an Odd Union: Evangelical Attitudes Toward the Arts." In *Evangelicalism and Modern America,* edited by George Marsden, 135–49. Grand Rapids: William B. Eerdmans, 1984.

MacDonald, Shari, et al. *Restoration and Romance: For the Love of an Old House.* Colorado Springs: Waterbrook Press, 2001.

Mach, Zdzislaw. *Symbols, Conflict, and Identity: Essays in Political Anthropology.* Albany: State University of New York Press, 1993.

Manning, Christel J. *God Gave Us the Right: Conservative Catholic, Evangelical Protestant, and Orthodox Jewish Women Grapple with Feminism.* New Brunswick: Rutgers University Press, 1999.

"The Market is Still Increasing for Religious Books and Bibles." *Publishers Weekly* 161 (February 16, 1952): 879–82.

Marsden, George. *Fundamentalism and American Culture: The Shaping of Twentieth-Century Evangelicalism, 1870–1925.* Oxford: Oxford University Press, 1980.

————, ed. *Evangelicalism and Modern America*. Grand Rapids: William B. Eerdmans, 1984.

Marshall, Catherine. *Christy*. New York: McGraw Hill, 1967.

————. *A Man Called Peter*. New York: McGraw Hill, 1951.

Marshall, Catherine, and Gretchen B. Rossman. *Designing Qualitative Research*. Thousand Oaks: Sage Publications, 1999.

Maxwell, Joseph A. *Qualitative Research Design*. Thousand Oaks: Sage Publications, 1996.

Maybin, Janet. "Death Row Penfriends: Some Effects of Letter Writing on Identity and Relationships." In *Letter Writing as a Social Practice*, edited by David Barton and Nigel Hall, 151–77. Amesterdam and Philadelphia: John Benjamins Publishing Company, 2000.

————, ed. *Language and Literacy in Social Practice*. Clevedon: The Open University, 1994.

McCourtney, Lorena. *Betrayed*. Sisters, Ore.: Questar, 1996.

McDannell, Colleen. *Material Christianity*. New Haven and London: Yale University Press, 1995.

McHenry, Elizabeth. *Forgotten Readers: Recovering the Lost History of African American Literary Societies*. Durham, N.C.: Duke University Press, 2002.

Meehan, Chris. "Zondervan's Mission and Marketing Goals Translate into Retail Expansion." *Publishers Weekly* 225 (March 9, 1984): 90–93.

Miller, J. Hillis. "Narrative." In *Critical Terms for Literary Study*, 2nd ed., edited by Frank Lentricchia and Thomas McLaughlin, 66–79. Chicago: University of Chicago Press, 1995.

Modleski, Tania. "The Disappearing Act: A Study of Harlequin Romances." *Signs* 5 (1980): 435–48.

————. *Loving with a Vengeance: Mass-Produced Fantasies for Women*. Hamden, Conn.: Archon Books, 1982.

Moore, Julia, ed. *The Bowker Annual 30th Edition*. New York: R. R. Bowker, 1985.

Moore, R. Laurence. *Selling God*. Oxford: Oxford University Press, 1994.

Morgan, David. *Visual Piety: A History and Theory of Popular Religious Images*. Berkeley: University of California Press, 1998.

Morris, Aldon D., and Carol McClurg Mueller, eds. *Frontiers in Social Movement Theory*. New Haven and London: Yale University Press, 1992.

Morris, Gilbert. *The Valiant Gunman*. Minneapolis: Bethany House, 1993.

Multnomah Publishers. <http://www.multnomahbooks.com>.

Multnomah Publishers. "Palisades Pure Romances: Writers' Guidelines." <http://www.multnomahbooks.com/PublishersGuidelines/Palisades .asp>, May 12, 2000.

Munce, Robert. *The Grace Livingston Hill Story*. Wheaton: Tyndale House, 1986, 1990.

Mussell, Kay. *Fantasy and Reconciliation: Contemporary Formulas of Women's Romance Fiction*. Westport, Conn.: Greenwood Press, 1984.

———. "Romantic Fiction." In *Handbook of American Popular Culture*, vol. 2, edited by M. Thomas Inge, 317–43. Westport, Conn.: Greenwood Press, 1978.

Nabors Baker, Carolyn. *Caught in a Higher Love: Inspiring Stories of Women in the Bible*. Nashville: Broadman and Holman Publishers, 1998.

Nerdrum, Odd, et al. *On Kitsch*. Oslo: Kagge Forlag, 2001.

"New Books for Adults." *Publishers Weekly* 227 (March 8, 1985): 55–68.

Newell, A. G. "Early Evangelical Fiction." *Evangelical Quarterly* 38 (January–March 1966 and April–June 1966): 3–21, 81–98.

"News and Trends of the Week." *Publishers Weekly* 171 (March 4, 1957): 41–42.

"News and Trends of the Week." *Publishers Weekly* 173 (February 17, 1958): 37–38.

Noll, Mark A., and Cassandra Niemczyk. "Evangelicals and the Self-Consciously Reformed." In *The Variety of American Evangelicalism*, edited by Donald W. Dayton and Robert K. Johnston, 204–21. Downers Grove, Ill.: InterVarsity Press, 1991.

Nord, David Paul. "Systematic Benevolence: Religious Publishing and the Marketplace in Early Nineteenth-Century America." In *Communication and Change in American Religious History*, edited by Leonard I. Sweet, 239–69. Grand Rapids: William B. Eerdmans, 1993.

Oke, Janette. *The Calling of Emily Evans*. Minneapolis: Bethany House, 1990.

———. *Love Comes Softly*. Minneapolis: Bethany House, 1979.

———. *Love's Long Journey*. Minneapolis: Bethany House, 1982.

———. *When Breaks the Dawn*. Minneapolis: Bethany House, 1986.

———. *When Calls the Heart*. Minneapolis: Bethany House, 1983.

———. *When Comes the Spring*. Minneapolis: Bethany House, 1985.

———. *When Hope Springs New*. Minneapolis: Bethany House, 1986.

Orsi, Robert A. "The Center Out There, In Here, and Everywhere Else: The Nature of Pilgrimage to the Shrine of Saint Jude, 1929–1965." *Journal of Social History* 25 (Winter 1991): 213–32.

———. "The Cult of the Saints and the Reimagination of the Space and Time of Sickness in Twentieth-Century American Catholicism." *Literature and Medicine* 8 (1989): 63–67.

———. *Thank You, St. Jude: Women's Devotion to the Patron Saint of Hopeless Causes*. New Haven: Yale University Press, 1996.

Ostling, Richard. "Evangelical Publishing and Broadcasting." In *Evangelicalism and Modern America*, edited by George Marsden, 46–55. Grand Rapids: William B. Eerdmans, 1984.

Packer, J. I. "Leisure and Life-Style: Leisure, Pleasure and Treasure." In *God and Culture: Essays in Honor of Carl F. H. Henry*, edited by D. A. Carson and John D. Woodbridge, 356–68. Grand Rapids: William B. Eerdmans, 1993.

Page, Carole Gift. *In Search of Her Own*. New York: Steeple Hill Books, 1997.

———. *Rachel's Hope*. New York: Steeple Hill Books, 1998.

Papshvily, Helen Waite. *All the Happy Endings*. New York: Harper and Bros., 1956.

Pearlin, Leonard. "Social and Personal Stress and Escape Television Viewing." *Public Opinion Quarterly* 23 (Summer 1959): 255–59.

Perry, Marta. *The Doctor Next Door*. New York: Steeple Hill Books, 2000.

Peterson, Eugene H. *The Message*. Colorado Springs: NavPress, 1993.

Peterson, Tracie. *My Valentine*. Uhrichsville, Ohio: Heartsong Presents, 1997.

Phillips, Susan Elizabeth. *Dream A Little Dream*. New York: Avon Books, 1998.

Pilkington, Joseph. "Backlist Best Bets among the Books for Protestants." *Publishers Weekly* 157 (January–February 1950): 986–89.

Price, Deborah Evans. "McCready Stays True to her Voice." *Billboard* 109 (October 11, 1997): 35–37.

Rabey, Steve. "No Longer Left Behind." *Christianity Today* 46 (April 22, 2002): 26–33.

Radway, Janice A. "Reading is not Eating." *Book Research Quarterly* 2 (1986): 7–29.

———. *Reading the Romance*. Chapel Hill: University of North Carolina Press, 1991.

Ramsdell, Kristen. "Romance 2000." *Library Journal* 126 (August 2001): 86.

"Religious and Inspirational Novels Continue to be Popular." *Publishers Weekly* 159 (February 3, 1951): 764–65.

"Religious Best Sellers." *Publishers Weekly* 213 (February 13, 1978): 88–90.

"Religious Best Sellers." *Publishers Weekly* 231 (March 6, 1987): 43.

"Religious Book Publishers Expect Another Year of High Sales." *Publishers Weekly* 159 (February 3, 1951): 755–56.

Reynolds, David S. *Faith in Fiction*. Cambridge: Harvard University Press, 1981.

Rivers, Francine. *A Fire in the Heart*. New York: Charter Books, 1987.

————. "Hooked on Romance." *Today's Christian Woman* 17 (May/June 1995): 38–41.

————. *Outlaw's Embrace*. New York: Charter Books, 1986.

————. *Rebel in His Arms*. New York: Ace Books, 1981.

————. *Redeeming Love*. New York: Bantam Books, 1991.

————. *Redeeming Love*. Chicago: Multnomah Books, 1997.

"Romancing the Novel." *U.S. News and World Report* 124 (February 16, 1998): 10.

Romanowski, William D. "Behind the Eyes." *Christianity Today* 41 (December 8, 1997): 44–46.

Roof, Wade Clark. *Spiritual Markektplace: Baby Boomers and the Remaking of American Religion*. Princeton: Princeton University Press, 1999.

Rosen, Judith. "Special Delivery: From Fan Mail to Letters of Complaint." *Publishers Weekly* 245 (February 16, 1998): 124–25.

Ryken, Leland. "In the Beginning God Created." In *The Christian Imagination*, edited by Leland Ryken, 55–67. Grand Rapids: Baker Book House, 1981.

————. "The Creative Arts." In *The Making of a Christian Mind: A Christian World View and the Academic Enterprise*, edited by Arthur Holmes, 105–31. Downers Grove, Ill.: InterVarsity Press, 1985.

————. "Literature in Christian Perspective." In *God and Culture: Essays in Honor of Carl F. H. Henry*, edited by D. A. Carson and John D. Woodbridge, 215–34. Grand Rapids: William B. Eerdmans, 1993.

Schaeffer, Franky. *Addicted to Mediocrity: Twentieth Century Christians and the Arts*. Westchester, Ill.: Crossway Books, 1981.

Schultze, Quentin, ed. *American Evangelicals and the Mass Media*. Grand Rapids: Academie Books, 1990.

Seiter, Ellen, et al., eds. *Remote Control: Television, Audiences, and Cultural Power*. London and New York: Routledge, 1989.

"Serenade/Saga: Inspirational Romances . . . Set in an Earlier Time." *Publishers Weekly* 225 (March 9, 1984): 62–63.

"Serenade/Serenata: Romance with a Difference." *Publishers Weekly* 225 (March 9, 1984): 54–55.

Shaw, Susan M. "Gender, Leisure, and Constraint: Towards a Framework for the Analysis of Women's Leisure." *Journal of Leisure Research* 26 (Winter 1994): 8–15.

"Shop Talk." *Publishers Weekly* 157 (January–February 1950): 577–78.

Sicherman, Barbara. "Sense and Sensibility: A Case Study of Women's Reading in Late-Victorian America." In *Reading in America*, edited by

Cathy N. Davidson, 201–25. Baltimore: Johns Hopkins University Press, 1989.

Sidey, Ken. "Once in Love with Amy." *Christianity Today* 35 (October 7, 1991): 17.

Simora, Filomena, ed. *The Bowker Annual 25th Edition*. New York: R. R. Bowker, 1980.

Simpson, Clarence. "Or Why Evangelicals Have Failed the Arts." *Eternity* 14 (1963): 10–11, 28.

Smith, Christian A., et al. *American Evangelicalism: Embattled and Thriving*. Chicago: University of Chicago Press, 1998.

Smith, Murray. "Film Spectatorship and the Institution of Fiction." *Journal of Aesthetics and Art Criticism* 53 (Spring 1995): 113–27.

———. "Regarding Film Spectatorship: A Reply to Richard Allen." *Journal of Aesthetics and Art Criticism* 56 (Winter 1998): 63–65.

Snitow, Ann Barr. "Mass Market Romance: Pornography for Women is Different." *Radical History Review* 20 (1979): 141–61.

Solomon, Robert C. "On Kitsch and Sentimentality." *Journal of Aesthetics and Art Criticism* 49 (Winter 1991): 1–14.

"Spring Religious Titles: New Books for Adults." *Publishers Weekly* 223 (March 4, 1983): 49–63.

Steeple Hill. <http://www.steeplehill.com>.

Stowe, Harriet Beecher. *The Minister's Wooing*. Hartford: The Stowe-Day Foundation, 1978. First published 1859.

———. *Uncle Tom's Cabin*. New York: Bantam Books, 1981. First published 1851–52.

Suleiman, Susan, and Inge Crossman, eds. *The Reader in the Text: Essays on Audience and Interpretation*. Princeton: Princeton University Press, 1980.

Sweet, Leonard I., ed. *Communication and Change in American Religious History*. Grand Rapids: William B. Eerdmans, 1993.

Thurston, Carol. *The Romance Revolution*. Urbana: University of Illinois Press, 1987.

Tompkins, Jane P. *Sensational Designs: The Cultural Work of American Fiction, 1790–1860*. New York: Oxford University Press, 1985.

———, ed. *Reader Response Criticism*. Baltimore: Johns Hopkins University Press, 1980.

Tuan, Yi-Fu. *Escapism*. Baltimore: Johns Hopkins University Press, 1998.

Tyndale House Publishers, <http://www.tyndale.com>.

Tyson, John R., ed. *Invitation to Christian Spirituality: An Ecumenical Anthology*. Oxford: Oxford University Press, 1999.

"Voice of the Industry: CBA Marketplace's Top 10 Best-Selling Fiction Books of 2000." <http://www.cbaonline.org/voice/a_fiction.html>.

Walkworthy Press. <http://www.walkworthypress.net>.

Warner, Susan. *The Wide, Wide World*. New York: The Feminist Press, 1987. First published 1850.

Waterbrook Press. <http://www.randomhouse.com/waterbrook/>.

Wellman, Barry. *Networks in the Global Village: Life in Contemporary Communities*. Boulder: Westview Press, 1999.

Wellman, Barry, and S. D. Berkowitz. *Social Structures: A Network Approach*. Cambridge: Cambridge University Press, 1988.

Welter, Barbara. "The Cult of True Womanhood: 1820–1860." *American Quarterly* 18 (1966): 151–74.

Wick, Lori. *A Gathering of Memories*. Eugene, Ore.: Harvest House, 1991.

———. *Sean Donovan*. Eugene, Ore.: Harvest House, 1993.

———. *Whatever Tomorrow Brings*. Eugene, Ore.: Harvest House, 1992.

Wilbee, Brenda. *Sweetbriar*. Eugene, Ore.: Harvest House, 1983.

———. *Sweetbriar Bride*. Eugene, Ore.: Harvest House, 1986.

———. *Sweetbriar Spring*. Eugene, Ore.: Harvest House, 1989.

Wilmott, Peter. *Friendship Networks and Social Support*. London: Policy Studies Institute, 1987.

Wolverton, Cheryl. *For Love of Mitch*. New York: Steeple Hill Books, 2000.

Woodiwiss, Kathleen. *The Flame and the Flower*. New York: Avon Books, 1972.

Zoba, Wendy Murray. "Take a Little Time Out." *Christianity Today* 44 (February 7, 2000): 86.

Zondervan. <http://www.zondervan.com>.

Banks, Leanne: *The Lone Rider Takes a Bride*, 77–78
Bantam Books, 159–60
Baptism: in evangelical romance novels, 112
Barbour Books: Heartsong series, 30, 82, 92; submission guidelines for, 82, 99, 112
Barton, David, 126
Baym, Nina, 20
Benson, Angela, 54
Bestsellers, religious, 25–26, 33, 200 (n. 24)
Bethany House Publishers, 24, 27, 30, 200 (n. 24); holistic gospel publications, 25; submission guidelines for, 82, 86
Bible: authority of, 9, 153; inerrancy of, 21; *The Living Bible*, 25; competition with evangelical romances, 152–55; as love story, 182–83. *See also* Gospel, holistic
Blackstock, Terry, 167; readers' letters to, 145; on divine romance, 183
Book clubs: evangelical women on, 62–63; African American women in, 68–69, 71–72, 91, 151, 172; Oprah model, 69
Bookstores, Christian: number of, 25; women customers of, 6–7, 9, 32; evangelical romance novels at, 52, 204 (n. 52); Steeple Hill novels at, 54
Boren Denny, Louisa, 3, 176, 186, 195
Boyle, Elizabeth: *One Night of Passion*, 3–4
Brand, Irene: readers' letters to, 48, 120, 121, 122–23, 125, 155, 168; in Love Inspired series, 54; on God's plan, 181; on marriage in Bible, 182
Breckus, Catherine: *Strangers and Pilgrims*, 110
Bunn, T. Davis: *Return to Harmony*, 33
Burch Brown, Frank, 101, 102
Butcher, Samuel: and Precious Moments Chapel, 101

Cana: wedding at, 182
Carothers, Merlin, 26
Carpenter, Joel, 22
Catholicism: women's devotional culture in, 101–2; immanence of God in, 190
Childrearing: and evangelical romance reading, 48–49, 52; in evangelical romance novels, 135–36, 150
Christian Book Distributors, 173
Christian Booksellers Association, 23–24, 108; marketing by, 29, 54, 74
The Christian Family, 25
Christianity: material, 22, 26; manly, 23
Christianity Today (magazine), 34
Christy (television series), 33
Church libraries, 64, 65; function of, 66–67
Cleary, Beverly, 52
Cohen, Anthony, 156
Coleman, Lyn, 89, 183
Commodities: evangelical, 74–75, 107–8, 190; in construction of identity, 117. *See also* Consumers;

Marketing; Popular culture—
evangelical
Communities, interpretive, 117–18;
female, 125, 126
Community: through evangelical
romance reading, 61–72, 128,
156, 159, 192; through secular
romance reading, 204 (n. 46)
Consumers: evangelical women, 9,
32–33; isolation of, 61; evangelical, 97. *See also* Commodities;
Marketing; Popular culture—
evangelical
Conversion: in evangelical romance
novels, 5, 87, 88, 106, 116; in
evangelicalism, 9, 103; through
romance reading, 108, 170; of
heroines, 193
Cover art: of evangelical romance
novels, 78–79; of secular romance
novels, 79
Curtis, Brent: *The Sacred Romance*,
172–73

Daily life: evangelicalism in, 10–12,
14, 106, 191, 192; coping with, 61,
72
"Dear Reader" letters, 54, 125
de Certeau, Michel, 98, 127, 190
Denny, David, 3, 186
Devotionals, nonfiction, 52. *See also*
Fictional devotion
Dickens, Charles, 108
Dispensationalism, premillennial,
21
Divine love, 158–63, 166; and
heterosexual love, 164, 167–68,
171; Jesus as, 179
Divorce: evangelical beliefs on, 97;

in evangelical romance novels,
113, 146, 147; evangelical women
on, 180
Dobson, James, 33

Earekson, Joni: *Joni*, 26
Eldredge, John: *The Sacred Romance*, 172–73
Elitism, artistic, 36, 101
Ellingsen, Mark, 9
Emotion, 139, 143, 148, 155–56, 174;
manipulation of, 37, 100
Escape: through romance reading,
38; through evangelical romance
reading, 45, 47–48, 59–61, 72, 92–
93, 102, 143; culture of, 60; from
stress, 60; through media, 60–61;
Radway on, 202 (n. 8)
Evangelicalism: beliefs on marriage, 5, 151; conversion in, 9,
103; salvation in, 9; witnessing
in, 9; in daily life, 10–12, 14, 106,
174, 191, 192; womanhood in,
11; gender ideology of, 12, 13,
21, 35, 56–57, 150–51, 187; use of
media, 13, 18–19, 27, 32, 110, 113,
200 (n. 23); use of the arts, 18–
19; attitude toward fiction, 19–20,
198 (n. 7); conflict with popular
culture, 21; and modernism, 21;
moderate leadership in, 23; theology of the arts, 35–37; fun and,
45, 47, 56, 72, 117; view of millennium, 55; racial barriers within,
72, 91; and sexuality, 82; diversity
in, 87; on divorce, 97; political
engagement of, 103; and the arts,
108; male leadership in, 135;
cross-generational, 51–52, 136;

individualism in, 143; forgiveness in, 148; romantic image of God in, 172–73; importance of love for, 180. *See also* Fundamentalism; Protestantism: conservative

Evangelicals: stereotypes of, 143, 189. *See also* Women, evangelical

Family, 48–49, 51–52; in religious identity, 135

Ferré, John P., 26, 32

Fiction: falsehood of, 18; evangelical attitude toward, 19–20; sentimental, 20, 27, 37. *See also* Romance novels
—religious, 108; of 1950s, 24–25; male-authored, 34; African American, 54–55. *See also* Romance novels, evangelical

Fictional devotion, 8, 106–7, 195; reader-text relationships in, 12, 41, 174; and entertainment, 44; in evangelicalism, 48; among family members, 48–49, 51–52; pleasure through, 52; boundaries on, 58; consequences of, 103; factors affecting, 126; community through, 128, 159, 192; mistrust of, 128; revitalization through, 137; confidence through, 139; effectiveness of, 148; spiritual tension through, 149; effect on marriage, 151–53, 165; romantic God in, 171; relationship with God in, 184; cycle of, 186–89

Films: evangelical, 52, 191; addiction to, 60

Fish, Stanley, 118

Fiske, John, 66, 107, 117, 191

Flint, Kate: *The Woman Reader, 1837–1914*, 19–20

Forgiveness: in evangelical romance novels, 87, 89, 145–48, 158; in evangelicalism, 148

Foster, Sharon Ewell, 54, 62; *Ain't No River*, 69, 70, 71, 77, 92

Foulkes, David, 56, 60–61, 139

Frank, Rene, 99

Fuller Theological Seminary, 23

Fun: through evangelical romance reading, 44–61, 76; and evangelical faith, 45, 47, 56, 72, 117

Fundamentalism: twentieth-century, 22; and popular culture, 23; political power of, 29. *See also* Evangelicalism; Protestantism: conservative

Gaebelein, Frank, 37; theology of the arts, 35, 39, 179; on leisure, 55

Gallagher, Sally, 135; *Evangelical Identity and Gendered Family Life*, 56–57; "Symbolic Traditionalism and Pragmatic Egalitarianism," 150

Gender roles: in evangelical romance novels, 6, 12–13, 137–38, 149–50; in evangelicalism, 13, 21, 35, 56–57, 110, 113, 150–51, 187; in nineteenth-century fiction, 20

Genesis, book of: leisure in, 36; creation story in, 181, 182

God: personal relationships with, 5, 9, 13, 16, 32, 103, 114, 164, 188, 193; action in history, 13, 174–84; providential nature of, 114, 174, 175; unconditional love of, 159, 163–67, 174–84; relationship with humanity, 166, 194; romantic vision of, 166, 171, 172–73, 183–84, 194, 195

Gospel, holistic, 23, 24, 29, 74; publications spreading, 25; women's commitment to, 32, 86

Graham, Billy, 23; *Peace with God*, 24; *Angels*, 26

Grant, Amy, 97, 192

Greaves, Arthur, 110

Greeley, Andrew, 189–90, 194

Griffith, R. Marie, 10–11, 174

Gunn, Robin Jones: "Christy Miller" series, 110; *Summer Promise*, 110; vocation of, 110–11; readers' letters to, 169; on romantic image of God, 172; on divine romance, 183

Hamilton, Michael, 32

Harlequin Enterprises, 6; Steeple Hill imprint, 53–54

Harlequin Romances, 38; evangelical readers on, 79

HarperCollins: purchase of Zondervan, 53

Harrison, Nick, 6

Harvest House (publisher), 30

Hatcher, Robin Lee, 115; divorce of, 113; *The Forgiving Hour*, 113, 125, 146, 147, 148, 163, 169; readers' letters to, 117, 119, 121, 146; *The Shepherd's Voice*, 117; *Whispers from Yesterday*, 120, 123; secular romances of, 163; *A Gathering of Memories*, 166–67; on God's plan, 181

HeartQuest series (Tyndale House), 30

Heartsong series (Barbour), 30; submission guidelines for, 82, 99; storylines of, 92

Hein, Rolland, 99

Henry, Carl, 23, 74

Heroes, evangelical romance, 149–53; physical stature of, 149; concern for wives, 150; religious lives of, 150; competition with husbands, 151–53

Heroes, secular romance, 4, 149

Heroines, evangelical romance: Oke's, 29; identification with, 132–38, 139, 141, 144, 149, 155, 156, 159; pregnancy of, 134; flawed, 135; resemblance to readers, 135–37; strong, 136; qualities of, 137; reassurance through, 140; forgiveness by, 145; conversion of, 193; evaluation of, 89–92, 94

Heterosexual love: and divine love, 164, 167–68, 171

Heterosexual relationships: and relationship with God, 5; friendship in, 78, 145

Hetherington, Kevin: *Expressions of Identity*, 62, 155, 204 (n. 51)

Hill, Grace Livingston, 15–18, 52, 116; *The Finding of Jasper Holt*, 15–16, 18, 21; influence of, 16, 22–23, 27, 108, 192; career of, 17; literary output of, 17, 22; vocation of, 17–18; and sentimental fiction, 20; heroines of, 21; optimism of, 39–40; marriages of, 40; *Patricia*, 49, 50, 51; popularity of, 49; criticism of, 92; biography of, 198 (n. 2)

History: cosmic view of, 9, 10; romance readers' enjoyment of, 174–78; sacred, 174–84, 195

National Association of Evangeli-
cals, 23
Nerdrum, Odd, 116
Neville, James M., 17
Niemczyk, Cassandra, 103
Noll, Mark A., 103
Novel reading: evangelical view
of, 19–20, 55. *See also* Reading,
evangelical romance

Ockenga, Harold, 23, 74
Oke, Janette, 26–30, 47, 79, 110, 177;
Love Comes Softly, 27, 28, 29, 40,
48, 89, 136; success of, 27, 29; witnessing in work of, 27; heroines
of, 29; prairie romances of, 29,
52; theological support for, 29–
30; *Drums of Change*, 33; *A Gown
of Spanish Lace*, 33; *Love Takes
Wing*, 33; *Return to Harmony*, 33;
When Hope Springs New, 33; *Winter Is Not Forever*, 33; *A Woman
Named Damaris*, 34; *Love's Long
Journey*, 40, 43–44, 61, 89, 175,
176; *Love's Unending Legacy*, 40;
teenage readers of, 66; *The Calling
of Emily Evans*, 83, 84; "Canadian
West" series, 89–90; criticism
of, 92, 95; popularity of, 94, 175,
192; on controversial topics, 100;
defense of romance novels, 109;
"Love Comes Softly" series, 124,
136, 187; readers' letters to, 124,
125; "Women of the West" series,
137–38
Oprah Book Club, 69
Orsi, Robert A., 202 (n. 12); *Thank
You, St. Jude*, 101–2

Packer, J. I., 18, 55
Page, Carol Gift, 110; vocation of,
25; in Love Inspired series, 53–
54; "Dear Reader" letters, 54; on
divine romance, 184
Paperbacks, mass-market, 26, 92
Patriarchy: reconciliation with, 38
Peale, Norman Vincent: *The Power
of Positive Thinking*, 24
Pearlin, Leonard, 60
Perry, Marta: *The Doctor Next Door*,
125
Peterson, Eugene: *The Message*, 108
Peterson, Tracie: *My Valentine*, 88,
92; vocation of, 111; readers'
letters to, 124
Piety, popular, 93; visual culture of,
109
Popular culture: beliefs relating
to, 7; evangelical women and,
16; conflict with evangelicalism,
21; and fundamentalism, 23;
redemptive potential of, 29; as
agent of pacification, 37; leisure
in, 56; isolation of consumers in,
61; as "making do," 127, 190
—evangelical: mediocrity in, 36–
37, 97–98, 190–91, 195; racial
divide in, 40; recreation in, 46;
secular elements in, 74; consumers in, 97; balance in, 97–99;
women's consumption of, 107; as
kitsch, 116; stability in, 192–93;
teaching through, 192–93; sentimentality in, 194; emergence of,
199 (n. 23). *See also* Commodities,
evangelical
Pratt, Maureen, 114

Precious Moments Chapel (Carthage, Mo.), 101
Prison inmates: evangelical romance reading by, 155; letters of, 122–23, 211 (n. 46)
Promiscuity: evangelical women on, 180
Prostitution: in evangelical romance novels, 160, 163
Protestantism: in nineteenth-century fiction, 20; conservative, 21, 198 (n. 7); feminized, 21, 22, 23. *See also* Evangelicalism; Fundamentalism
Publishing industry, romance, 5–6
Publishing houses, evangelical, 18, 22–26; rationale for fiction, 30, 32; submission guidelines for, 82, 86, 96, 99–100, 112

Racism: African American readers on, 69; in evangelicalism, 72, 91; portrayed in evangelical romance novels, 73, 74, 99
Radway, Janice, 6; *Reading the Romance*, 4, 7, 38; on Avon Books, 26; on escape, 202 (n. 8); on community, 204 (n. 46)
Random House: Waterbrook Press division, 53
Rapture: in film, 192
Reader-response theory, 115
Readers, evangelical romance, xi, 6; narratives of, 7–8; church attendance of, 8, 9; demographics of, 8–9, 197 (nn. 10, 11); consumer patterns of, 32; relationship with texts, 12, 41, 174; gender socialization of, 13, 48–49; rela-

tionship with God, 13, 188; view of leisure, 13; experience of the divine, 13–14, 166–72; African American, 40, 62, 68–69, 71–72, 91–92; white, 40; motives of, 41, 44, 45–49; leisure time of, 44–61, 94, 187; reading choices of, 45; book swapping among, 51; self-restrictions on, 57–58; communities of, 61–72, 118–28, 142, 155–56, 159, 192; friendships among, 63–69; teenage, 66; expectations for novels, 75; and secular romances, 79, 83, 85–86; critiques by, 90–98; selection of novels, 94–95; relationship with authors, 119, 125; influence on authors, 124–25, 211 (n. 50); criticism of, 127–28; relationship with heroines, 135–37; evaluation of spirituality, 143; hyper-individualism of, 143; on marriage, 151–53; enjoyment of history, 174–78; on Jesus, 179; stereotypes of, 195; geographical breakdown of, 197 (n. 8)
Readers' letters, 7, 48, 118–25; prayer in, 142; from inmates, 155, 211 (n. 46); affirmation in, 169; on sequels, 187; choices in, 210 (n. 45)
Reader-text relationships, 115, 132; in evangelical romance, 12, 41, 174
Reading, evangelical romance: purpose of, 7, 11–13, 95, 104, 108–9; role in religious identity, 12, 103–4, 117, 143, 188; fun through, 44–61, 76; escape through, 45, 47–48, 59–61, 72, 92–93, 102,

143; as coping mechanism, 46; enjoyment of, 48; during illness, 48; during loneliness, 48, 139; and childrearing, 48–49, 52; introduction to, 48–49, 51; fellowship through, 52; guilt in, 57–58; compulsive, 58–60, 72; solitude in, 65; validation of, 66; immaturity in, 101, 102; spiritual change through, 104, 128, 132, 138–48, 167, 170; conversion through, 108; experience of divine through, 115, 166–72; frequency of, 126; insight through, 138–39; as ministry, 139; confidence through, 140; prayer in, 142, 144; unintended consequences of, 149–56; competition with Bible reading, 152–55; ambivalence toward, 154; by inmates, 155; emotion during, 155–56; relationship with God through, 164; cyclical, 186–89; hope through, 188. *See also* Fictional devotion

Realism: in evangelical romance novels, 92–93, 95, 133, 151–53

Religious books: bestsellers, 25–26, 33, 200 (n. 24); marketing of, 199 (n. 21). *See also* Fiction—religious; Romance novels, evangelical

Retailing, Christian, 26. *See also* Commodities; Marketing

Rivers, Francine, 67; "Mark of the Lion" series, 59, 138; themes of, 93; Bible in works of, 153; "Hooked on Romance," 201 (n. 38)

—and *Redeeming Love*, 33, 84, 157–

66, 189; rewrite of, 159–60; self-worth in, 160; covers of, 161, 162; readers' responses to, 163–66

Roberts, Oral, 190

Romance: evangelical women's view of, 76, 78, 179–80; theology of, 182; divine, 182–84. *See also* God: romantic vision of

Romance novels, evangelical: formulas of, 3, 6, 22–23, 38, 187; historical figures in, 3; plot structure of, 4; conversion in, 5, 87, 88, 106, 116; religious components of, 5, 87–104, 112–13; evangelical prescriptions in, 6; gender roles in, 6, 12–13, 137–38, 149–50; popularity of, 6, 33, 35, 191; settings of, 6, 53, 174–78; marketing of, 6–7, 9, 53–54; purpose of, 7, 95, 104, 108–9; emergence of, 13, 25–30; theological aesthetics of, 13; publisher's rationale for, 30, 32; evangelicals' perception of, 34, 127–28; mediocrity in, 36, 38, 191; sentimentality in, 39, 99, 100–101, 132, 143, 194; racial homogeneity of, 40, 54; stigmatization of, 34, 40; private collections of, 51; demand for, 52; crossover marketing of, 53–54; variety in, 55, 85; addiction to, 58–60; friendships in, 61–62; vocabulary of, 64; African American, 68, 91; depiction of racism in, 73, 74, 99; reader expectations for, 75, 97; religio-romantic issues in, 75; sexuality in, 75–87, 97; cover art of, 78–79, 162; anger in, 87; forgiveness in, 87, 89, 145–48, 158; loneliness in,

87; self-esteem in, 87, 140, 170; betrayal in, 89; spiritual growth in, 89, 90–91, 93, 94, 137–38; salvation in, 90; spiritual gifts in, 90; dissatisfaction with, 90–98; character development in, 92; librarians on, 92; storylines of, 88–90, 92, 112–13, 126; realism in, 92–93, 95, 133, 151–53; readers' selection of, 94–95; happy endings of, 39, 95, 100, 177, 194; imagination in, 96; controversial topics in, 99–100, 112; optimism in, 39–41, 100; individualism in, 103; as ministry, 107–18; Oke's defense of, 109; utility of, 109, 111, 115, 117, 139, 193; baptism in, 112; adultery in, 113, 125, 146–48, 160, 163; divorce in, 113, 146, 147; international adoption in, 134; childrearing in, 135–36, 150; emotional impact of, 139–45; prostitution in, 160, 163; abuse in, 163; divine history in, 174–84, 195; West in, 175–78; sequels to, 124, 136, 187; diversity in, 55, 85, 191; travel through, 202 (n. 12). *See also* Heroes, evangelical romance; Heroines, evangelical romance

Romance novels, secular: themes of, 3–4; cruelty in, 4; heroes of, 4; reconciliation in, 4; popularity of, 6, 27; rise of, 26; sexuality in, 26, 29, 76–78; cover art of, 79; evangelical readers and, 79, 83, 85–86; communities of readers, 204 (n. 46)

Romance Writers of America, 163

Roof, Wade Clark, 7

Ryken, Leland, 36, 180; on leisure, 55

St. James, Rebecca, 75

Sallman, Warner: *Head of Christ*, 179

Salvation: in evangelicalism, 9; in Hill's fiction, 22; in evangelical romance novels, 90

Schaeffer, Francis: and theology of the arts, 35

Schaeffer, Franky, 37; *Addicted to Mediocrity*, 36; on kitsch, 116

Self-esteem: in evangelical romance novels, 87, 140, 170

Self-help books, 52, 137, 173

Sentimentality: and romance novels, 37; in evangelical romance novels, 39, 99, 100–101, 132, 143, 194; in evangelical art, 99, 101, 102, 194–95; in evangelical aesthetics, 190, 194

Sexuality: in secular romance novels, 26, 29, 76–78; in evangelical romance novels, 75–87, 97; evangelicalism and, 82, 85, 86–87; secular views of, 82; imagination in, 86; in religious identity, 86; social constructions of, 180; God's plan for, 181

Shaw, Susan: "Gender, Leisure, and Constraint," 55–56

Sicherman, Barbara, 202 (n. 5)

Smith, Christian, 12, 76, 103, 190; *American Evangelicalism*, 8–9; "Symbolic Traditionalism and Pragmatic Egalitarianism," 150

Smith, Murray, 60

Snitow, Ann Barr: "Mass Market Romance," 86

Women, African American: knowledge of evangelical romances, 40; romance authors, 54–55; evangelical, 55, 62; in Christian book clubs, 68–69, 71–72, 91, 151, 172; on racism, 69

Women, Catholic: devotional culture of, 101–2

Women, evangelical: as consumers, 9, 32–33; feminist critique of, 10–11; devotional lives of, 11, 106, 117; socialization of, 13, 56, 61, 113; and popular culture, 16; and holistic gospel, 32, 86; influences on, 39; leisure of, 44–61, 62, 94, 187; African American, 55, 62; in workplace, 57; networks of, 61–72; identity formation among, 62; on book clubs, 62–63; view of romance, 76, 78, 179–80; view of sexuality, 85, 86–87; passivity of, 103; relationship with God, 103; consumption of evangelical popular culture, 107; religious roles of, 110, 113; spirituality of, 116, 138, 140–43; constraints on, 127; family leadership by, 135–36; in mission groups, 137; singleness of, 144–45; forgiveness by, 145–48; gender beliefs of, 150–51; acceptance of scripture, 153; role in history, 177–78, 181, 184; on romance, 180; and evangelical aesthetic, 189; de-emphasizing of Jesus, 216 (n. 49)

Woodiwiss, Kathleen, 29; *The Flame and the Flower*, 26

Zoba, Wendy Murray, 97

Zondervan (publisher), 24; Serenade romance line, 30; advertisements of, 31; purchase by HarperCollins, 53